Bird Hunting with Dalrymple

Bird Hunting
with Dalrymple

The Rewards of Shotgunning
Across North America

Byron W. Dalrymple

Stackpole Books

Copyright © 1986 by Byron W. Dalrymple

Published by
STACKPOLE BOOKS
Cameron and Kelker Streets
P.O. Box 1831
Harrisburg, PA 17105

The author and publisher express their gratitude to the publications listed for permissions to reprint from
articles by Byron W. Dalrymple. Some of the articles were originally published in a somewhat different form.

"Everything You Need to Know to Limit Out On Doves," *Outdoor Life*, March 1975.
"Picking a Perfect Dove Stand," *Field & Stream*, August 1984.
"The Most Elegant Pigeon," *The American Hunter*, August 1977.
"Paloma Morada," *Field & Stream*, October 1962.
"Bobwest," *Field & Stream*, January 1986, under byline "Christopher Michaels."
"Canine-less Quail," *Field & Stream Hunting Annual*, 1978.
"Another Way to Hunt Quail," *Southern Outdoors*, October 1983.
"Blue Racers," *The American Hunter*, January 1985.
"Sand & Sunshine Quail," *The American Hunter*, September 1980.
"It's Easy to Grouse," *Outdoor Life*, November 1952.
"Wild Flight," *Sports Afield*, September 1953. Copyright © 1953, The Hearst Corporation. All rights reserved.
"The Best of the Last," *Field & Stream*, March 1985, under byline "Christopher Michaels."
"A Sound to Remember," *Field & Stream*, September 1985.
"Bull Grouse of the Sagebrush," *The American Hunter*, January 1983.
"The Unringneck," *The American Hunter*, December 1979.
"Outwitting Fall Turkeys," *Field & Stream*, October 1981, under byline "Christopher Michaels.
"Lady Henrietta's Lovers," *Field & Stream*, February 1980.
"How to Find & Hit Woodcock," *Field & Stream Yearbook, Hunting '83*.
"The Other World of Woodcock," *Field & Stream*, January 1980.
"Wanted! Snipe Hunters," *Pennsylvania Game News*, September 1970.
"Game Bird of History," *Field & Stream*, November 1961.
"No Game Bird Like It," *Outdoor Life*, June 1970.
"The South's Wackiest Game Bird," *Southern Outdoors*, December 1981.

Printed in the U.S.A.

Library of Congress Cataloging-in-Publication Data

Dalrymple, Byron W., 1914–
    Bird hunting with Dalrymple.

    Includes index.
    1. Fowling—North America. I. Title
SK313.D35   1986   799.2'4'0973   86-19164
ISBN 0-8117-0252-9

For Michael, Rebecca, Joshua, and Phillip
— grand kids!

Contents

Introduction

If you're looking for technical details about wingshooting, or a treatise on guns and loads for the purpose, you'd best put this book down. Over a long career as a writing outdoorsman, I've always been bored by the technical aspects. I remember with amusement a young man, a technical type, who once sent me a stack of charts he had evolved that, he claimed, would take all guesswork out of wingshooting. If you memorized each detail of his equations, however a bird took to the air, you had only to put into play the correct one, and at your shot the bird would fall.

"Don't you agree," he asked in his covering letter, "that attention to my system would make master wingshooters of us all?"

In reply I simply inserted between "make" and "master" the word "soulless."

Another gentleman, obviously a far-gone gun-and-load nut but not remotely a bird hunter, sent me one time a list of a dozen or more varied shot and powder combinations for stuffing several gauges of shotgun shells, and asked me to note after each what effect I thought it would have on ruffed grouse. I wrote my answer after the first, then jotted ditto marks for all the others: "If you hit the bird, this load will kill it."

My approach to bird hunting since boyhood has been that I sure hoped I'd hit the bird, but that the tools and shooting techniques were secondary. Bird hunting as a pastime or endeavor was for high drama, fine-crystal enjoyment, and a unique kind of animated interest in whatever target was being pursued. I honestly cannot recall ever comparing seriously the sporting qualities of game birds, or failing to enjoy sampling a new one. The spruce grouse won't win prizes for startling flushes, but its appearance and personality lend freshness to a hunt for it. That feeling of eagerness to experience with open attitude as many of our game birds as possible has led me over many years on uncounted thousands of miles of immensely enjoyed hunting travel.

Indeed, as I prepare this introduction to a collection of pieces, some written for several of the national magazines and others new writing, I cannot help feeling grateful for the unusual opportunities I've had to sample North American bird hunting. Most of that wasn't planned, and, looking back, it's a wonder I ever grew up to be a bird hunter at all.

In the days of my grandfathers and great grandfathers, very little bird hunting was done for sport. In most instances, when birds were bothered with at all, it was to put meat on the table. Recently my wife was combing through phonetically spelled letters my maternal grandfather wrote in the middle of the last century when he was young, and she found one in which he spoke of going out to set traps for "paterages." Gun and shells would have been far outside the possibilities of his frugal, primitive Canadian lumberwoods world. Food was the purpose.

My father was a country school teacher, never had a gun, never hunted. We lived on a small farm in the Thumb area of Michigan. Curiously, game bird opportunities were almost nil, though at that time the region was one of woodlots and weedy fence rows, of scruffy, ill-tilled fields and swales, and brushy, untilled swatches and creek bottoms. There were a few bobwhites, but they were considered song birds and weren't plentiful enough even to poach. Ruffed grouse, it was said, once had been abundant, but with cutting of the forests they had disappeared.

About the time I reached pre-high-school age, however, ring-necked pheasants, released a few years earlier experimentally in our region, simply erupted in population. Though no one then and there knew much about what the birds required, conditions were optimal for an explosion of those colorful birds. I still did not own a gun, but my brother and I set steel traps for them, traps we used to catch muskrats in our creek. There were then no regulations—at least that we knew of—pertaining to the birds. They decimated our garden, pulled up our sprouting corn, and were superb eating. Why kill a chicken?

Eventually I schemed to get hold of a gun. The first pheasant I downed awing was done in by a single-shot .22 rifle. The gaudy cock flushed and flew at right angles across in front of me. In wild excitement I shot from the hip, and it tumbled, shot through the *neck*. I presume that was the day I unknowingly became a bird hunter.

Lucky for me that I had been born an American. Nowhere on earth are there more varied bird hunting opportunities for average shooters. Most species are native, but there are several striking success stories of transplants—pheasants, chukars, Hungarian partridge. Nowhere, additionally, can the average hunter, if he determines to do so, sample at such modest cost hunting for each of the available species. Bird hunting licenses are still not exorbitant in cost. Although fee hunting for birds on private lands has become routine in many states, there are also vast expanses of public hunting lands with excellent game bird shooting. Further, modern game management keeps the highs and lows of game bird populations surprisingly well controlled. Most of the species are somewhere still shootably abundant each season.

I don't intend here to attempt to explain the magnetism bird hunting has for those of us to whom it appeals. One either knows or doesn't. One point, however, has always seemed important to me. Dedicated bird hunters are not the kind who equate "big" with "big thrill." In a long career of writing about all aspects of the hunting sports, I've known many individuals who, perhaps because of some deeply buried insecurity, dote on telling tales of the *large* animals they've bagged. If you pursue this fixation, an elk beats a deer, a moose beats an elk, and so on.

That brings to mind an invitation I received a few years ago to join a group going to Africa to hunt elephants. All my expenses were to be paid. How could I refuse? Well, I couldn't tell this group, all of whom meant well, how I felt about elephants. It wasn't that I had some quirky adoration for the huge beasts. I simply had no desire to shoot one.

That same year I'd gotten wind of the fact that after closure for several decades, a season was to be allowed on band-tailed pigeons in Arizona. I wouldn't for the world have divulged to the elephant group that since I didn't have time or inclination to do both, I'd chosen the pigeons. They'd have considered me cracked. Maybe so. Nevertheless, I passed up the free elephant and spent my own money going after wild pigeons. Possibly that's a fair round-about

definition of a bird hunter!

Some of that feeling I hope is inherent in the experiences that follow. I've arranged the groups of game birds to keep relatives together, and the coverage of each species complete in one chapter or two consecutive ones. Thus you may begin anywhere you wish, read back to front or however it suits you, with no previous chapter or group of chapters needed for reference to any other.

As you read this book, and as you hunt, I urge you to pursue my tack of never comparing game birds. In Louisiana one time, a quail addict told me he hated to see the advent of winter, when woodcock swarmed on their southern wintering grounds. They were a nuisance, he said, interrupting and frustrating his bobwhite hunting.

I didn't try to convince him that woodcock were themselves marvelous game birds, deserving of as much attention in his bailiwick as quail. I thought as he talked, however, what a wonderful nuisance he was low-grading, and what delightful interruptions woodcock were to any quail hunt. Certainly it is legitimate to have favorites, but if you are an authentic bird-hunt enthusiast, each species and its surroundings excite you because of their differences from, not similarities to, your most loved.

Part I

THE DOVES AND PIGEONS

The first dove hunt I experienced—I picked off a few in random non-hunting escapades as a young fellow, and shouldn't have—occurred near Wichita, Kansas, over 40 years ago. For some reason I still don't quite understand, the mourning dove, and later many of its relatives, overwhelmingly intrigued me.

I began reading pertinent literature about the world's doves and pigeons. The more I read, the more my interest was fired. By 1948 I had amassed such a horde of information that I decided to write a book based on it and my continued annual dove shooting experiences. That book, titled *Doves and Dove Shooting*, was published by G. P. Putnam's Sons in 1949. It was to my best knowledge the first book on the subject, at least in America. It was also, of the numerous books I've written, one of my own favorites.

It must be admitted that sales were not what might be called even moderately brisk. Mourning dove hunting was a well-attended sport even then, but chiefly in the South, where "dove shoots" involving scores of hunters, with whiskey and food in abundance, often lasted several days. But apparently, not many dove shooters needed to read about it. Nonetheless, years later that book did acquire a smidgen of fame in a decidedly secondhand fashion. A modern author who in recent years did a book on the same subject confided to an editor, who was also a friend of mine and passed along the compliment, that he had, well, borrowed copiously from my old book as research for his. My interest in these handsome birds was at least modestly vindicated by someone who agreed.

The doves and pigeons of the world, I learned while writing that book, are extremely varied, beautifully styled birds. On this continent that variety and beauty are evident. They were even more so during the days of early settlement, when the passenger pigeon was here. Tales of its awesome abundance are still told, and often this bird is used by anti-hunters to illustrate how hunting brought a grand species to extinction.

Market hunting certainly did have a drastic effect on the passenger pigeon. I lived for some years near the Pigeon River—named for those birds—in the northern Lower Peninsula of Michigan, and heard from old-timers stories carried down from their forebears about the massive nestings in that region and the terrible toll of squabs the market hunters took.

But what actually did in the passenger pigeon was not market hunting but the cutting of forests and resulting removal of mast and other forage the birds required. The plain fact is that if the passenger pigeons were as plentiful today as originally, there would be poisoning programs and federal subsidies to get rid of the pests—egged on probably by the same antis, who would claim the despicable pigeons were crowding out some rare warbler.

Although that handsome pigeon could not cope with settlement, pioneering effects on the mourning dove were quite the opposite. The dove, unlike the extinct passenger pigeon, is not a colonial nester. Pairs nest in scattered, territorial locations. As settlement pushed into the West and Northwest, the mourning dove expanded its range. Today it is the most wide ranging of all our native game birds, nesting in each of the lower states, in portions of southern Canada and along the Pacific Coast clear to southern Alaska, and on down through Mexico into Central America. It has been a sensationally successful colonizer.

The mourning dove is also the most hunted of all native game birds, and the annual harvest of it far outnumbers that of any other. The dove receives basic management in the form of carefully regulated seasons and bag limits, but over many years of high harvest has required little more in order to sustain itself abundantly.

The popularity of the mourning dove hinges partially on its astonishing mobility, its speed and maneuverability under fire.

The fast action of heavy flights during a good "shoot" has immense appeal, and the exasperation born of too-numerous misses keeps even the worst shots going back for more punishment. The excellent table qualities of the mourning dove, even though it is small, add to its appeal.

These same attributes and qualities pertain to the several other American doves and pigeons that are legal game. Further, this wingshooting is for everyone, because these are the only game birds—excepting waterfowl, which are another situation entirely—that come to a stand the hunter has preselected. I even recall seeing publicity for a dove hunt somewhere in the Southwest for the handicapped. Everyone present was in a wheelchair.

The mourning dove furnishes by far the bulk of the available dove and pigeon hunting. The other species are present only regionally, and their habitats and therefore numbers are more limited. The white-winged dove of the Southwest and Mexico offers one of the most exciting and dramatic wingshooting experiences available. This sport is the closest approximation to what passenger-pigeon shooting must have been like. These birds are colonial nesters, and make daily feeding flights together. I've shot whitewings for two solid hours as the birds poured overhead, moving from mesquite roosting areas to vast grain fields.

During the latter part of such a flight, some birds were still flying out to feed while others were returning. Although habitat is nowadays meager in southern Texas and westward, flights farther down in Mexico are, for the first-time shooter, unbelievable. Some tyros say they'd as soon stand and stare for the first hour as to shoulder the gun.

Within whitewing range in the U.S. and southward, there are several common doves that are not considered game, or just barely qualify. The diminutive Inca dove and the like-sized ground dove, often in my area called the Mexican dove, are for bird watchers only. These dapper little dudes, with scalloped, scale-like feathers and underwing flashes of cinnamon, do well in towns and around houses. We feed and coddle a bevy of them year-round, and delight in watching perched pairs cuddle, always so close they're crowding.

Another dove just halfway "game" is the white-fronted dove of the brushy U.S.-Mexico border country and southward. This bird, nowadays called by the Texas game department the "white-tipped dove" because of its white tail corners, is as large as the mourning dove, some specimens being possibly an ounce larger. It has a white forehead and breast, is gray on back and wings, has the usual dove-pigeon nape sheen, and, like the smaller Inca and ground doves, flashes underwing patches of rich reddish-brown when in flight.

This dove is chiefly a ground dweller, and often runs off in brush when disturbed, instead of flying. It has long been pot-hunted by natives in Mexico. It was recently made legal in Texas as part of the bag (two a day) during that state's brief white-wing season and long mourning dove season along the border. This was done because the white-fronted dove is occasionally an "error" bird in that region—shot by hunters who mistake it for a mourning or whitewing. It's abundant enough so the small harvest has no effect. When it first became legal, some hunters spoke of it jokingly as a "trophy" dove.

Two other doves are of passing interest. Neither is native. These are the ringed turtle dove and the spotted dove. Scientists are unsure of the origin of the former. Original stock may have been native to Africa. The spotted dove originated in eastern Asia. Both birds long ago were domesticated,

and have been in the U.S. for many years. Both were released, or escaped, and have been able to sustain themselves in the wild in portions of Florida and southern California. There have been open seasons on them in California because hunters can't always distinguish between these and the mourning dove in flight.

The only U.S. game pigeon is the beautiful band-tailed pigeon of the West, a barn-pigeon-sized dweller of forests and mountain foothills. For those who have a fetish for new wingshooting experiences, this bird is worth a pilgrimage.

One of the most striking pigeons that we can claim as at least remnantly a native is the big slaty-blue white-crowned pigeon of the Florida Keys, actually a native of the Caribbean islands. These birds are not hunted here. I recall seeing a small flock, years ago, that had made a rare visit to the southernmost mainland of Florida, and wishing they were abundant and on the game list.

One other big pigeon not on the U.S. game list but occasionally seen along the Texas-Mexico border is the red-billed pigeon. This is a stunningly handsome bird, mauve and bluish with many-hued iridescences. Dove hunters along the border call them "bluerock," a confusing term because the bluerock of domestic pigeon fame stems from ancient stock of the blue rock pigeon along the Wales coast. The red-billed pigeon is hunted and abundant in a wide swath along both coasts of Mexico, and on down into Central America.

For the wingshooting enthusiast who seeks high-level challenges, the doves and pigeons are a prime choice. These birds offer tricky shots and ever-changing angles that have many a gunner wishing they'd be at least a bit more considerate. Indeed, no other American game birds can match their agility awing.

1

The Big-Shoot Bird—
What Hunters Need to Know

The mourning dove, as the introduction to "The Doves & Pigeons" suggests, is far out front as No. 1 U.S. game bird—even game *species*. Legal in over 30 states, its total annual bag averages at least 40 million. This shows how fond hunters are of this awesomely swift, spear-tailed, tricky target.

Ammunition makers love it. Estimates place the number of shells emptied annually at mourning doves at over 200 million. Among manufacturers of shotgun shells, the mourner long ago was dubbed "The Big-Shoot Bird." One wag on an outdoor TV show claimed that each season the space around every mourning dove was eventually shot so full of holes there wasn't room for another. The fast, concentrated shooting, including the myriad misses on this most difficult target, is the real basis for the high drama and excitement of the activity. Further, the infinite variety of shot

angles presented is unmatched anywhere in American shotgunning.

Maybe you've never thought about it, but dove hunting is without question our most unique field gunsport. It's the only one that can be, and usually is, a convivial group activity. Additionally, there's no need to arise early, travel far, expend much physical energy, suffer in low temperature, or get home late; and there's no endless wandering through difficult cover to flush game. You just select a spot, sit, and let the doves come to you.

All of this makes the dove sound like the perfect game bird, and hunting it, deceptively easy. It is indeed a virtually perfect game bird, but finding that magic place to sit and wait is often the Achilles heel.

The dove is unlike any other game species, bird or animal, on the continent in that it is not tied down to anywhere. Deer,

16

Mourning doves are graceful, swift-flying birds. In numbers annually bagged they are far out in front as the No. 1 U.S. game bird.

quail, pheasants, elk, sheep, and almost all other game inhabit very specific ranges and live out their lives within relatively small areas. Waterfowl, though migratory over vast distances, are inexorably tied to water everywhere. The migratory dove is the most mobile, wing-and-fancy-free of all creatures. Of course, it must have food, water, and perching places. That means it can be practically anywhere, at any time. A concentration can suddenly move, for its own whimsical reasons, to a spot 20 miles away in little more than 20 minutes.

This is the first basic the beginner must learn about doves. Only when food, water, or both are exceedingly scarce are dove gatherings wholly predictable. However, the birds take a great variety of food and can drink from the merest puddle. Roosting sites are never a problem. Although they usually utilize trees or shrubs, doves can make do. I've seen groups roosting among low-growing vines in Mississippi, and on the ground in a cover of catclaw in the southwestern deserts.

Nonetheless, even given their whimsical, unpredictable, and highly mobile lifestyle, a dove hunter who has spent years at the sport can still pin them down most of the time. To do so, he must understand another basic. The mourning dove is not actually a flocking bird, even though superficially it may seem to be. It does not nest in colonies, as do some other members of the family, such as the white-winged dove, and it does not travel in or consort in genuine flocks, as for example do ducks and geese. Ordinarily doves travel singly or in small groups—two or three to a dozen. These small groups are gregarious enough but by no means dependent upon group living for a feeling of well-being.

What brings doves into medium to large concentrations anywhere is a special abundance of a favorite forage, a watering place that especially suits their needs, or a combination of both in a particular area, plus suitable places to perch or roost in the same general region. However, another, even more important influence is responsible for concentrating the birds in a certain place, and especially for keeping them there or dispersing them. That is weather.

Doves are warm-weather birds. It never gets too hot for them, but it easily gets too cool. This is why they are early migrators. If you live anywhere in the northern half of the contiguous states where there is an open season, the early days of it are always best. In fact, if you wait and a chilly front blows in, almost all the birds may be gone. If there is rain or drizzle, you can be certain the preponderance of the birds will pull out. In the Deep South and Southwest, a windless, light, warm drizzle won't necessarily move them, if feeding conditions are good. On the whole, however, doves are sunshine lovers that won't tolerate chill days or suddenly lowered temperature.

The situation from the middle-south states and southward is moderately different. Many studies here have shown that the heaviest dove kill is invariably during the first week or so of the season. Some of this, of course, is because many young and rather naive doves are present at opening. You can easily recognize the late-raised youngsters in flight by their abbreviated tails. As more and more migratory adults pour into the southern areas, remember that they've been hunted on the way down and are therefore ultra-shy.

In the concentration areas of the southern half of the country, the majority of the birds, both locally raised and those coming in on migration, do have general regions that they annually favor. For instance, western Kentucky and Tennessee always have

the major share of birds in those states, and the Yazoo Delta gets the heavy influx in Mississippi. The reason birds gather in them is because feeding conditions are always better there. Within these large areas a hunter still has to pinpoint a hunting spot, and weather can cause many an upset.

For example, a heavy rainstorm during which the temperature drops only a few degrees may move every bird from what looked during preseason scouting like a surefire mop-up place. A hard blow from north or northeast will do the same. A weatherwise dove hunter won't necessarily give up. He'll check the weather reports for surrounding states and postpone his hunt. If weather in states to the north is also bad, it may be that a day or so later birds will come pouring in.

Doves don't always move south. Let's say you had a big concentration spotted just before the season, and a chill but brief rain moves in. The birds pull out. You check the weather and find that 100 miles to the east or west it was twice as bad. Birds from that area are likely to replace in a day or two those that left, especially if there is a quick warming where you are.

Heavy, continued rain, even though the temperature stays fairly stable, moves birds by the thousands. One fall I was invited on a hunt near Skidmore, Texas, where there were hundreds of birds—until a couple of days before I arrived. The area had received 15 inches of rain over those days. Fields where doves had been feeding were flooded. Except for a few hard-to-find pockets, there was no shooting. There are even times when flooding rains send doves flying north rather than south. This is not a result of temperature but of the need to locate dry feeding conditions.

All told, then, a careful weather check before and during the season can be most helpful to a hunter. Find out what's happening in every direction from you, and what is expected. Sudden quick drops of temperature, hard winds, severe or chilly rains will either send birds to you or send yours to better havens—or both. Warm, bright, moderately quiet, stable weather, provided food is available, will influence the birds to stay put.

Regardless of weather, available food, water, and roosting sites, doves don't have to and won't tolerate constant harassment. Even in states where shooting is legal both morning and afternoon (most allow only noon-to-sunset shooting) it's best to hunt any hotspot only half a day—morning or afternoon—and in any case only on staggered days, or certainly no more than three days a week. The birds would rather seek a new feeding ground miles distant than put up with heavy day-to-day shooting.

Food, especially in large quantities, is what most draws the birds. There are few places where finding either water or a roosting site is a problem for them. Food often is. The sharp hunter soon learns also that certain feeding grounds, given stable weather, draw birds year after year as long as land use does not change. Even in years and places where food is no real problem, certain feeding fields will gather birds every year. No one is quite sure why. Maybe they're easy to fly into and alight in. Anyway, it pays to find a few of these and always check them before the season. If the crop—of grain or weeds—changes, the birds won't gather there, unless, of course, another crop to their liking has been planted.

Also, if the seed crop is late and thus still green and not fallen, some hunters are perplexed because birds don't show up as usual. Mourning doves rarely feed from a stalk or head of a plant; they feed on the

The seeds of croton, shown here, which grows wild over a vast area of dove range, are a favored food. Wherever croton is abundant, so are mourning doves in fall.

ground, on fallen grain or seeds that are not covered. They do not scratch for food. Unripened or unharvested crops may not offer enough fallen forage to bring birds in. Such fields, however, may be sizzlers a week or so later.

The variety of dove food is extremely wide. Domestic crops make up a heavy portion of dove diet: millet, milo, corn, peanuts, maize, various field peas, wheat. A prime favorite is sorghum. Among wild foods, two are outstanding attractors: croton (often called "dove weed") and wild sunflower. Ragweed, foxtail, and pigweed are also eagerly sought. Among the wild foods, small seeds seem to be preferred.

Because croton often usurps a whole fallow or early-harvest pasture, and doves relish it, a stand of it is almost surefire.

Doves do not like to feed in dense ground cover. Croton, which grows with a spreading top up a foot or so in height, actually is open underneath. Wild sunflowers, hard for a hunter to push through, are also open at ground level for birds of this size. Corn fields through which a picker has moved, scattering waste grain between standing dry rows, commonly attract birds. In fact, both standing dry corn rows and lush stands of croton, beneath which birds may stay unseen, occasionally provide the unique thrill of walk-up or jump-shooting. By and large on harvested crop fields, however, doves prefer those that are clean-harvested rather than those with a tangle left on the ground.

Considering the variety of foods doves eat, it might seem confusing to select possible good feeding sites where you live. However, you need be familiar only with the favorite foods most abundant in your area. Where I live, for example, there is not much crop farming. But there are places where an abundance of both croton and wild sunflowers grow. These are the spots we check. A hundred miles south, in the edge of the south-Texas brush country, there are some heavily crop-farmed areas growing grains such as maize. Few of the foods found in my area are present there. Thus, the crop fields there often swarm with doves.

A general rule is that when food is abundant everywhere, doves will be scattered. When it is scarce, concentrations are easier to find. Nevertheless, even when food is abundant, doves tend to gather in certain spots, for unfathomable reasons. A good way to locate them is to drive around side-roads watching for lines of birds perched on telephone wires.

When food is everywhere, however, the birds will tolerate little heavy shooting at any given spot. In states that offer split seasons, hunting may be difficult in the late segments because the mature birds are very wary. But food late in the year is likely to be scarcer and thus concentrations, while sometimes tough to locate, may be large.

The same general rules apply to water. If it's standing everywhere, waterhole shooting is not likely to be as good as when water is fairly scarce. Yet doves are exceedingly whimsical about where they drink—or so it may seem to the hunter. There is a large ranch on which I shoot each fall that has 11 stock tanks. Two are always hotspots. The rest toll in only scattered birds. A hunter should constantly watch for this phenomenon.

It also pays to watch precisely where most birds drink at a waterhole. I know one, for example, that has steep sides, grassy banks, and a narrow, muddy draw running a short distance away on one side. Right at that draw is where almost every dove comes in. The reasons are simple. Doves like open, not heavily grassed, banks. They don't favor steep banks, because a dove drinks by squatting and thrusting its bill into the water, not lifting the head to swallow. The bare, muddy flat along the flooded draw makes it easy for birds to alight and walk to water. Doves don't hop and cannot walk well in heavy grass. Further, although doves will drink clear water, they prefer muddy, stagnant, and, if available, somewhat saline water. That knowledge can help you select a possible favored drinking place.

Two other considerations make either a feeding location or a drinking spot more appealing to doves. The birds must pick up sand and small gravel as grit to store in their gizzards to grind up their food. If a watering place has abundant grit around it, birds

Doves drink as shown here—by squatting and thrusting the bill into water and keeping it there—unlike many other birds, which raise the head after the bill is filled to let the water run down the throat. Doves like muddy and saline water better than clear water.

Waterholes that have open fringes where grit for the crop is readily available are often selected by doves. This dove is picking small gravel.

will often top off a full crop with grit and then go to the water. Grit-supplying road-sides or washes near a feeding field have the same appeal.

The other item to watch for is a scatter-ing of dead, leafless snags. Doves love to perch in these. Feeding birds may fly off to alight in a dead tree, stay a few minutes, then go back to feeding. Near a waterhole, doves habitually come circling in, perch for a bit, then drop down to water. A stand beside a graying snag, near either feed or water, is the best spot in the area for col-lecting a limit. If a series of snags surrounds the place, so much the better.

Leafless snags should not be confused with roosts. Snags are just resting places. The roost usually has leaves or else is in dense brush where large trees are unavail-able. It is a fairly protected place where doves spend the night. Shooting near a roost during the last legal hour can some-times be filled with wild-eyed action, but it is never a good idea. A roost is a haven

where birds need to feel secure during the hours when they cannot see. Coming-to-roost shooting has dispersed many a heavy concentration.

It does not happen often that food, water, grit, and roost are all together. Where they are, shooting may turn out poorer than expected. The birds are easily driven away. Mobile and fast as they are, doves think nothing of flying several miles from or to food, water, and roost. Where this occurs, good pass-shooting is offered. You may not know exactly where the birds are feeding, watering, or roosting. But if you study flight patterns closely, you'll see birds—singles, a few, or up to a dozen in a group—intermittently winging along the same general route. Getting under a flight offers high shots at birds flying swiftly. It's great sport. If you are some distance from a roost to or from which they're moving, pass-shooting does no harm.

When you bag a few birds on a pass, remove and open their crops. This may give

Dead trees near feeding or watering places have immense appeal to doves as perches. A stand near one may bring a limit right to you.

you a hot clue to where and on what they are feeding. Simply trace back the direction from which they came, and you may find an abundance of the forage the crop contained, and set up an excellent feeding-field shoot.

In fact, the major share of dove shooting everywhere is done at a feeding area. Second comes the waterhole. The routine of a dove's day is roughly as follows. The flight from roost to feed begins about dawn. When crops are full of seeds and grit, the birds fly off to water, and thence to a midday resting area, usually in leafy trees nearby. By midafternoon the flight to feed begins again. Late in the afternoon, with full crop, they move to water, and then at dusk back to the roost. Thus feeding-field shoots are best during the first half of the morning and the middle to late afternoon. Waterhole shoots pay off with most action late in the morning or later in the afternoon.

The number of hunters present may dictate where to get the fast action. If you find and plan to shoot at a large feeding field, it's just about mandatory to have several companions, in order to keep birds flying. This is what made old-time dove shoots in the South such festival affairs years ago. Sometimes 100 hunters took part. Unless hunters are stationed at numerous points around the field, the birds fly in, fill up, and fly out with very little shooting offered. Waterhole shooting is different because watering places are ordinarily much smaller. Birds fly within range even if only a couple of shooters are present.

If you intend to use decoys, place them in leafless trees so they show plainly. A few full-bodied decoys perched thus will definitely attract birds. A scattering of silhouette decoys on the ground beside water also may help. Observe first where most water-

Decoys may be helpful at times. These, placed in a leafless tree near a waterhole, drew the attention of incoming doves and brought them into range.

ing doves alight, and then place the ground decoys.

Although calls are sold by many firms, are fun to play with, and just may get the attention of flying birds, their value is questionable simply because hunting season is not "cooing season." Camouflage suit and cap, or at least drab clothing, are important. Young doves on opening day may not flare if they see you, but mature birds certainly will at any time. If possible, select a stand in the shade where you can see out and have a full 180 degree swing. If you can shoot from the sitting position, hunker among clumps of tall grass or bushes, in the open.

An important consideration is to select a stand where you have a "clean fall." Hundreds of doves are lost each season because shooters drop them into tall grass or brush. Doves are small and blend so well they're difficult to find. Further, forget about trying for doubles, unless you can drop birds onto a completely open field. Keep your eye on the spot where a bird fell, and go pick it up immediately. An exception, of course, is when you have a good retriever. Some dogs heartily dislike retrieving doves because the feathers come off in bunches in their mouths. A dove retriever, however, is a great help.

When shooting at a waterhole, if no open ground is available for shot birds to drop onto, the edge of the pond serves well. Doves that fall into the water won't sink. A retriever can get them, or perhaps the breeze will move them to shore. A gimmick I've used for years is to bring along a casting rod and surface plug. When a dove drops into a pond, I cast to it and pull it in.

Several casts may be required to hook a bird. Cast past it, then guide the plug back gently against it. Comically, one time I was casting for a fallen dove and instead had a rousing strike from a bass, which proved to be a five-pounder.

Much excellent dove shooting is annually missed because hunters look for the birds in obvious places but fail to check out not-so-obvious spots. As a classic example, one fall in New Mexico I hunted with a native who drove through uninhabited rangelands to an abandoned old house and outbuildings. On the north and west sides was a grove of big trees that had once been a windbreak in this flat country. Nearby was a windmill with a seep from a tank overflow. Yucca and grass seeds were abundant. Doves had gathered in this bleak place from every point of the compass. Every need was here. In an hour of fast shooting we limited out.

All of this should pretty well set you up to find and get shots at doves. Don't expect me to tell you precisely how to hit them. I doubt that anyone can do that. The exasperation of the misses, however, undoubtedly is what keeps us all going back, determined to do better next time.

2

Fine-Tuning for a Sure Mourning Dove Limit

A Texas friend of mine has for years bamboozled hunting buddies into believing he's an expert dove shot. "Always has a limit before anybody else," one acquaintance says enviously. "Yet hunt quail with him, and he's downright four-thumbed."

This amuses me. I know him, have hunted with him, understand his approaches, and couldn't agree with them more. As a great dove *shot*, he's a fake; as a successful *hunter*, he's an expert. There are three reasons. He's astute at appraising a feeding field or waterhole and accurately judging where most birds will fly. He figures where they'll break speed. He picks his position so the most likely shots will be the ones he's best at.

"A dove hunter's wingshooting expertness," he once confided, "is secondary, in terms of success, to his expertness at picking a stand that gives him advantages."

Unlike other upland birds, which hunters walk up or hunt with dogs, doves are almost always hunted from a stand. They come to the hunter, or don't, depending on how astutely he's chosen his position. The more that come into range, the more shooting chances. The slower they're moving, the easier the shots. The more shot angles presented that the hunter is good at, the fewer bangs per bag limit.

The ultimate demonstration I recall involved the Texan just mentioned, and illustrates how craftily a limit can be arranged by a sharpie. The focal point of this shoot was a ranch windmill where cattle were fed livestock cake in large pellets. The many stray pellets scattered over the area were prime pickings for doves.

Three hunters and I drifted off to stand under nearby scrub liveoaks. Doves were coming in, circling, and trying to alight, but without pattern.

Off at one side was a small board-fence

corral where several horses were penned and fed each night. Tex made a beeline for it, having seen several doves swirl down and alight in it. He climbed over, leaned against a post, and was limited out while we were still muttering and missing.

"Here was the one spot," he told me later with a grin, "where feed was concentrated, certain to draw birds pinpoint. As they dropped in, they had to brake hard. I stood where I'd get mostly incomer shots, always easy for me. These were almost too easy. The doves were practically standing still."

For doves, wingshooting expertise is secondary to astuteness in picking a stand that offers advantages. This lefthanded shooter, for example, does best at birds crossing from right to left, and has selected his stand where most incoming birds are following that flight pattern.

Some hunters wouldn't want it that easy. Nevertheless, most of us like shooting we can handle without frustration and still put a limit in the pot. Doves perplex many hunters because they're the most highly mobile wanderers among U.S. game birds. Regardless, wherever doves gather, they evidence specific preferences. All aspects of selecting a sure-limit stand are based on dove habits that are identical everywhere.

Consider a hypothetical feeding field. Three sides are open. One is bordered by trees. The surrounding country is flat and featureless. Birds arrive from almost every angle. If feed is well distributed, some may drop in anywhere. A majority, however, will circle and come along near the tree line. That's an ingrained dove habit. They'll slow down as they decide where to alight. Somewhere here is the easy-pickin's stand.

If the field is in a valley, doves come to it almost without fail up or down the trough, seldom over hemming ridges. Their approach speed usually is swift, and the difficult shots are presented on stands under the approach. Doves like to look over a field before alighting. Once over the field, they'll cut speed. On a given day, most come from the same direction and then circle—right or left—in a distinct pattern. The pattern may switch directions on another day, due to wind direction or reasons only the birds know.

Only a few minutes are required to dope out the general pattern the majority of birds is following, and observe points where flight is slowest. Now comes the fine-tuning of stand choice. I recall one field where I've often shot limits, hunkered beneath a tree out in the middle. Doves have a penchant for veering to pass close to a lone tree or clump of them set apart.

Another field I hunt has several lone green trees, and at one end, on the fence

Doves never alight in weeds or swale growth as thick as this. However, if a point or line of such growth thrusts into a feeding field, they'll often fly along it. Such spots make good stands.

line, a single tall, dead tree. I pass up the "pretty good" live trees, and head for the snag. Doves are mesmerized by dead trees, large or small. They love to perch in them, before or after feeding.

Those that don't perch may fly slowly past or circle a snag. Perchers routinely make a partial circle—from the left one day, maybe from the right the next—then flutter down onto a limb. Knowing this maneuver alerts a shooter to time his best opportunity. Approaching a perch, birds cut speed up to 25 yards away. Doves flying off a perch are tricky. They don't launch upward. They drop off, possibly a foot, then climb steeply with a rattle of wings.

As a long-time snag lover, I've experimented time and again with how best to select my position. My rules go like this. If the snag or a lone green tree is on a fence line, I take a position within range in grass along the fence, on the side most birds are coming from or circling. However, if I wear camouflage with headnet and sit against the snag, I often get beautiful shooting. But I must sit still and wait out birds, letting them get close.

When shooting under a large, spreading, green tree, watch how birds are flying. Pick the side most birds pass. Forget the others. You can't shoot both sides. Don't take a stand under a tree with low, spreading limbs. You may be able to see doves, but you won't be able to successfully follow them with your gun. You might better stand quietly right out in the open than run out from under limbs to get passing shots.

Checking for potential payoff stands at any feeding field somehow reminds me of bass fishing. You look for structure. I recall dove shoots I've had in four different states where there has been a creek running either across or beside the feeding field. In all instances, most of the doves regularly flew along the creek, coming or going. I also remember a narrow swale running out into a cutover grain field. In this moist depression, weeds and tall grasses grew. Doves never alight in such thick stuff, but for some reason they often turn and fly along it. I hunkered right on the point, where it petered out in the cultivated field. Practically every bird coming in or leaving veered to pass that point or fly along the swale.

Pipeline rights-of-way and power-line swaths offer excellent stands. Doves like to fly "slots." Power poles and lines have some inexplicable fascination for doves. On our own ranch we have a small field where we occasionally get shooting. In one corner a power-line pole stands. For some reason doves make a point of passing it, coming in or leaving. Is it some sort of guide, or simply an object taller than its surroundings? Only the birds know.

Dove hunters who want the best and fastest shooting should pay attention, too, not just to what doves eat in their areas but to which foods they relish most and to where those favorites are concentrated in the smallest areas. Here's an example. One recent season I was invited to an afternoon shoot where a group had located a large dove concentration using a 200-acre harvested cornfield. Even with a number of hunters to keep birds moving, a large field presents difficulties.

I watched one crafty gentleman head for a dead tree I'd hoped to use. Another hunkered near a patch of bordering woods. A third chose a tree near a stock tank. Many doves coming to a feeding field that has a pond nearby will veer to fly near it or over it, even though it's not watering time. For a while I was stumped. Birds were all over the place, but no spots in the field seemed to draw large numbers, except the few well-chosen stands mentioned.

I walked around the perimeter and suddenly noticed a welter of birds moving in and out of one corner. Reaching there, I instantly knew why. Waste grain over the field was not abundant. Birds had to work hard and widely to fill up. Here, in a small

At a waterhole, a hunter places decoys on a wire fence, then sits near the pond edge. Birds following the valley to the pond, slow as they come in, and don't see the hunter until it's too late.

area, the corn crop had failed. Dense cro-ton had sprung up. This plant, aptly named "dove weed," is irresistible to mourners. I nestled into the fence corner and filled out in a hurry.

That illustration should serve to make the point. Know the favorite foods in your region. Look for the best crops covering the smallest spaces. Even if birds are not as nu-merous in those restricted spots as they are over an entire large field, you can maneuver to have them in your pocket. You don't need a lot. You just need a limit flying where you can hit 'em.

A modest-sized patch of concentrated feed that draws doves is comparable in some respects to waterhole shooting. Doves are drawn to a compact area. Further, sev-eral aspects of stand selection at waterholes are similar to those at feeding fields. The dead snag near a watering place is a mag-net. The tree clump near an otherwise open waterhole will cause doves to veer and pass close. A creek running into or out of a watering place invariably serves as a flyway. The place for your stakeout along such a creek, for birds either coming in or leaving, is usually about where the creek and pond meet, either inflow or drainage. The rea-son: doves may fly swiftly along the creek—often at moderate altitude, some-times very low. But they brake as they come to the broader water.

Certain objects at a small pond will draw incoming birds. I remember a Kansas cattle tank that was smooth-sided but had a single big boulder at the narrow drainage end. On several hunts I watched a majority of doves come up the drainage trickle to the boulder and either make a tight circle or simply flutter down. Some even perched momen-tarily on the rock. A small bush 25 steps distant made a sure-limit stand.

If there's a choice between a muddy inflow and clear pond water, always stake out near the discolored water. Doves pass up clear water for silty or salty water every time. One end of a pond tracked up by cattle, the tracks full of muddy water, is often a mesmerizer for incoming doves. Some that have been drinking here regu-larly will head straight for the muddy portion. Others will circle the waterhole perimeter but wind up at the muddy part.

If a watering place is still and stagnant, with no inflowing water or drainage, it probably is an almost dry pond. These are selected routinely as favorites by doves, and most are small enough to shoot across. The stand position isn't important in such a place, except as related to shots you like best.

One most important observation to make when you locate a waterhole doves are using is which portions of the bank are grassy or weedy and which are clear. As mentioned, doves won't alight in heavy, tall grass or weeds. We have a pond on our place that well illustrates the point. One portion of the perimeter has dense grass bordering a steep bank. The rest is small gravel, bare of vegetation, and with baked mud down to water's edge. Every dove coming here, from whatever direction, heads for the open gravel or mud. Some alight and pick grit, then walk down to water. A few alight right on the baked mud. I can sit under a tree in the tall grass and shoot across the small pond, picking off doves as if I were shooting ducks drop-ping to decoys.

Wherever you decide to stand or sit, tak-ing advantage of the shots easiest for you is seldom any problem. I've always had more difficulty with crossing shots left to right than vice versa. When I take a stand where most birds will be crossing at right angles, I select a position where my swings will be

A classic example of a dove's drinking place—the rim is clear of dense weeds; there is ample room to alight on open ground; grit is available.

right to left. I'm not very good at incomers, but I like level going-away shots. If I choose a stand where most birds pass over in the same direction, I turn my back to the flight and take 'em going away.

There's only one other consideration in choosing a sure-limit stand—the sun's angle. It's especially important during last-hour waterhole shoots. In Arizona one fall, an experienced shooter told me, "If you observe closely, doves flying from feed to water in late afternoon usually have the sun behind or across them as they near the waterhole. They can't see facing a low sun any better than you can. But their angle may tempt you to try to watch them coming, and blind yourself for shooting."

How true! I'd done it many times until he called it to my attention. The obvious cure is to arrange a stand that puts your back or shoulder to the sun. If birds circle water, you'll still have crossing targets, well lighted. If they come from directly behind over your head and let down without circling, they'll be so easy you'll almost be ashamed to shoot. Indeed, as that Texan said, what counts most toward banging a bagful is not so much how slick a shot you are as how crafty you are at picking a place to do the banging.

3

Bird Shooting's Fastest Action — White-Winged Doves

The September afternoon was bright and blistering. We hunkered in a vast cut-over maize field that stretched away toward the southern horizon. Behind us several hundred yards was a muddy irrigation diversion as large as a small river, and across it and flowing northward toward the Rio Grande River and the Texas border was an enormous, feathery-leaved, pale green mesquite forest. A stream of birds had begun to flow out of it, moving high and southward over our heads. The afternoon feeding flight of the white-winged doves had begun.

We moved briefly a couple of times to dodge venomous, outsized red ants that love to poison humans. All five of us were sweating profusely but paying no attention to the heat and humidity. The flight of the birds was so fascinating that no one yet had even thought about shooting. Several Mexican kids who'd attached themselves to our group, wanting to pick up birds for us in return for a U.S. dollar per hunter, squatted grinning in the stubble, eager for action.

By the time the flight was well under way, hundreds of birds were in the air. There is no gunning experience on this continent remotely similar to shooting whitewings when you are in an area where they are abundant. Here in Mexico possibly 20 miles south of Reynosa, no one had estimated the whitewing population except the farmers, who sometimes massively poison them because of their grain-crop depredations. There were undoubtedly several *million* in this region.

I had seen them on another occasion in Mexico descending on a standing crop of ripe maize in such swarms that their wing sounds were a steady roar, and it would have been impossible to pick out a single

South of Reynosa in northern Mexico, two Mexican youngsters eager to pick up downed birds for tips watch while a hunter tries for birds flying out to feed. Thousands pass over during a good flight.

bird to shoot at. Unlike mourning doves, which seldom alight on heads of grain but feed on fallen grain and seeds on the ground, whitewings do both. They are therefore, in some seasons and places below the U.S. border, an utter scourge to farmers.

A group of birds suddenly swept over low enough for us to try them. Three of us arose; the others shot from kneeling. Whitewings are determined in their flight. Mourning doves commonly dart and twist, veering and sideslipping when shot at. Whitewings bore right on. The barrage means nothing to them. Those coming on behind follow the same pattern. From our burst of fire they certainly had nothing to fear. We made a clean sweep—everyone missed.

No one was perturbed. Under a flight like this there was only one concern over collecting a limit, which in Mexico at that time was 20 birds—all we were allowed to take back into the U.S. That concern was whether or not the shells held out. Birds would continue to pour over for at least a couple of hours, and by that time the early contingent, full-cropped, would be heading back to the mesquite roosting haven, so that heavy flights in both directions would offer more shooting than we could use.

White-winged dove flights are moderately comparable to what the great flights of passenger pigeons must have been like. The whitewing is an exceedingly gregarious bird. It is also colonial in its nesting habits. Conversely, the mourning dove nests in scattered locations. Although male whitewings are territorial, and engage in small battles during mating when one's territory is invaded by another, each bird's required territory is smaller than a mourner's. In southern Texas summer studies have shown as many as 500 nests to an acre.

Actually, southern Texas, and westward across the Southwest to California, is only the northernmost nesting fringe of the white-winged dove. It is basically a hot-weather bird of Mexico and Central America, but spills northward for summer nesting across the Rio Grande and meagerly into portions of southwestern New Mexico (wherever the country is not too high), over much of Arizona north to the rim country, and along the Colorado River on the Arizona-California border.

The best opportunities for hunters within the U.S. are the Lower Rio Grande Valley in Texas, and a broad swath across southern Arizona. In both states, however, the whitewing is in trouble today. Many years ago this fringe nesting range swarmed with birds. During one early period wealthy sports from as far away as the eastern U.S. cities trekked to southern Arizona in summer to shoot the daily flights, each hunter commonly averaging more than 100 birds per day.

Whitewings also went through a period of severe market hunting, in Arizona especially, where they were slaughtered by thousands at scarce springs to which they daily flew long distances for water. Later, as the mesquite and other desert growth was cleared, farm crops at first enhanced whitewing habitat. Eventually, the clearing of nesting habitat for farming upset the delicate balance between food and cover. Whitewing numbers, though still substantial in the U.S., were reduced.

In Texas the birds declined drastically. Then, as citrus growing in the Lower Valley increased, they adapted surprisingly, nesting in citrus trees. They even spread northward in modest numbers as far as Corpus Christi and San Antonio. Then, some years back, hard freezes destroyed Texas citrus trees. The summer — and early fall — whitewing populations plummeted. Presently, with assistance from the game department, which has bought nesting tracts, Texas whitewings hold on, and to date there has been a brief season almost every fall. How long there'll be whitewing shooting in either Texas or Arizona is difficult to guess. Birds are still reasonably abundant, but everywhere north of the border they face continuing problems.

They're tough and surprisingly prolific desert birds, however. The whitewing is slightly larger than the mourning dove, averaging up to six or seven ounces. Delicately colored in grays, olive-browns, and black, with pinkish-buff and blue-gray showing in certain lights across the breast, and with the crown, nape, and part of the back glistening in purplish sheens, it is a strikingly handsome creature. The name derives from the wide swaths of white across the upper wing surfaces and the thin white border along the trailing edge of the secondary wing feathers.

The tail is squared at its tip, in sharp contrast to the spear-shaped tail of the mourning dove. Where both birds are present, the tail quickly identifies either in flight. The flying whitewing appears shorter because of its squared tail, and plumper, than the mourner. Its wingbeats seem in slower rhythm. The illusion lulls inexperienced hunters into believing it is a slower flyer than the mourning dove. Actually, both birds fly at about the same speed, averaging 35 miles per hour when lazing along, 50 to 55 when hurrying.

The whitewing tail has white feathers at

White wing patches—seen also in flight—easily identify the whitewing. The body is more compact-appearing than that of the mourning dove, and the tail is squared.

the end on either side. Males show a naked patch of blue skin surrounding the eye. The profile of the bill is quite different from that of the mourning dove. It is dark, appears longer, and is slightly down-curved. The white wing swath, however, is the telltale key for identification. It shows as a white edging along the wing, even when birds are perched.

I have made exciting hunts for whitewings a number of times in both Texas and Arizona. I've also been flat skunked on a couple such hunts because of weather. The whitewing will not tolerate even moderately cool temperature. It is strictly a desert dweller. North of the Mexican border, if a cool or chilly front blusters through as the season opens, the whitewings change their address in a hurry. There have been times in Texas when a substantial nesting population stayed north of the border right up to a day or two before the season opening—and then overnight were gone, south of the border.

Even birds in northern Mexico will drift south if cool rains occur or an early norther whistles through. Anyone planning to hunt whitewings in the northern portion of their range, especially in the thin strip of range in the U.S., should not wait for that "uncrowded second weekend." It may be uncrowded by birds, too!

The point is, all of the whitewing's northern range, on both sides of the border, is simply temporary—summer nesting range. The bird is migratory. The vast concentrations in the first hundred miles of range in Mexico clear out as fall progresses. Nowadays some hunters book winter trips down into Central America, where game laws are iffy and the doves are packed in unbelievable concentrations. Some resorts advertise that you can shoot all the doves you wish. This seems distasteful.

That day south of Reynosa, although thousands of birds passed over, we couldn't have made large kills if we'd wished to. Where we were, most flew too high. That, however, made it sporty and dragged out the enjoyment. It also proved that we had not astutely selected our stand. The first important chore of a whitewing hunter is to locate a flight lane. The more important second chore, however, is to wisely select your location under it.

Whitewings concentrate in such numbers that they must have within flight range a guaranteed supply of food, throughout nesting and on into the few weeks before they drift south. The huge fields of grain crops in northern Mexico and some in the

Shooting singles on the Texas side of the border. Current law allows a specified number of "mistake" birds during mourning dove season.

U.S. offer what they need. Forested roosting and resting sites in desert growth hold the birds at night and during midmorning to midafternoon. Thus, unlike the far less concentrated flights of mourning doves, these birds daily make en masse beeline trips back and forth. If forage remains ample, the flight lines vary not at all day after day, sometimes for weeks.

Area hunters spot a flight lane before the season opens. For example, I was invited one fall to southern Texas and assured by my host that abundant birds were traveling along the course of a dry wash every day to grain fields near the Rio Grande. This hunt was one of those grand experiences that

every hunter should experience. It was something of a social event. Out in the thornbrush and mesquite, local hunters and their wives had set up tables groaning with food. Abundant cold drinks were stashed in ice chests in the dappled shade.

We gathered a bit past noon, ate too much, drank cold beer, and then lounged contentedly, telling tall tales and waiting for the flight to begin. We were picnicking on the perimeter of a huge resting and roosting area. When whitewings began flying, they rose from cover a couple of hundred yards from us. They came sizzling low over the chaparral, beginning to rise just before they reached us. This placed most of them within a 30- to 40-yard range, with scattered birds barely skimming the brush and whistling past so close we couldn't swing fast enough to catch up.

The locals had craftily selected the perfect place for our stand. Farther on toward where the flocks fed, which was some miles distant, the doves rose to high flight. Most would have been out of range. Whitewings will fly long distances if necessary to both food and water. Twenty miles for them requires no more than half an hour. We were limited out all too quickly, and sat in the shade plucking our birds while hundreds more whistled above us.

That shoot was more or less standard procedure in whitewing country. However, the other end of the flight, at the feeding location, is as good, and in some ways a bit easier. I shot one September about 70 miles

south into Mexico with Charlie Schreiner III, owner of the famed YO Ranch in Texas, and Enrique Guerra, scion of an illustrious border family with ranches in both the U.S. and Mexico. Enrique drove us in a pickup across thornbrush country to the edge of an enormous recently harvested maize field.

In the pickup bed were a group of Mexican youngsters who would retrieve birds and pass shells to us. The location Enrique had selected placed the resting region of the doves far behind us, and the sun at our backs. Birds coming into the feeding field either skimmed the brush or scaled down from high flight to dip into the feeding area. They came in from behind and over our heads, offering straight-away or, as some turned, crossing shots.

There was a case of shells near me. As I

Shooting in a harvested milo field in northern Mexico. Texas whitewing hunting is good some years, poor during others. Mexico offers the best opportunities for this bird.

burned them, one of the grinning youngsters kept scurrying for more. Those kids were whooping it up, eagerly racing to pick up birds and instantly starting to clean them. They indicated not very subtly that they'd like some birds to take home with them. All of them came from poor *campesino* families, most unlanded, some of them squatters on Guerra's large ranch. It may have been bending the law a bit, but we used our sympathy and understanding as a valid excuse to pop an extra batch for each

youngster. Somehow our consciences were quiet.

At Enrique's La Nutria Ranch headquarters that evening I watched his head cowboy, who doubled occasionally as cook, build a big fire in a huge barbecue pit where half a steer was often roasted over coals for guests. Another cowboy was busy shaking salt and pepper inside and over our birds, drenching each with lemon juice, and wrapping it in a square of foil. Whitewings are always much fatter than mourn-

A white-winged dove perches in a mesquite. Whitewings are invariably fatter than mourning doves and are superb eating.

ing doves; the yellow fat, the cook knew, would baste them. Soon, with only the two cowboys plus Charlie Schreiner, Enrique, and me to eat them, 60 whitewings were spritzling inside their foil cocoons.

While the cowpoke chef slapped out scads of tortillas, kept the coals ardent and the flames down, we three sat flat on the patio tile, backs against a wall, enjoying what seemed a cool evening after the scorching afternoon. Although I am not a lover of tequila, for some reason sipping it with abundant ice and a squirt of squeezed lime seemed to underline the total enjoyment of that simple meal of whitewings and tortillas. It was superb, and eating a dozen plump doves each proved no problem.

Flight-lane shooting of whitewings, with the best of it at one end or the other, is the standard approach. Seldom are they shot nowadays at waterholes. Interestingly, some famed flights probably have followed the same routes for centuries. Modern man has changed land use in whitewing range, and that has sometimes changed the ancestral flight lanes. Some of the ancient ones, however, persist unbelievably.

I recall, for example, that while writing my book about doves and dove shooting in the 1940s, I ran upon material about what was called in pioneer times, and still was in the '40s, "The San Xavier Crossing," a famous whitewing gunning site. This was outside Tucson, near the beautiful old San Xavier Mission, built several centuries ago. There are old records indicating that even during its building and early use, massive whitewing flights occurred at this point daily. Tens of thousands of birds flew out of the forests of huge and venerable mesquites into the surrounding deserts to feed on cactus fruits and drink at remote springs.

It is interesting to imagine that the rugged fathers and their native Indian followers, who built San Xavier with the most primitive tools—fashioning its massive carved mesquite doors and altar and painting its murals with dyes gathered from the surrounding desert—watched those unbelievably abundant flights almost in awe. Undoubtedly the swift desert doves were also a staple of their diet. For modern hunters, the white-winged dove is a one-of-a-kind gunning experience that should not be missed.

4

The Most Elegant Pigeon

The small pond was delightfully lost somewhere off an unmarked trail in the uninhabited wilderness of the Coconino National Forest, between the highway fork of Clints Well and Winslow, Arizona. Awesomely tall pines mixed with oaks brightly dressed for fall ringed the pond and marched over the high mountain ridges below which it lay.

As I came to the edge of the water, I swept a glance across the surrounding forest and noted a deep saddle that gouged the ridge to the west, and another one to the east, both possibly a quarter-mile distant. Just right, I decided. Abundant food, water, and favorite flyways.

There were elk tracks imprinted in the soft earth around the pond, and like a dolt I was studying those when the birds came in. I shouldn't say they *came* in—that's too weak a word. I glimpsed the movement out

of the tail of my eye and jerked my head erect. They *hurtled* in like missiles through the saddle to the west, possibly 30 of them, limned against the vivid blue of the sky. They shot down steeply toward the pond, and before I could react they were overhead, swirling in a stunningly beautiful maneuver to bank and circle the pond, then rising and turning so sharply there was a multiple clap of wings—and off they went through the far saddle to the east.

Band-tailed pigeons! I stood with my mouth open. Trembling. Feeling foolish. Irked and embarrassed. I had driven a thousand miles for this—well, not really for this. I was supposed to have made the long trip to shoot bandtails, and here I stood, caught with my gun and my guard down while I looked at a scattering of elk tracks. Then the birds suddenly reappeared, sizzling in from the east, the morning sun

During banding operation in Arizona, a trapped and banded pigeon is about to be released.

and then somehow, my cheek having been belted from the near-vertical angle of the shot, I managed to calm down.

"They're too far," I thought with a mental groan. But I pulled above a rising bird anyway until I could see ample sky and touched off. The pigeon cartwheeled and plummeted, feathering an oak branch and bringing a flutter of yellow leaves down with it to the forest floor.

Quickly marking the tree, I ran over and presently had the handsome creature, an adult male, in my hands. Without even thinking about others that might come in, I sat on a log and looked at it, turning it so that the light touched and flashed from the iridescent and subtle greens of the neck nape and from the pale mulberry mauve of the head, throat, and breast. I ruffled the crescent slash of white across the back of the neck just above the nape, touched the yellow feet and the yellow, black-tipped bill. The eye, I reflected, was not really at all as the books usually describe it. It was a bright orange-red, with a yellow center and dark pupil, not simply yellow.

I smoothed the gray-blue back with its quiet touches of browns, and spread the tail from which the bird acquired its name. Some say that the end of the tail has a wide gray band. Others say that the gray portion is separated from the bluish upper portion by a narrower black band. Regardless, the banded tail, whichever band you wish to designate—it's present also on the moderately smaller and somewhat less colorful female—is this pigeon's identifying banner.

As I looked at the bird, I decided that only one word properly describes the smooth, tasteful design and coloring of this bird: *elegant*—the most elegant pigeon. The fact that it is also basically a bird of the western big-forest wilderness—except where man's crops temporarily tempt it to

spilling off their long wings as the flock wheeled almost as one, lowering, heading to sweep in an arc to match the curve of the water's edge, directly over me.

I was conscious of swinging up my shotgun, selecting a bird and trying to get out ahead of it. I was also conscious suddenly of the fact that I was gripping the gun as though I intended to bend it into the proper lead, and in my haste and anxiety I amateurishly jerked the trigger. The birds flared at the burst of sound, untouched, forage—lends it an aura of primitive mystery that is immensely appealing.

For a moment I was taken back to the first bandtail I had ever seen, as a youngster, on a trip with my father to Oregon. And how I had vowed that someday I would follow this wild pigeon on its migrations and see it and hunt it at home in other places. Well, that I had done. I was remembering flights of bandtails in the pine-oak highlands of the Sierra Madre in Mexico, and I chuckled to recall a certain group of bandtails that had led me astray in New Mexico.

I was directing and scripting a TV trout-fishing film, on location far back on the Costilla River in northern New Mexico. I saw a small bandtail flock course down the valley and alight on a high, timbered ridge beside it. I eagerly splashed out of the stream, seized a long-lens camera, and raced for the ridge, stumbling in my hip boots. Climbing that slope with those boots on wasn't easy. I crawled, I sneaked, I bumbled. I laid my $40 western hat on the ground so I could better make my stalk. I got the pictures, too. And that night there was a deluge. Next day I discovered that my hip boots had holes punched in them. And my fine hat? Still up on the ridge, soaked to a cow-pie-flat blob, I discovered, when I remembered and climbed up to retrieve it.

As I stowed that first Arizona bird and went back to my stand by the pond, I recalled that nobody in New Mexico had seemed excited about those pigeons. Nor have very many hunters shown enthusiasm for the bandtail during the years since 1968 that it has been legal game in the Southwest. And that is unfortunate for all those who either aren't aware of the bandtail seasons there or else have shrugged them off as not worthwhile. This wild pigeon is without question one of the most dynamic and sporting of upland and migratory game-birds. The band-tailed pigeon requires craft and diligence to find and offers some of the most sporty, difficult, and unusual wing-shooting in America.

To be sure, bird hunters along the Pacific Coast have long made their annual bandtail pilgrimages. Band-tailed pigeons are usually plentiful there, and in most seasons the three coastal states account for a kill of perhaps a half million birds. That is another story, and an entirely different band-tailed pigeon population. The birds also

Bandtails come in to perch in a tall dead tree beside a pond. Dirt around the pond is salty, from salt blocks put out for cattle. The birds eat the dirt to get the salt.

sustain a separate and substantial nesting and migratory population in the mountains of Colorado, Utah, New Mexico, and Arizona. For a good many years, up through most of the 1940s, bandtails were hunted there. Then the season was closed to give the modest population full protection, and it remained closed for 20 years.

In the '60s Arizona decided there were enough birds available for hunting. They started pressing for a regional season. New Mexico was only lukewarm at the time. However, in 1967 Arizona began a trapping and banding study program; then

The tail shows how the name "band-tailed pigeon" originated.

game-department personnel from the four states met to discuss a cooperative study project to establish the true population status of the wild pigeons in the Rockies flock. In the fall of 1968 an experimental season was allowed in both New Mexico and Arizona, and New Mexico also launched a banding program. Later the season and the study were enlarged to include Colorado and Utah.

A friend of mine with the U.S. Fish & Wildlife Service who was involved in the study work in Arizona had pointed me to the forest pond. It proved to be an excellent location. It had been used by cattle grazing on the forest lands, and for that reason salt had at one time been placed beside it. The salt had leached into the dirt around the water. One of the first rules to be learned about searching for bandtail concentrations in a forest area is that the birds are exceedingly fond of salt, as are all doves and pigeons.

Some of the most successful trapping and banding—and hunting—has been done at sites of saline springs and seeps. The previous day, we had discovered such a seep. There was enough water to drink, but the birds apparently had been coming into the place in a small forest valley primarily to pick at the salty mud. At that location, also in the Coconino National Forest, a fine flight of birds had sliced in, making several periodic passes that offered us heady shooting. One of our hunters that day had his dog along to retrieve birds. Watching the work of the excellent little dog was almost as enjoyable as the shooting.

The limit, when I made that particular hunt, was five birds daily, 10 in possession after the first day. I hate to admit that even with ample opportunity at the saline seep I failed to collect a limit. I hate even more to admit the amount of shooting I did. I sure

Bandtails feeding on piñon mast in New Mexico. Note the bird silhouetted on the ground, another in flight. Acorns are one of the main diet items in fall, but the pigeons also feed on berries and even raid domestic fruit orchards.

didn't give the dog much retrieving practice! Regardless, the passes of the bird were thrilling. They habitually fly through saddles in mountain ridges. One of our hunters climbed up and took a stand in a saddle above the seep. His gun kept booming steadily. Presently it ceased. He came down, grinning, limited out.

Because five hunters all told had been shooting the salt spring, a partner and I decided next day to rest it and try a new location. That's when we ferreted out the forest pond. After my first kill I hunkered down and waited for more birds—or the same flock—to appear. I suspected they

wanted to come down to drink, and to consume the salty dirt. If undisturbed, bandtails will gather at a source of water, or of water and salt, after dawn feeding. The first birds in will alight in a dead snag, if one is available. As others gather, small groups fly down to lower trees, and finally to the salt and then to water. After this routine, they fly off to perch and rest, then repeat later in the day.

Without question there is easier shooting, often larger concentrations, and less difficulty in locating birds if you go the route of shooting over or near cultivated forage. Migrating birds often gather in swarms wherever grain fields have been cut near the foothills that hold pigeons, or where orchards of fruit such as cherries are available, as in California, or around truck gardens such as the pea fields on Whidbey Island in Washington.

Landowners invariably are aware of the flocks, and often irritated by them. Hunting permission is seldom difficult to obtain. Or, a good stand for pass-shooting can be found where the birds move from resting and roosting areas in the tall timber to valley feeding fields. Even wild forage attracts and holds large gatherings occasionally, if the feed is abundant and concentrated over a modest-sized area. For example, stands of pinyon heavy with nuts draw birds. Oak mast is a staple food.

The problem with oak, however, is that it is usually available over vast expanses of bandtail habitat, making bird concentrations unpredictable. Nonetheless, a stand of oak that bears heavily may get special attention. But you must keep in mind that the bandtail, like the mourning dove, is an extremely mobile bird. It may shift forest feeding sites often. A flight of 10 miles to feed is no strain. Wild berries as well as tame ones draw birds, although in fall seasons, which usually are set in September or early October, some wild berry crops may be depleted. Chokecherries, elderberries, and cascara, all favorites, may be available.

Although I'll grant that the drama of shooting a grain field to which scads of pigeons flock is strong tonic, my own pref-

Hunters show excitement as a bandtail crosses within range. These birds are exceedingly swift, strong flyers, among the most difficult of targets.

erence is for forest shooting. The bandtail is by nature a wide-roaming bird of the true wilderness, a personality of the vast mountain distances and pine-forest fastnesses. In those settings it is at its most appealing, presenting its most sporting qualities. That is why I have a fixation on the southwestern shooting. To be sure, there are a few places even there—in northern New Mexico, for example—where flocks come to domestic feed, but unlike some West Coast bandtail hunting, you shoot mostly in the hush of the mountain forest, where the bandtail truly belongs.

We had decided to concentrate chiefly on waterholes, because food was almost literally everywhere in the form of acorns. Every bird shot had its crop stuffed with them. I recall reading with amusement several times that bandtails feeding on acorns were not fit to eat, because the flesh took on a bitter hint of tannic acid. Possibly. I suspect, however, this was just a tale passed around by people who'd never eaten any but had heard it from "an old-timer" who knew about such things. I've never eaten an acorn-fed bandtail yet that was anything but delicious.

At any rate, we knew that in the high forests water is not to be had just anywhere. We also knew that the bandtail is selective about watering places. Unless water is exceedingly scarce—in which case the mobile birds can simply drift on—they seldom select clear streams, lakes, or ponds. All doves and pigeons are fond of muddy water, often still and stagnant, and of saline seeps and springs. Bandtails will pass up crystal water to swarm to a muddy puddle with a soft mud bank. Like others of the family, they drink continuously with head down and bill in the water, not tilting the head up and back as most others birds do to let a billful run down the throat.

The pond with the elk tracks around it was perfect. I watched several birds, two to a half-dozen at a time, swing over the surrounding forest and alight in trees. This, I reflected, would be a great place to try decoys. An acquaintance in Oregon tells me he makes bandtail decoys out of cork, and that they work very well.

I could hear my companion occasionally booming away farther back in the forest. I, too, moved away, thinking perhaps the big flocks wanted to come in to water and I was inhibiting them.

It proved a good scheme. A large band coursed through the eastern saddle and sliced at smoking wingspeed over the pond. I made no attempt to fire when they came into range, so as not to spook away so many. But when they had passed on behind the far mountain, a pair of birds came lilting in, drifting lazily—for bandtails. Standing motionless, back against a big oak, I let them come head on toward me. When they presented a perfect target framed momentarily in a sky-filled hole through an opening among the trees, I swung to blot out the first bird and fired. Swiftly I turned to take a going-away try at the other, hearing the first one plop upon the leaves behind me. But No. 2 was screened now by branches, offering no target.

For some years, a special permit has been required in addition to the hunting license in the southwestern mountain states. It is free, obtainable as a rule from any game-department office. The purpose of the permit is to give biologists a chance to tally hunter participation and kill. Only certain specified portions of each state may be open, so hunters must check carefully.

When the next pigeons appeared, I dropped a brace out of a trio flying together. Swinging broadside on them, I fired three times, thinking one bird better than I shot. But two were a thrill—and more so when I picked them up. Each wore a leg band. I knew banding had been done somewhere in this general region earlier, but what a coincidence—two out of three and both banded. Naturally I wondered if the third had also carried a band.

I had made a trip earlier with a pair of game-department pigeon trappers, far back in the wilderness of the Apache Indian Reservation south of Show Low, over 100 miles from my present location. I had shared with them the exasperations of lying endlessly in wait, hidden near a salt lick beside a pond. They had set up a cannon net with a remote detonator. We watched birds fly down, but then flush nervously when an Abert squirrel ran across the area before the net could be fired. Later we had counted 40-plus birds on the ground, well within net range, and in elation congratulated ourselves—but when the electric contact was made, nothing happened. There was a short in the detonator connection.

Eventually we did gather several dozen birds, and the biologists banded them. I came away from that interesting experience with new respect for the field work of biologists. Setting a cannon net for wild pigeons in the middle of a vast forest and waiting for birds to come precisely where you want them in order to boom the net over them is to say the least a game for gamblers with stoic dispositions. However, from diligent trapping, banding, and return of bands by hunters, much has been learned about the movements, habits, and numbers of the pigeons. The study resulted in continuing seasons.

One important rule of bandtail hunting I had learned from West Coast experience was not to go undergunned, particularly in forest hunting, where you must put birds down for keeps if you hope to find them. Anyone who has ever tried shooting semi-

wild "barn" pigeons knows those birds are tough. An adult bandtail is as large as the domestic kind, and somewhat tougher because of its wholly wild existence and long flights.

The adult bandtail weighs about three-fourths of a pound, with some males close to a pound. Overall length may be as much as 16 inches, with wingspan approximately the same. I was shooting a full-choke 20 gauge, using high-base No. 6 shot. Actually, for this work I prefer a 12 gauge with high-brass shells in either No. 6 or No. 7½. I have found that pigeons of this general size, all strong fliers, require plenty of punch. The modified barrel is all right, but numerous shots are certain to be long, and the full choke in my estimation is better.

My last shot proved that point well. With one bird to go for my five-pigeon limit, I strolled slowly through the timber, circling the pond. I could hear the booming owl-hoot-like calls of two or three birds up on the ridge. Then there was a sudden sharp clap of wings above me. I had startled an unseen perching bird. Often when they take wing, the first deep stroke slaps the flight feathers of wings sharply together, perhaps as a "flush" signal to others. The bird revved up instantly to high speed, heading toward the eastern saddle. Then it changed direction and flew to my right down the pond, circling.

From down there somewhere another bird arose to join it. The two wheeled far over the valley to the south and then turned back. They appeared to be coming in a continuing circle right toward me. By the time they came into range they were really smoking, almost as if this was a speed contest between them. I swung on the lead pigeon and managed to get ahead of it in what I felt was perfect execution. But the shot was a clear miss.

Exasperated, I turned and quickly got my

feet placed, determined to try again. This time the rear bird was clearly the only possible chance. It appeared to be a straightaway level-flight shot. I got on its tail, dropped the barrel to show light below the bird so I could send the charge under it and hope to intercept flight and shot lines out ahead. Somehow the scheme jelled. The bird folded at what I guessed to be an honest 45-plus yards.

I smoothed feathers on my birds, laid them on a rock surrounded by fall-colored scrub oak, and photographed them. The elegant pigeon, I thought. An experience in the Southwest and also along the Pacific Coast that is savored by too few. Later I plucked and quickly seared the birds, then gently allowed them to simmer until they were squab-tender. The same word, I reflected as I sampled them, applies to the bandtail as table fare. Elegant indeed!

5

Paloma Morada

The trees along the river were startlingly large, towering above the matted thorn, but they dwindled quickly to low jungle growth in the arid soil stretching away from the rushing stream. Through this jungle, tough Mexican cattle had cut a maze of permanent trails and openings, and it was in one of these that we had camped. Along here, a Mexican had told us, we'd find *paloma morada*, literally the mulberry-colored pigeon.

We had made camp just at dusk so we'd be awake and ready when the flight started, and now I put the coffee on. The Mexican, whose thatch-roofed shack slumped beside the trail a couple of hundred yards away, must have smelled it, for as it came to a full boil he appeared out of the dawn dimness and without a word hunkered down beside the fire.

One of my Texan partners grinned at him and said, "Bueno."

His face was impassive. "Bueno."

That single word sometimes does service as "hello," "goodby," "okay," and "good." I was about to utter it too when from down by the river there came a deep, booming *coo*, a sound that seemed to fill the trees. Then there was a chorus of *coos* along the stream.

I looked at the Mexican. "Paloma morada?" I asked.

"Sí."

I quickly stepped to the jeep, got my gun, and loaded it. The two Texas-rancher sportsmen with me did likewise. Now hundreds of yellow-headed parrots in the big trees by the river let go with their dawn serenade. Then there was a sudden, sharp clap of wings at the river. That was the signal we'd been listening for. The beautiful

The red-billed pigeon is a native of Mexico but appears occasionally along the Rio Grande River on the Texas side of the border. It is a handsome bird.

bird that ornithologists call the red-billed pigeon was awing.

The swift shapes of the pigeons were dark against the dawn sky, sweeping high above the thorn jungle, coming straight toward us. They were the size and build of barn or park pigeons in the U.S. They side-slipped, swerved, and dipped with that characteristic dove-pigeon flight that makes all the tribe such difficult targets. As they approached, we stepped out and swung our guns.

I tried to swing fast enough to catch up with a group of six. Their speed fooled me; it was most deceptive. They appeared to be lilting along without effort. I shot behind and tried again, only to see the birds keep right on. Then I heard the others shooting and saw the birds racing away out of sight. I picked a single and missed again. Suddenly we were all frantically reloading.

The sky was momentarily empty. I glanced at the Mexican. He was grinning. It half annoyed me. Still, I couldn't blame him. Nine shots among us—and not a feather.

"Cafe?" he asked. He was not in the least interested in our hunting.

I nodded and motioned him to the cups and the coffeepot. As he rose to pour himself some, I saw another group of pigeons coming. This time, at my first shot, I was gratified to see a bird tumble. I had got their number—maybe. Out of the tail of my eye I saw one dropping above the Texans and then two more. But I had lost all notion of shooting again. I was running to pick up my bird, the first red-billed pigeon I'd ever shot or even seen close up.

It was a beautiful bird, plump and compact, yet gracefully and smoothly fashioned. It appeared to me to be a little heavier than the average semidomestic pigeon in the U.S. The sun, now breaking over the low jungle, struck my prize, and the wines, mauves, deep blues, purples, violets, and varied iridescences of the feathers made a beautiful display. I noticed immediately the startling color of the iris of the eye. It was bright red-orange, with a scarlet circle around it and a dark pupil. The base of the rather large bill was scarlet, and the legs and feet a deep red-pink.

Behind me one of the boys ribbed, "You come all this distance just to shoot *one?*"

Their guns began to boom again, so I put down my bird. The sky was full of pigeons, all of them in sizzling flight, hurtling like jets across the sunrise.

We shot steadily now, none of us doing very well. Soon I was through almost a box of shells. By the time I trotted to the jeep and got more ammunition, not a bird was in the sky. The morning flight from the roost was over.

The sun, though barely up, was already hot. We gave the Mexican several birds and quickly cleaned the rest. Traveling light and without refrigeration, we had to eat our game as we killed it. We washed the birds in carefully hoarded "good" water, then rolled them in flour, salt, and pepper, seared them in hot grease, added water, turned the camp-stove fire low, and covered the big skillet. We had been told that quite often the redbills are tough, possibly because a hunter cannot select only young birds. After a breakfast of eggs and canned sausage, we fished and scouted around a couple of hours while the birds gently simmered. The morning seemed quite satisfactory.

We had left Texas three days earlier for this pigeon shoot. Because we went into Mexico not knowing just where we'd find our targets, it had taken us three days to get operating. One day had been spent traveling only 50 miles. At that time, even via

four-wheel-drive jeep, you did not move far or fast over some of the trails that probe into the thorn jungle of the vast area between Victoria and the Gulf. Along the coast almost all the way from Matamoros to Tampico, there were only occasional mud-hut settlements. It was while traveling this desolate route that we'd seen, in the distance, what looked like wild pigeons flying. We turned in their direction and presently found the big river on which we were camped, and our new Mexican friend.

Now, prowling along the river and fishing, we saw small bands of pigeons intermittently skyrocketing over the towering trees. We hurried back to camp for our guns. I needn't have bothered. By the time I would sight a flock above the trees, I couldn't swing fast enough to get in a shot before they'd be out of range or sight.

Then a small group swung over the river, hurtling downstream. This was better. I caught them precisely on the turn and managed to drop one onto the gravel—the gravel on the other side of the river. Next I saw a fluke shot I still don't believe. One of the Texans shot twice at a group of six pigeons, missing both times. With one more shell in the gun, he fired a final wild shot as a gesture of disgust.

By then the birds were not only across the river but beyond the first of the tall trees. I figured they were somewhere between 75 and 85 yards away. So we all stood gawking as a bird peeled off and went spinning down into the jungle.

We were determined to get the two dead birds. Perhaps I should draw the curtain on what followed. Against the dawn chill, I was wearing light longjohns. My Texas buddies were not. Now, as the long-range man and I prepared to wade the river, I had to strip from the waist down, whereas he could wear his shorts. Carrying our boots, we started across. Behind us we heard chuckling and shutter-clicking.

We got across, found the two birds, and started back. I fought the current and the harsh stones of the bottom while carrying boots, pants, and bird—and trying to achieve some modesty in the face of the camera. The Texans thought it hilarious. The long-shot bird, incidentally, had been struck by only one pellet. The photo, I found out later, had been printed and sent to numerous magazine editors of mine!

The birds had apparently fed out over the thinner jungle and were now returning in scattered numbers to settle among the stream-course trees during the midday. The sun was really hot. Not all the pigeons selected high, leafy trees. Many of them perched singly, a few minutes at a time, atop a small bush or on a low limb of a scrub. Here and there one even alighted on the ground. Others, as is usual among doves and pigeons, made straight for bare, dead stubs and perched on them, sometimes in fair-sized groups. I noticed that flying pigeons, seeing the perching birds, decoyed readily. I believe some of the oversized full-bodied mourning-dove decoys used in the States would bring these redbills in nicely.

We tried stalking the perched birds, both with shotguns and a .22. They were exceedingly difficult to approach. A few gave us some shooting with the little rifle, but we never succeeded in getting within shotgun range—at least we weren't successful in collecting any as they flushed. They'd drop off a limb and then swoop up as their wings caught air—a trick that made them tough targets. The real sport, of course, was to get under a flight, as we had at dawn. We were to learn more of this on another day.

We took our jump-shot pigeons to the Mexican's hut and gave them to his wife and cluster of children. They smiled and

Like all doves and pigeons, the redbills love to perch in dead trees. Scanning old snags like this is a good way to locate flocks.

gabbled happily. Then we hunted some camp shade and made the usual tick inspection. Ticks are one of the hazards of this area; the thorn jungle is alive with them. The cattle ticks are bad enough, and one should spray constantly against them and make thorough inspections. The real menace, though, lies in the clusters of tiny seed ticks that fall from bushes onto one's clothing. They spread swiftly over the body. Even the natives fear them. About the only preventive is to watch for a gob of them dropping on a sleeve or pants leg and instantly brush them off.

Aside from ticks and snakes, there is little to harm a person in this jungle. It pays to take along snakebite kits and to be careful. We killed a few very large rattlers. But usually the weather is so chilly in midwinter—at least during the night and at both ends of the day—that few snakes are crawling.

If you go on a pigeon hunt in eastern Mexico in winter, take warm clothing, as well as the average-weight stuff. And rainwear, too. If you're on jungle trails, be prepared to get out fast when the rains come, for much of the area—even many miles inland from the coast—may become a bog. The word is, "When the first raindrop hits—git!"

For the adventuresome gunner who wants to go on his own, a 4WD vehicle is practically mandatory. For others, guided package hunts can be arranged. That's the sensible route to take. Getting guns and ammunition into Mexico, buying licenses, and understanding the often vague game laws, as well as U.S. game import laws, is too often a welter of endless red tape. There are several clubs or resorts operated by U.S. citizens in the pigeon country, as well as guides along the border who will make all arrangements, acquire licenses, and furnish transport. Obviously, these ser-

vices change from time to time. Contacts with Chambers of Commerce on the U.S. side of the border in cities from McAllen to Brownsville, Texas, will be helpful in locating current ones. So will contacts with local Texas game wardens. Most experienced hunters claim that December is a top month for this shooting.

The Mexican states of Tamaulipas and Nuevo Leon are both within easy range of the Texas border, and both are within prime red-billed pigeon habitat. First-timers shouldn't be confused if they hear Texans refer to these birds as "bluerocks," or speak of going into Mexico for "bluerock shooting."

This term, though few Texans are aware of it, originated centuries ago with the blue rock pigeons native to the coast of Wales, which nest on the Welsh seaside cliffs. The same name was brought to America in Colonial days, and referred to the blue-colored common domestic pigeons the colonists brought with them. Eventually these pigeons, of mixed breeding, became the common semi-wild barn and city pigeons of today. Red-billed pigeons occasionally are seen on the Texas side of the border, and are invariably referred to as "bluerocks," even though that is a misnomer.

We drifted on down the wild coast, looking over the possibilities. We had a boat with us and, taking our guns, made a run up one of the rivers. We got shooting that was unusual. We'd fish until a flock of pigeons came racing across the river. Then we'd reel up, gun the motor, and try to get near enough for shots. Or we'd sit tight and wait for them to come within range.

None of the coastal area was as good as the region inland and farther up the rivers. So we took a new trail and headed back. The first morning we awoke to an awful

Shooting a pass near the Rio Soto la Marina in Tamaulipas State, Mexico, I bring down a redbill. They are among the most beautiful of the wild pigeons.

clatter of parrots. They are great pests to growers of crops, and the Mexicans beg hunters to shoot them.

A middle-aged Mexican came along the sand trail near our camp, greeted us, saw our shotguns, and motioned to the flying horde of yellow-headed parrots, as if he was shooting.

"*Buena comida*," he said. "Good eating."

They were tricky targets, faster than they looked. We dropped several as he watched. They're beautiful birds, mostly green, with bluish wing tips, and several scarlet feathers on the shoulders and wing surfaces and bordering the tail. The head is yellow.

We indicated to the Mexican that he could have the ones we'd shot. He smiled. "*Papagayo.*" he called them. He also used a word that sounded as though it might be spelled "*parrico*" as he felt the end of the breastbone of one old parrot, and then smiled as he tested other breastbones and called these "*parraquito*" – young parrots. Tender ones.

While we were engrossed with the parrots, there was a sudden rush of wings to the left. A group of redbills came swirling in and settled in a tall tree. Over near the trail another group braked to a stop and alighted upon a branching dead stub. Then suddenly the sky was full of pigeons. I knew I should have been taking pictures, but I forgot the cameras as we rummaged frantically for more shells. Then we hunkered back at the edges of various brush clumps and started shooting.

We were all getting a bit better at it now. Also, many of the birds swept low above the thornbrush. Their speed was still awesomely swift, and their effortless flight deceiving. Each bird swerved and sideslipped as it bored along. Those that saw us either flared wildly or, if at a distance, simply drifted imperceptibly out of range. Nonetheless we accounted for one here and there.

Now two Mexicans appeared. They have a way of emerging from seemingly no-where. They scurried around collecting downed birds. What I did not realize was that the Mexicans' fingers were flying, for they were plucking birds as fast as they found them. Then they'd run a thumb under the lower end of the breast, break the body cavity open, and, in one strike, clean the plucked bird.

Eventually the main flight subsided, and none of us wanted to bother with stragglers. After all, we had some heavy eating to do, besides sharing with the Mexicans who had picked up for us. We counted up and were still shy a limit, but it didn't matter. It had been a good shoot, a good trip, and the game was well worth the effort. Paloma morada, I had decided, is one of the sportiest birds on the continent.

Part II

THE QUAIL

This country is richer in quail varieties than is any other nation. Quail are actually diminutive members of the large and extremely diverse non-migratory pheasant family, which even includes domestic chickens. A quail smaller than the bobwhite, common in Europe and often called the migratory quail, is one of the very few family members that does migrate. At one time in the Mediterranean region these birds were caught in nets during their southern migration, and marketed. This is the same quail, the Coturnix (or a close relative), that was stocked numerous times in the U.S. The idea didn't work. The bird just wouldn't stay put.

When the word "quail" is used in the U.S., most hunters think of the bobwhite. No doubt this is because the bob, in the past and presently, always has had the broadest range of any American quail. Natively it blankets more than half of the U.S. from east to west. It is missing only in the northern extremes of that vast region.

Although the bobwhite's range is im-

mense, it is fair to say that in tradition and hunting importance, this quail has always been considered chiefly a southern bird. There it has always been especially numerous. In early days the bob was called a "partridge" throughout the South. A few older hunters still stick with that quaint name. For many years "bird dogs" were virtually synonymous with bobwhite quail dogs. Still today, when one speaks of "bird hunting" to any southerner, the inference is that this means bobwhite quail hunting. Even worse, you don't need to qualify it with the word "bobwhite." What other quail are there?

There are quite a few. There are six species abundant enough to be annually huntable at least in most of their ranges. When you begin to count subspecies, the numbers zoom. I don't suppose one in 100 bobwhite hunters would be able to differentiate positively among the half dozen or more subspecies of that bird within the U.S. Others occur southward throughout Mexico and Central America, 20-plus in all. In Texas alone there are three different bobwhite subspecies—the Texas, Plains, and Interior races.

However, quail transplants and releases from game farms and shooting preserves have rather thoroughly mixed up the bobwhite varieties. Identification of each is not especially important to the hunter anyway, although some might not agree. When Texas bobwhites were introduced some years ago into Georgia and other southern states, where they were often referred to as "Mexican quail," dedicated quail hunters wanted nothing to do with them. They were, it was said, runners, and besides, they were runty and no-account. Texans don't agree, but then, quail hunters with a fix on their local birds are an opinionated lot.

Bobwhite hunters' cranky opinions indicate how important the bob has always been on the American gunning scene since the days of the Colonists. No one knows how many bobwhites go into the annual bag. It is probably a figure somewhere in the 20 millions. Even so, over much of their range today bobwhites have difficulties. Most are caused by habitat loss and changes. Undoubtedly there'll be excellent bobwhite hunting ahead for many years. But the birds will need constant help and careful management.

One bobwhite that has been getting a lot of that is a variety many quail hunters are not even aware of and, it's safe to say, few will ever see. This is the masked bobwhite. When the Spanish were first in what is now Arizona several centuries ago, the masked bobwhite was an abundant bird of the southern border grasslands. It teemed in similar country of northern Mexico, and indeed still survives there in remnant coveys. Changes in land use and overgrazing decimated much of the masked bobwhite range. It was placed on the endangered species list in 1969.

I have a color photo of a male masked bobwhite, part of a group discovered and trapped in Mexico some years ago for U.S. reestablishment purposes. You would hardly believe it is a variety of bobwhite. The head is black. The breast and flanks appear much the color of the breast of a robin. The back is black and brown with light speckles.

Much effort and money have been poured into attempts to bring this handsome bird back to relative—even huntable—abundance. Recently a 21,000-acre ranch near Tucson was purchased by the U.S. Fish & Wildlife Service as a refuge for these quail. An additional 90,000 acres of state land adjoins. Masked bobwhites have been reared captively by the Service for at least two decades. Some of these will form the basis for what is hoped will be a wild, self-sustaining population. Whether masked bobwhites will ever be hunted again is questionable.

Other western quail—tough birds all, some of them dwellers in patches of the country's least hospitable terrain—all appear to be doing well. Among these are several of our most beautiful game birds. Western bird hunters have often resented the fact that their favorites receive so little positive publicity and are so routinely downgraded by eastern hunters, particularly bobwhite hunters. These several quail species are commonly lumped together and tagged derogatorily as "the running quails."

In truth, the term is not wholly undeserved. Blue or scaled quail, that name deriving from the dark-scalloped feather edges that give them a scaled appearance, certainly deserve the name, although they can be grand flyers when they take the notion. Most of the scaled quail population is in western Texas, New Mexico, and eastern Arizona. Fringe populations appear in the Oklahoma Panhandle and southwestern

Colorado. They've been transplanted with no great success elsewhere in the West.

Plumed Gambel's quail headquarter in southwestern New Mexico and southeastern Arizona, with spillover into adjoining states. These tough and beautiful desert birds make do at times in some of the most barren terrain imaginable. As long as it remains so uninviting to developers, the birds will probably continue to frustrate hunters. California quail, sometimes called valley quail, appear at a cursory glance much like the Gambel's, but close inspection shows distinctive differences in color patterns. California quail are abundant all along the West Coast and also in eastern Oregon and Washington and in parts of Idaho and Utah. These two quail are *the* important quail species over most of the quail range of the West, replaced in importance by the blue only in New Mexico and Texas.

Intermingled over California quail range, but usually in quite different terrain and cover, is the country's largest species, the mountain quail. Oddly, this tall-plumed, exceedingly sporty bird gets so little hunter attention over most of its range that often hunters who've lived nearby all their lives have never shot or even seen it. It is one of the most strikingly handsome—and often to the hunter exasperating—of all American game birds. One of its curious traits is that in certain parts of its range it makes vertical seasonal migrations. During summer it stays on the mountain slopes; when oncoming winter gives it a gentle hint, it moves down into the foothills. The trek is casually slow, and afoot. Some mountain quail groups have been known to stroll as much as 25 to 30 miles in fall and spring.

Last and least known of the hunted U.S. quail species is the Mearns or Harlequin quail. This comical little bird is the most quirky of all our quail varieties, and also

the most restricted in its huntable U.S. range. There are a few in western Texas, and a few more in southwestern New Mexico. The most abundant birds, and the only one presently on the hunting list, are those in southeastern Arizona.

Male Mearns remind me of miniature guinea fowl. Their white-speckled sides and dumpy appearance, enhanced by the short tail, set them apart from any other U.S. quail species. The female is quite different, pale pinkish buff and brown. The white and black face mask of the male sparked the name "Harlequin" quail.

This bird has long been called "fool" quail. The late Jack O'Connor, renowned outdoor writer, claimed to have picked one up in his hand. My introduction to the Mearns came after it had been hunted a few seasons in Arizona. I suspect from my experience with it that anyone who approaches a Mearns hunt thinking of this as a "fool" quail may come away finding the real fool in the mirror. Though hunted by few, mostly locals, the Mearns quail is in my opinion just possibly the sportiest of all U.S. quail.

It is interesting that birds the size of quail quickly became the most important and most loved, and indeed most hunted, of the gallinaceous or chicken-like birds of this continent. Part of their popularity, of course, is due to the sit-tight qualities of bobwhites, especially before a hunting dog, and the same trait among the so-called running quail of the West, once a covey has been scattered. Part also stems from their direct but swift flight. Quail are shotgun targets one thinks of as being—well—proper, dignified, predictable, yet with a whole lot of space to shoot into around each. They are also, all of them, simply superb hunt climaxes when they appear before hungry shotgunners on a table.

6

Upland Classic – the Bobwhite

The pointer, Doc, was a mean and independent one, old and crotchety, and scarred from fighting with other dogs in the kennel. He was also tough and so long-experienced that it was halfway annoying to hunt with him. He knew everything.

We had just shot, both Gene Burke and I, at a single bobwhite and had seen it scale down but weren't certain of its fate. The dog made no move whatever to retrieve it, so Gene said, "Dead bird."

Doc sat on his rump and turned his head away. He wouldn't look at us.

Burke, who often borrowed and worked out Doc and other dogs from the local sheriff's big kennel and thus knew the old pointer well, muttered and said sharply, "Find that dead bird, you cantankerous old devil!"

Doc got up and wandered off, made a disinterested, cursory round, and came back and sat down, head again turned away. What he was saying was: "There isn't any dead bird, you dumbbells. You both missed that single."

As Burke kept browbeating him, the dog presently arose and walked away. Shortly he was swinging wide out in the grass and gallberrry bushes along the edge of a stand of Georgia pine, continuing the hunt. "I guess you can see who's running this hunt," Burke chuckled. The younger dogs, two setters and a pointer, flanked Doc, waiting for him to find scent. Then they'd back him and do whatever he did. Doc *knew*.

This hunt took place in southern Georgia almost 40 years ago. I was experiencing some of my first southern bobwhite hunting then – what residents would have called *"authentic* bird hunting." The bobwhite everywhere throughout its large range is unquestionably the classic American game

Male bobwhite perches on a fencepost, acting as sentry while the remainder of the covey feeds nearby.

bird. But in the South, where the bob since early settlement has been the epitome of hunting tradition, it has significance akin to hard-shell religion.

I recall with amusement an old gentleman from Albany, Georgia, telling me, "Certainly there is excellent bobwhite hunting in many states. Why, even the Yankees have some. Here in the South, however, is the only place where quail hunting's done *right*."

It's difficult not to agree. I've been on southern quail hunts during which several of us rode on a mule-drawn wagon driven by a black sharecropper who had trained the dogs. They worked ahead, and he called to them to keep them swinging where he wanted them. When they stiffened and set up, we'd get down and move in, while he held the mule and offered advice. Other hunts were even fancier, the hunters riding in a 4WD vehicle, with dog handlers mounted on high-toned horses. Entire southern plantations for the past hundred years or more have been given

over primarily to raising and managing quail.

Indeed, much of the South is ideal bobwhite habitat. Crop fields with weedy or brushy borders, plus the ever-present stands of pine, create perfect edge cover for quail, which is what they utilize most. On this bright fall morning we had gotten out early, to catch the coveys as they moved out of brushy roosting places to feed in field edges. Here we'd get open shooting. By midmorning they'd have filled their crops and sought water, then drifted back into the edges to dust and rest till midafternoon, when the feeding period would begin again and continue almost into dusk.

Now Doc was stiffened out two shotgun ranges from us, in a patch of grass belly-deep on him. We had to admit grudgingly that Old Doc never lied. The other dogs were uncertainly backing him. Suddenly Doc broke point, circled wide, turned, and came to a tense point again, facing toward us. The covey, he knew, had run. He had craftily circled it and cut it off. The younger dogs kept creeping in now toward the hotseat the birds had left. We walked past them and toward Doc. With a swirling burst of wings, the covey buzzed up in a blizzard.

I was trying to force myself to pick a single bird and stay with it. After pheasants and ruffed grouse earlier that fall in the North, these covey birds were confusing. I wanted to shoot the whole flock with one bang. Most beginning bobwhite hunters have this urge. Some even believe if you shoot into the flock, something is bound to happen. Indeed it is. Seldom will a feather be touched!

Burke calmly downed a quail, swung on a second farther out, and took it, too. The general bobwhite-covey shooting rule is: two successful shots are possible for a precise shooter, but three is stretching it. Bobwhites get up in a rush and usually fly along a fairly predictable getaway route. They do not rise very high in the air, so shooting angles in general are not especially steep. Nevertheless, the birds rev up to full speed swiftly. By the time you get off that second shot, your target is probably traveling 35 to 45 miles an hour. Range lengthens in a hurry. After the speed burst, wings working fast, quail start a long cupped-wing glide to the cover they've aimed for. When the glide starts, they're far out of range.

I managed my first shot as though I knew what I was doing. I got on track with a second bird and touched off, knowing I was stretching. At the shot the quail towered straight up, a sure sign that a single lucky pellet had struck the head. It fell. Old Doc was running and made a bounding grab for it in the air. I moved up and took the bird and started to pat his head.

Burke warned, "Don't do that! Doc hates everybody." Just so. The old dog growled and shifted out from under my hand.

Some of the finest bobwhite shooting is had by following a covey that has been scattered, and hunting the singles. The individual birds usually sit very snug. Whenever possible, they also fly when covey-flushed in the direction of heavy cover. Thus the shooting one gets on singles is often in cover that makes it tricky and difficult. I've followed dogs into pine and palmetto where every rising bird was screened by a grid of trees and chances of hitting one in 10 were slim. Additionally, you never know what direction a flushing single will take in such cover. Now and then one explodes practically in your face and flies back over your head.

On southern lands where quail are meticulously managed, some owners don't favor pursuing singles. You hunt covey rises and leave the scattered birds to regroup without further disturbance. Whichever way it's done, the great joy of bobwhite hunting when, as the old gentleman said, "It's done right" is as much in watching the work of good dogs as in shooting at quail.

Numerous breeds handle bobs well. In southern kennels—I recall hosts I've hunted with who owned a dozen or more dogs—pointers are a majority. Southern hunters favor them for their short hair because weather is hot and burrs don't stick in their coats. Many also claim the pointer, usually a wide-ranging breed, covers more ground in less time and is exceedingly staunch on point. Nonetheless, setters are common in the South, and certain setter strains have been purposely developed for southern quail hunting. The German shorthair also has had spotty southern popularity, and the Brittany, for those who like a close-in worker that's not too fast, makes an excellent bobwhite dog.

Any of the pointing breeds work bobs successfully, mainly because the bobwhite holds so well not only as singles but also in coveys. It's interesting to note that this is one of the few U.S. game birds that can be hunted consistently in true coveys that lie close for pointing dogs. That's another reason for its American classic status.

To some extent, hunters across the enormous range of the bobwhite have selected favorite dog breeds according to the habitat where their hunting is done. Needless to say, it differs widely throughout such a vast sweep of country. On one occasion in the Midwest, I hunted heavy weed cover in large fields, with only spots of edging brush. Don't think bobwhites won't run if they take a notion! They can make good time, and some do, both coveys and singles, in any kind of cover. In this case, it seemed they all ran. The landowner I hunted with used a springer spaniel. We had to trot some of the time to keep up. The dog was

fast, and without its tactic of rushing, I doubt we'd have gotten many quail into the air.

It would hardly seem that a bird as small as the bobwhite, and one with such a delicate, even fragile appearance, could have been so successful a colonizer and so adaptable. Average weight of the bobwhite is only five or six ounces. Undoubtedly the settlement of the country, clearing of land, and planting of crops assisted bobs in spreading their range and becoming more abundant than they were originally. For many years, however, they've been present in a welter of contrasting situations. They live in swampy edges in Florida and other locations in the South. They are the favored game of numerous hunters in crop fields of the Midwest. They manage to cope with severe winters in portions of the

The start of a bobwhite hunt, along the edge of a harvested crop field bordered by woods.

Great Lakes country. They are found in astonishing abundance in some of the most arid, miserable cactus and thornbrush expanses deep into eastern Mexico.

Indeed, they've learned to live in every kind of cover imaginable. Nevertheless, the edges of dense vegetation are always the places bobwhites select. They are not forest birds, except when they dive into wooded terrain to escape. They are not swamp birds, except when a swamp is handy to disappear into when pursued. Bramble patches, weedy margins, and brush near open areas where food is abundant are where bobwhites live.

That food may be of wide variety. In some instances in farm country, it is almost entirely waste grain. Ragweed, wild sunflower, dove weed, and beggarweed are wild favorites. In the South, sorghum, corn, soybeans, and various field peas all furnish high living for certain coveys. Acorns and peanuts seem large portions for quail, but they eagerly manage those, too.

One of the prime reasons the bobwhite became the classic American uplander is that these birds are strictly homebodies. This makes covey location, to one familiar with the hunting ground, fairly predictable. Every bobwhite hunter has heard coveys named for the places where they hang out.

There is the "home covey" that lives within sight of the house and is taboo to shooters. I recall a hunt where the landowner spoke of "the east fence covey," "the back pond covey," "the swale covey," and "the corn patch covey." I once asked a sharecropper on land strange to me in Alabama if he knew where any coveys might be. "A covey's been usin' rat yonder in that pecan bottom serval years," he said, pointing, "an' then there's the clover patch buhds way beyond—big bunch, an' fairly gentle."

Obviously the same pair of bobwhites

doesn't continue to raise a brood year after year at the same location. Studies show that natural attrition, even without hunting, takes upward of 80% of bobwhites annually. Certain progeny raised in a certain area that furnishes needed amounts of food, water, and cover have a home-bailiwick imprint and will replace parents that disappear. Not all can stay at the original homestead, but a dominant pair of offspring will take over, while others, in what is known as the "fall shuffle," will be driven out and will find other places to set up housekeeping.

The heavy annual loss of quail assures that they seldom become overpopulous and crowded. When several seasons occur that are conducive to high survival of young, bobwhites do become temporarily too abundant and saturate their habitat. Inevitably a debacle occurs and a low cycle begins. In the South especially, bobwhite managers strive to avoid these drastic ups and downs, and to keep a stable quail population tailored to the habitat.

Optimum habitat can sustain an astonishing number of bobwhites. On a southern plantation managed for hunting by clients who came from many states for plush hunts, I once rode with the owner, who was proud of his heavy crop. In a single morning he showed me over 50 coveys.

This indicates that each covey of bobs requires only a very modest range. That's another reason the bobwhite is a classic. Not only are the coveys homebodies, but each home is small. On prime grounds, numerous coveys may live out their lives within a single square mile. Under optimum conditions, a covey of bobs may never roam outside an area of 25 acres. Where feeding conditions are somewhat less bountiful, perhaps they'll cover 50 to 100 acres. Seldom do bobwhites range,

For many years "bird dogs" meant quail dogs. The interest in and use of pointers and setters in this country was sparked originally by the bobwhite's abundance, especially in the East and South.

even under severe habitat conditions, over one mile away from where they were hatched.

That is one of the built-in joys of hunting them. Wherever they're known to be present, they're never very difficult to find. The difficulties come later. How can it be, many a bobwhite addict has complained, that a hunter can know in general where the birds are, and his dog can tell him exactly to the square yard where he has them pinned down, but somehow everything comes apart in getting them up before the gun?

In most instances there are simple explanations. How hunters approach a pointed covey holds the secret of success or failure. This is a facet of bobwhite hunting seldom considered. First, the dog owner must

know what his dog's reactions will be. Some dogs are jumpy, too eager. Some are "creepers," edging in. Some are like statues. I've hunted several times behind dogs that were belled, because if one got out of sight in cover and on point, it would stay there as long as the birds held. Some of these extra-staunch dogs are "distant" pointers. They set up the moment they scent birds, and so are not close enough to make the quail nervous.

Even a rock-steady bobwhite dog can be upset by hunters who rush in or talk noisily as they approach. Conversely, a steady dog can be disturbed when hunters move in too slowly. A point is a very tense few moments for any dog. The point is a disciplined interruption of its natural urge to flush the birds. The most successful bobwhite hunters as a rule are those who know precisely how their dog or dogs will react, and who move in with quiet words of reassurance, at a steady pace, never crossing in front of the dogs. Some hunters never learn. They excite their dogs, causing them to jump coveys prematurely or even chase birds.

The bobwhite hunter with dogs also should practice reading the intention of the birds. Which way will they fly? Almost without fail, because the birds know their homestead down to every tuft of grass, they will flush and head arrow-straight toward safe cover. The astute hunter instantly sums up the situation as the dog comes to point, then makes his move to place himself in the best position for shots.

That day with Gene Burke and old Doc and those younger dogs presented an excellent illustration of how it goes when it goes right. The dogs picked up scent possibly 75 yards out in a fallow field. Grass and weeds were short, but high enough to hide bobs. The young dogs both came to pretty points, but we watched Doc. The mean old

Along a levee beside the lower Mississippi River, a pointer delivers a bob and gets a pat in return. In the Deep South especially, the bobwhite has been a much loved game bird for the last couple of centuries.

scoundrel paid no attention to the others. At the field edge, pines and undergrowth began abruptly, and here also was a swampy place with small pools of water. Grass and gallberry tussocks were scattered in these puddles.

Doc knew very well that those quail, this late in the morning and caught so far out in the open, would be nervous. He also knew which way they'd fly—straight toward the woods and swampy area. In a marvelous display of craft, he circled and came in to point from a quartering position in front of where his nose told him the covey squatted. I like to think he knew that his stance at left front would force the quail to rise and veer right, giving us at least a first broadside opportunity before they turned straight toward the timber.

It was as if Doc had told Burke and me where to move. He was still running this hunt. We went halfway around and came in opposite Doc, right shoulders toward the timber. Instantly Doc crowded gently, two steps, then went poker stiff. That did it. The nervous covey swirled up in a mini-roar of small wings. Momentarily confused, they started toward us, then began to veer toward the distant cover edge.

For an instant the whole covey seemed to hang in the air. We fired, and two birds tumbled. Then they went speeding on a beeline toward timber, but still in beautiful range. We took two more and, because all was open before us, sent off third shots.

One bird wavered but kept going. The younger dogs were bounding around, joyfully picking up quail. Doc didn't. He turned his head and watched that wavering bird all the way to the line of timber. As it disappeared, he trotted away. We took the birds from the other dogs and followed after Doc. When we got into the edge, we saw old Doc belly-deep in an expanse of swamp. He waded toward a small grass tussock, very gently picked a quail out of it, and brought it back.

Not to me. He ignored me. I was a stranger, and maybe Doc knew I was also born a Yankee. Burke took the quail and said, "Good dog, Doc." A classic bird hunt. A classic scene. A classic old pointer, too. He liked his work. Hunters, however, were just one of those necessary annoyances linked with it. He growled at Burke and shook himself, throwing muddy water in Burke's face.

7

Bobwest

Since the U.S was young, whenever the average hunter spoke of quail hunting it meant bobwhites and conjured up mental pictures of dogs on point and coveys bursting before them somewhere across the South, the Atlantic and lower Great Lakes states, or the middle-south hillbilly belt. Where else could you find bobwhites in numbers worth a well-trained dog's attention?

To this day, virtually every addicted bird hunter east of the Mississippi River has that same notion. Thousands of upland gunners *west* of the Mississippi smile knowingly when they hear about eastern and southern quail hunting, but say nothing. To them there seems little reason to push the facts of the excellent and nationally rather obscure west-river bobwhite hunting.

The facts are that for many years the annual harvests of bobwhites west of the Mississippi have matched and sometimes exceeded those east of the river. And the intriguing clincher statistic is that the eastern kill is spread over exactly twice as many states as that west of the river.

Even numerous westerners—on the Pacific Coast, in the mountains, and some within the bobwhite belt itself—have little idea of the quality of this hunting between the big river and the eastern foothills of the Rockies. This places bobwhite hunting west of the Mississippi in a kind of "discovery" category.

It was certainly a startling discovery for me when some years ago I found myself in Nebraska looking for pheasants but incessantly bumbling into bobwhites. I hadn't realized they were there, and I didn't especially like it. Every time a quail covey buzzed up, I jumped and swung my gun. A partner did likewise, both of us muttering

To the east-of-the-Mississippi bobwhite hunter, this doesn't look much like quail cover. But bobs are about as plentiful west of the river as east of it, often in habitat that seems incongruous compared to "classic cover."

about these little birds that were bothering us when we were after big birds. I had hunted intermittently for years in the "quail states," chiefly Tennessee, the Carolinas, Georgia, and Florida. That was *real* quail hunting. That was where bobwhites belonged, not way out here halfway across the continent.

Presently, however, we had flushed, collected, and frozen to take home our possession limit of pheasants. The hunt was over almost before we'd gotten started. When I anguished out loud about this, wishing there was more to come, our host said, "Well, the quail season's open, but you fellows don't seem to care for quail." Lightning struck us! Over the next several days of wonderful shooting it was the *pheasants* that made us jump and mutter.

The ancestral range of the bobwhite might surprise many quail hunters. It was vast, stretching from Maine westward across a slice of Ontario and much of the Great Lakes states to the upper Mississippi valley. It reached south to the lower tip of Florida, blanketed all the eastern and central interior, and stretched into the Southwest and over most of Texas. Various subspecies even reached south, and still do, over eastern Mexico and far into Central America. As settlement and farming pushed across and westward from the Mississippi, bobwhite range and population spread by 1850 into most of the west-river plains clear into eastern Colorado and New Mexico. Transplants eventually were made to Idaho, Wyoming, Washington, and Oregon.

Although changes in land use in this century have shrunk the fringes of the range everywhere to some extent, and the introduced West Coast bobwhites have not been able to sustain themselves, the western range is still large. There have been token harvests in recent years in Idaho, fair to good hunting in a few places in eastern New Mexico and Colorado as well as southeastern South Dakota, and truly sensational shooting elsewhere. The big-time bobwhite hunting west of the Mississippi is located in a total of eight states. The state-by-state harvests in peak years are startling to one not aware of them. Even in low-cycle years they are higher than those in many east-river quail states.

Nebraska and Louisiana each account during up-cycle years for at least 750,000 birds, Iowa a million. In Arkansas and Texas estimates run at least two million each, Kansas gathers 2½ million, Oklahoma and Missouri each claim at least 3½ million. Seasons in all those states have run from six weeks to as long as three months, with recent daily bag limits of six in Nebraska, eight to 10 in most other states, 12 to occasionally 20 in Texas. As in the South and East, western bobwhites have been having some habitat problems, and some declines. However, over most of the western range, habitat deterioration seems not as accelerated as it is east of the river, due partly to lower human population.

For those used to hunting southern-plantation style, or around crop fields and fence rows of the lower Great Lakes states, quail cover west of the river can offer some startling surprises. To a Pennsylvania, Illinois, or Virginia bobwhite hunter, for example, a hunt in the cactus and thornbrush of southern Texas might be quite a jolt. It would open eyes, however, to just what an adaptable bird and excellent colonizer the bobwhite has been over the centuries.

I was introduced to south-Texas quail hunting well over a quarter century ago when we moved to the state. Texas also has abundant blue quail in its arid regions. Many of my Texas hunts have been where blues and bobs range the same lands. You never know which will get up. Several years ago I was on a bobs-only hunt in the thornbrush country. The ranch where we

were had no blues. Five of us spread out to walk 'em up. This cactus country is rough on dogs, especially because it is the primest of the prime snake range. All of us routinely wore snake leggings.

When bobwhites are at peak in Texas their numbers are simply unbelievable. There is a veritable eruption of birds. That was a peak year. The daily limit had been boosted to 20, to allow harvest of as many as possible, for a heavy die-off was certain in that harsh country. The five of us, hunting dogless about three morning and three afternoon hours, cleaned 100 bobs that evening—and removed about as many cactus spines.

Of course, much western bobwhite range is somewhat similar to eastern habitat—the Iowa farm country, for example, the brush and pineywoods of eastern Texas and western Louisiana, the farmland hills of Missouri and Arkansas. In portions of Nebraska, Kansas, and Oklahoma, however, bobwhites are birds of tall-grass prairies as well as brushy stream courses.

Some west-river bobwhite hunters believe the bird failed to receive early recognition and attract many hunters there because other, larger uplanders were so abundant. East-of-the-river hunters had *only* bobwhites, with the exception of ruffed grouse, which were seldom found in bobwhite territory. Conversely, west of the river the region was renowned for its awesomely abundant prairie chickens, and in some areas sharptails also. Prairie chickens were originally abundant from the Dakotas clear down through Kansas, Oklahoma, and much of Texas and eastern New Mexico. These larger birds, right next door to the bobwhites, were more appealing.

Those who are convinced this is why the bobwhite for so long played a low second here point out that in the late 1800s and early in this century, hundreds of quail dogs from the Atlantic and southern states, owned by well-to-do sportsmen, were taken to the western plains to be trained on prairie grouse. Then, following the decline of the grouse, the introduced pheasant exploded in population and grabbed attention. Today some bird hunters aware of the excellent quail hunting in several of the top pheasant states think a new focus is coming. As pheasants have declined in numbers from their early massive populations, more and more nonresident visitors as well as natives west of the river are excited about combo bird hunts.

Robert Barratt, Wildlife Superintendent for the Iowa Conservation Commission, told me in a letter, "We have many nonresident hunters coming here for pheasants. Most are surprised at the excellence of Iowa's quail hunting. Many return as much for the quail as the pheasants. The two make a great combo where their ranges overlap." By careful season planning, any bird hunter can arrange a combo trip to Iowa, Nebraska, South Dakota, or Kansas during which he can shoot two or more species of uplanders, chosen from among bobwhites, pheasants, Huns, prairie chickens, and sharptails.

West Coast and mountain-state bird hunters do have other quail species—valley, Gambel's, scaled—often dubbed the "running quails" because they are difficult for dogs to handle. But numerous western hunters who can afford it take their dogs to Alabama, the Carolinas, or elsewhere to have a go at bobwhites, or make guided

Bobwhite dogs range wide and fast in brushy edges along a stream in Kansas. Even some westerners are unaware that they have close-to-home bobwhite hunting better than they can find east of the river.

plantation-type hunts east of the river to sample the bobwhite experience, unaware of what's closer.

I have friends in Utah who were eager to hunt bobs. I told them about another friend who owns a big expanse of land in eastern Kansas, in the middle of wonderful bobwhite shooting, and agreed to meet them there. They were skeptical. They flew instead to Georgia. That season the southeastern quail population was at a low level. I made the Kansas trip. The landowner had two excellent pointers. The limit was eight per day, 24 in possession after the third day. We had a delightful hunt; then he drove me a couple of hours west where we worked over the pheasants. The Utah hunters had leapfrogged right over the top of a better hunting ground a third as distant as their destination.

Certainly bobwhites have severe ups and downs in the west-river states. Indeed, year-to-year populations may fluctuate more than they do east of the Mississippi. Therefore it pays, when planning a trip, to check with game-department personnel. The hard winters in Iowa, South Dakota, Nebraska, and Kansas often decimate bobwhite populations. Farther south, in Oklahoma and Texas, drought commonly causes massive losses. The south-Texas ranch where I told of five of us bagging 100 bobs had its quail all but wiped out by drought a year later.

As with most wildlife native to areas of severely fluctuating weather influences,

Although much west-river bobwhite habitat is in farm fields, many other areas contain plagues like thorns and snakes. Here a hunter removes spines from a dog's foot.

In several areas of Oklahoma, Texas, and eastern New Mexico, bobwhites and blue or scaled quail are found on the same ranges. Here hunters show bobs and blues shot in the same cover.

however, when a good season does arrive, production is overwhelming. Bobwhite managers in the western states agree in general that loss of optimum habitat is causing slow declines in numerous places. Nevertheless, discounting the short-term fluctuations that are self-adjusting in time, they all pretty much agree that the bobwhite is fairly stable here. It also is under less pressure than east of the river, where solid pine plantings and vast soybean acreages in many places have destroyed enormous expanses of bobwhite habitat, and continue to do so.

Happily, in the areas of best bobwhite populations in the west-river states, there

are few problems in finding places to hunt. In my home state, Texas, where public hunting lands are all but nonexistent, there are large acreages open to the public in one of the major bobwhite zones, the eastern third of the state: several National Forests and timber-company holdings, roughly a million acres in total. In Louisiana, the best bobwhite range blankets thousands of acres open to public hunting, numerous blocks of National Forest, vast timber-company lands, plus several state wildlife-management areas.

In Oklahoma, Arkansas, and Missouri the situation is similar. High quail populations are found on National Forest lands, open timber-company acreage, numerous state-owned public hunting areas or wildlife areas. In these southern states west of the river, incidentally, clearcuts on all forest lands, after they've started growing low cover in one to five years, offer some of the best quail hunting.

In Kansas and Nebraska, the cover situation is somewhat different. National Forest and timber-company lands are lacking. However, there is a welter of state-owned tracts—game-management areas, special-use areas. There are also large tracts of National Grasslands in these two states, and also in Oklahoma and Texas. Iowa has numerous public hunting areas, and for that matter, here and in other plains states permission to hunt private lands is not especially difficult to get.

It is enigmatic that the western bobwhite is so little known outside its range, and even sometimes inside it, especially because it is just as plentiful as its eastern cousin. An amusing incident that occurred recently at our house well illustrates the fact that it's time the western bob was publicized. A friend from Kentucky was visiting us for an afternoon, passing through, a gentleman descended from a long line of bluegrass bird-dog men. As we sipped a drink he happened to look out the window and spotted a covey of bobs strolling across our backyard.

"Quail!" he exploded, spilling his drink on the rug. "Bobwhites! Where the devil did *they* come from?"

I was as amazed at his not knowing bobwhites had been here for eons as he was at seeing them. So I just said between sips, "They knew you were coming. They flew down from Lexington."

8

The "Other" Way to Hunt Quail

The story is told of the aristocratic old southern gentleman showing his large kennel of dogs to a nonhunting Yankee visitor. When the visitor asked why on earth anyone kept all those dogs, the Old Colonel replied, "Why, suh, they're *buhd* dogs. For *buhd* hunting. Every southana keeps buhd dogs. Of coase." And when the unlettered Yankee asked what kind of birds, the testy reply was, "Why, suh, quail. Of coase. What otha kind of buhds *ah* there? Every southana hunts buhds with dogs. There's no otha way."

No one could deny that quail hunting over professionally trained dogs, or even behind the old pointer or setter that for years has been the family combination pet-and-hunter, is classic sport. Quail dogs and quail hunting with them has been an American tradition since Colonial days. Trouble is, as dramatic and enjoyable as this

sport may be, nowadays only a relatively few hunters own quail dogs, or have hunting companions who do.

Should lack of a dog keep a prospective beginner from becoming a quail hunter? By no means! Long ago, when the population was heavily rural, keeping quail dogs out in the country was easy, and the dogs got lots of practice. In today's world there are tens of thousands of prospective quail hunters in urban and suburban situations that make keeping a quail dog, or a pair of them, virtually impossible. In addition, those who do try it seldom can spend enough time afield to train dogs properly and keep them in shape. A few are financially able to keep dogs in a kennel, with a professional trainer, or to farm out bird dogs to country friends. The average hunter who yearns for a day now and then with quail can't afford that.

When hunting dogless, watch closely where each bird falls. Here a bobwhite has dropped into a grass clump, and might have been missed except that the hunter paid close attention.

The dog tradition relating to quail is so ingrained that all too many hunters seem to think hunting without a dog is a waste of time. I leaned toward that opinion myself when I came to Texas to live over 25 years ago. I had often hunted bobwhites in Georgia, Florida, the Ozarks, and elsewhere, invariably over dogs. During my first Texas fall I was invited quail hunting. At the camp where I arrived late one afternoon I could smell the delicious aroma of quail broiling over mesquite coals, but there wasn't a dog in sight.

To my question about that, my host said,

"Oh, we never use dogs here. Just never have. Too many thorns, cactus spines, and rattlesnakes." Then, reflecting, he added, "Maybe it's simply tradition with us to walk up our birds. Anyway, we never have trouble finding and bagging enough."

Now this is not to say that quail dogs are never used in Texas. Many are, in the eastern pine woods and farm country, in the north and the Panhandle. But traditionally in the southern "Brush Country," which has some of the best quail hunting in the nation—mixed-bag often, bobwhites and blue or scaled quail—almost everyone hunts dogless.

That fall, birds were awesomely abundant. The limit was 12 a day, 36 in possession. Four of us hunted three days, and all filled limits. I had learned emphatically that though dogs are a wonderful addition to the sport, they are by no means mandatory.

You should be aware that if you do hunt without a dog, many a dog owner will bristle at you and criticize you. The claim is usually made that without a dog you lose many quail. There is certainly some truth in this. Actually, some are lost either way. A careless dogless hunter may lose cripples and even birds that fall dead. A careful one, I have found, loses very few, no more than the average hunter with a dog. Not all dogs, remember, are efficient bird finders. Only the most highly trained and experienced are infallible.

The first rule I learned about hunting quail without a dog is to match my caution to the cover. If grass is short, for example, and there is no brush, then it's all right to try for two birds on a covey rise. You have a good "fall" for downed birds. If cover is dense, get on one bird and make sure of it. Don't try for doubles. And never take your eye off the spot where a hit bird falls. Go straight to it. When you get to the spot, hang your cap on a bush or drop it if you don't immediately see the dead bird. Keep circling until you find it. As a general rule, a quail flying over tall cover will be farther away than you thought. Practice restraint, and make determined searches for dead or crippled birds, and you'll seldom lose one.

To be consistently successful in hunting without a dog, you must learn to know your quarry intimately—the favorite quail foods in your area, and the feeding, resting, and watering routines of the birds. Knowing how quail spend their day allows you to pinpoint with surprising accuracy where birds will be at any given time.

Quail are homebodies. Where habitat is optimum, bobwhites live out their lives on as little as 20 acres, sometimes less. On our home place in Texas, not really good quail country, in high-hatch years we have two coveys living on 27 acres and its neighboring fringes. If food is not abundant, a covey may be forced to range more widely, per-

haps over 100 or more acres. This usually causes overlapping of area use with other coveys.

The western quails—blue or scaled, Gambel's, Valley, mountain, Mearns—usually must range more widely. In arid regions food is often not as concentrated. Nonetheless, each covey has its very specific home and can always be found somewhere within home boundaries. The western species in general are for obvious reasons much more dependent upon specific watering places than are bobwhites, which commonly have several choices.

All quail species are covey birds. Among bobwhites, the covey is almost always the family of that year. Blue (scaled) quail, which range chiefly in the Southwest, sometimes gather late in the season into groups of more than one family. Gambel's quail, a southwestern bird, and valley quail, with their heaviest concentrations in the Pacific Coast states plus Nevada, Idaho, and

Hunter slowly combs a brushy creek bank. Knowing the habits and daily routines of quail enables you to hunt where birds are most likely to be.

Utah, are renowned for gathering in late fall and winter "packs." These contain several coveys, and the drove may number as many as 100 birds.

The gregarious and homebody nature of quail has advantages for dogless hunters. You may have to search hard, but you know that when you find birds there'll be a group together. Then, after they flush and scatter, you have two choices: to go after a few singles, which is not easy without a dog, or to let them alone so they'll soon regroup and perhaps find them again later in the day. Also, when you locate a covey, you know that it probably uses this specific area every day. Very often the same covey will be right there another day at about the same time.

A sharp hunter will know *why* they are at any given location. This requires knowledge of the daily routine of quail, and is the main secret of success for the hunter who walks them up. On bright days, even if it is chilly, quail move from their roost site to feed shortly after sunup. They may fly, but quail walk or run far more than they fly. Flying is mostly an escape tactic. The birds make amazingly good time afoot. I have watched bobwhites moving along through grass — undisturbed, picking up seeds — cover 100 yards in less than 10 minutes.

If forage is concentrated, they may feed in a small area. And they don't necessarily require very long to fill up. For example, I have fed quail in our yard several winters so I could observe them. They are usually prompt and predictable, appearing at around 8 or 9 a.m. and again at 4 to 5 p.m. However, when eating maize at the feeding spot, they needed only five minutes to fill crops. This, of course, is an artificial situation. In a waste-grain feeding location they may require 30 minutes. Easting small grass seeds may require an hour or more.

By and large, the early feeding period lasts up to about 9 a.m. The second one begins around 3 p.m. and often continues right up until dusk. Some of the best mixed-species hunting I've ever experienced with bobs and blues has occurred during the last shooting light. But I advise dogless hunters not to stay too late where brush cover is present. It's too difficult to find downed birds.

Overcast, drizzly weather or bitter winds change the feeding routine. Birds leave roost sites later, and may put in an extra feeding session to keep filled because they are uncomfortable. On days of cold wind, always look for birds in the lee of cover or on a protected slope. Cold, sunny weather will send birds out into open spots where they can get the warmth of the sun. Edges of ranch and farm roads in any quail country are perfect locations. I've sat on a deer stand early in the morning and observed a covey nearby pecking casually at gravel and fluffing feathers in the sun. All species do this.

As all experienced quail hunters know, once you discover the domain of a covey, you should mark it well. Given amenable reproductive cycles, a covey will be there not just during the current season but year after year. A friend of mine in North Carolina told me that he had pinpointed a number of prime bobwhite spots where he had found a covey every year for 30 years. Such spots obviously furnish everything quail require. Year after year a pair nests in the vicinity and replenishes the stock. The important point is that you don't need to seek new hunting grounds constantly. Get intimately acquainted with one that has a substantial population, and you're in business for years — always knowing precisely where birds will be.

Roosting and resting places are not al-

Bringing in a skilletful after a foray. Late afternoon is a prime time for the dogless hunter. Birds must fill up to tide them over the night.

ways easy to find, but they usually all have definite distinguishing attributes. Bobs feed out into grain or weed fields. They retire to brush or taller, denser weed cover to rest, and for night roosting. Whether they are actually in the cover or not, they will seek refuge on its fringes. Fence rows, clumps of brush, weedy areas around abandoned buildings, stream courses—these are rest and roost sites.

When bobs rest during the day they simply laze around in a loose group. At night they generally sit huddled closely. Always keep an eye out for a small, matted place with copious droppings. These are clues to where bobwhites have been spending nights, and where to find them at dawn. Sometimes western quail roost in trees or brush. I have watched blues many times up

15 feet in a big mesquite. These quail have a curious habit—sometimes practiced by bobwhites also—of resting beneath a bush or beside a fence in the daytime, with one bird perched in plain sight atop the bush or atop a fence post. I've even used binoculars to scan brush in the Southwest, looking for a perching blue. Without fail the group will be below.

Of all the clues to quail, water sources are probably the most important. In some portions of bobwhite range, to be sure, choices of watering places are numerous. This is true in the Deep South and portions of the central states. Over vast areas of the central and midwestern states and Texas, however, all of the very best bobwhite hunting is based on available water.

For example, in Kansas and Oklahoma

the fringes of the water courses, from rivers down to tiny creeks, encompass the major share of the quality hunting. In addition, every farm and ranch stock pond or tank is a magnet to which a covey or two is drawn. Illustrating the point even more emphatically are the quails of the West, where water is more scarce.

I have hunted, for example, in several areas of Texas, across New Mexico, and in Arizona where all quail varieties were found by the simple expedient of first checking water sources. Many of us hunt blues and bobs on south-Texas ranches simply by driving from tank to tank and hunting the area around each.

Near these dug ponds—or small creeks where they occur—food is likely to be more abundant than elsewhere. So is cover. Thus the birds have all their needs in one location. Commonly a covey will spend resting hours within a few yards of a tank, will roost near it, and will forage out not over 100 to 300 yards in any direction from it. Find water and you'll find quail—it's a rule the walk-'em-up-hunter should follow anywhere.

A nugget of quail hunting lore very few dogless hunters even know about is the importance in some places of *tracks.* Because quail walk and run more than they fly, and are covey birds, they leave a myriad of tracks—if the terrain is such that tracks of birds so light are readily imprinted. Sandy loam, the dust of farm or ranch roads, and soft, moist earth near a spring or a windmill overflow all record the impressions.

Another most helpful technique is using a call. Many quail hunters scoff at the suggestion. Don't! The idea is not to call quail *to* you—although some will at times actually move toward the source—but to locate coveys or singles. It isn't difficult. There are calls available for bobwhites, Gambel's, and

valley quail. Blues can be imitated by practice, using even a common predator call.

The sound needed for all species is a "get-together" call. Bobwhites often whistle—*whee-eet*—when scattered and when spreading out to feed in the morning or afternoon. It is a stay-in-contact call, to keep a group in touch or used by strays to locate the others. The valley quail says *cha-quí-ta,* the Gambel's *cha-quí-ta-ta,* both easily mimicked by using a call available in stores. The blue says *kip-kerrr.* Bite the very end of a predator call in teeth and lips, and say this into it, using throat muscles.

The western quails are more talkative than the bobs, and have broader vocabularies. The sounds noted, however, are all you need. I have a southern bobwhite hunting friend who drives out at dawn and makes a quick tour of the farm country where he hunts. He stops here and there and, using his call, whistles several times with pauses between, listening for replies. I've seen him pinpoint three or four coveys in 15 minutes. Then he begins hunting. On countless occasions in various states I have walked up a bobwhite covey, got a covey-rise shot, stayed quiet for 10 minutes, and then located singles by giving the rally whistle. Sometimes you can stalk one, calling and getting replies, until you know precisely where it is.

With the desert and western quails, calling is even easier and more effective. These talkative quail often start calling when they hear a vehicle door slam and hunters begin talking. Friends and I have stalked whole coveys, talking to them and getting answers, right to the bush they're squatting under. When scattered, they begin calling almost at once.

Because the western quails are exasperating—and astonishingly swift—runners, a careful hunter without a dog can often have better success than a gunner with one. Scattered singles of all the westerners often sit tighter than single bobs. But alerted coveys sometimes are difficult to get into the air. Locating them by listening for them, and allaying their suspicions by using a call, allows a good prowler to sneak up and force a flush.

Whatever the quail variety where you hunt, there is no valid reason for missing out on this sport because you don't have a dog. You can enjoy excellent shooting without one, and you will wind up know-ing more about your quarry than a great many hunters who use dogs. Without a keen canine nose to depend upon, you must compensate by studying the habits and personality of birds in fine detail. Granted, using a dog is a grand experience, and just watching a well-trained dog work can be the biggest thrill of the hunt. Using your own knowledge of quail, however, to make your own success is nonetheless a very satisfying accomplishment. Indeed, the dogless hunter can enjoy great sport, too!

9

The Runningest Quail

When we came to Texas to live, it didn't take me long to find out about blue quail. Books call them scaled quail because of the feather pattern on breast and throat, each feather gray-blue edged with black, so the area looks scaled. But to ordinary hunters and country people in Texas and nearby Mexico, they're blue quail—*codorniz azul*.

The late Paul Young Sr. of Laredo introduced me to the birds. He had a large hunting lease near Laredo and an old camp, Camp Howdy, on it. He kept a pair of ancient cleated track shoes hanging on the wall. Many an out-of-state visitor, myself among them, after a bit of tippling would happen to squint up at the shoes and ask about them.

"They're my blue quail shoes," he'd explain.

This invariably led to questions about blues. "Are they hard to hit?"

Paul would say, deadpan, "In all this brush? You bet! You have to go like blazes to get close enough, then drop down to see 'em underneath."

The startled newcomer would say, "Not on the *ground*—on the wing!"

Paul would shrug. "Never tried that. Why spoil sporty ground-sluicing at those speed demons by settling for easy wing shots?"

Paul was a masterful wingshot, and of course he had shot hundreds of blues in flight. No one in blue quail range except a visiting "elitist" east-of-the-Mississippi bobwhite hunter, however, would deny letting off an occasional skillet shot at blues. Nor would any hunter of experience, born or long schooled in blue quail range, criticize anyone given to such intermittent moral breakdowns. It's routine. There are, in fact, times and situations in which you might see several hundred blues in a day of hunting and not once get a chance to shoot one awing fair-and-square. Other days are quite the opposite. I explained that patiently a couple of years ago to a magazine editor from New York City who was visiting me. "Take 'em as they come," I told him. He nonetheless clung to "the code." He didn't kill a single blue. You can bet *I* did! And I didn't notice any reticence on his part about eating them!

Over many years hundreds of bobwhite hunters born to that sport have refused to have anything to do with blue quail. Some will grudgingly grant you that other western quails—Gambel's, valley, Mearns—have at least *some* sporting qualities. But they'll pass off the blue as not worthy of any true sportsman's attention. They claim it's the most exasperating, runningest quail ever invented. Several old books in my personal library refer to the scaled "partridge" or "cotton-top"—a colloquial name referring to the whitish small crest or tuft atop the head—as lacking or wholly inferior in sporting qualities. One also notes that they are virtually tasteless, stringy, and unfit table fare. Even a couple of modern volumes parrot the same nonsense, their authors obviously lacking experience and with their blue quail material possibly plagiarized from older east-river writers.

The fact is, the blue is a superbly delicious table bird, often an ounce or two larger than the bobs with which it commonly consorts over portions of its Texas, Oklahoma, and New Mexico ranges. It is also dynamically sporty and often exasperatingly difficult on the wing because of its unpredictable flight habits. And—yes—it can be downright difficult sometimes to shoot running, as it zigzags expertly through dense thornbrush, for those who choose that approach. I place some truth in

Scaled, or blue, quail perches in a mesquite. The name derives from the breast, throat, and nape feathers that are gray-blue with dark edging, giving them a scale-like appearance. The dark belly of this one identifies it as the chestnut-bellied subspecies.

the old wheeze about how the man aiming at a fleeing group but holding fire had no intention of shooting them on the run, but was waiting for them to stop. H.L. Betten, in his delightful old (1940) book titled *Upland Game Shooting*, says it best: "After designing various kinds of western partridges that can run, the Great Architect may have been dissatisfied. So maybe He concentrated on a final effort, and the scaled quail or cotton-top resulted."

The blue quail is strictly a southwestern arid-country bird. The center of its abundance is in New Mexico and southern and western Texas. It spills westward into southeastern Arizona and north into southeast-

Much of the range of the blue quail, colloquially called "cottontop" because of its whitish crest, is a welter of spines and thorns.

ern Colorado. There are a few in southwestern Kansas, and a good supply in panhandle Oklahoma and along the Red River to about opposite Wichita Falls, Texas. A few have been transplanted elsewhere, as far away as Washington, but have not done especially well. Southward the range reaches deep into Mexico. In fact, the type species is named from there.

The blues over most of the U.S. range are of the Arizona subspecies, quite pale in color. In my estimation the most interesting subspecies of the blue is the second one dwelling in the U.S., the chestnut-bellied scaled quail. Few hunters, even among blue quail enthusiasts, are aware of the existence of this bird. It is present only in a few counties of extreme southern Texas. Its range continues south across the border into northern Mexico in the same region. This quail is darker than other blues, and in mature birds the male has a large, round

belly area that is rich chestnut in color. The belly of the female is of similar hue but not as pronounced.

The first blues I hunted, in the vicinity of Laredo, Texas, were of this subspecies. I met hunters from that area who didn't realize they were hunting a "different" blue. It was all they'd ever seen. My next forays were in the Big Bend region of western Texas, then in New Mexico, and finally in southeastern Arizona. The distinction was quickly apparent. The chestnut-bellied blue is one of the most handsome quail on the continent.

The problems most hunters face with blues are caused by their going after the birds with preconceived notions of what quail hunting should be like—generally what bobwhite hunting is like. Blues became one of my favorite uplanders simply because I accepted them as they are rather than trying to force them to comply with bobwhite standards. One reason the blue learned eons ago to trust its speed rather than to hide and lie still as a group is that over almost all its range the desert cover may be dense above but during most years there is no great amount of grass at ground level to hide in. So it runs.

It is most intriguing to hunt blues in brush country like that of southern Texas, where tens of thousands of acres are a tangle of thornbrush and cactus. You hunt it during normally dry years, and you think nothing ever will cover the grazed-down, bare ground again. However, millions of seeds are lying dormant, awaiting water. That's the way of the desert. When rains arrive at last, the ground beneath the spiny brush and cactus simply explodes in greenery. Suddenly a thick carpet of grass and forbs is paving what was barren ground.

This just as suddenly places perplexing barriers to blues that are programmed by nature to run. I vividly recall such a fall in the south-Texas Brush Country. A wet year also invariably means an explosion in quail numbers. Blues were everywhere in unbelievable abundance, but they couldn't do much running. We'd drive a 4WD along ranch trails. Every couple hundred yards or so a large pack of blues would swirl into the air. Running away was too difficult. They'd fly off in a close-packed group, and we'd watch where they came down. Ordinarily they would have hit the ground running. That year, all we had to do was converge on their alighting area and walk them up. No quail ever offered finer wingshooting.

When you manage to scatter blues—sometimes dogs can do it, although not many hunters use dogs on blues, because of the thorny country and the too-common rattlesnakes—the singles sit just as snugly as bobwhites, and sometimes more so. A dog

has to be trained to rush a covey, then slowly, meticulously hit singles. The ingrained habit of the blue, however, where there is little ground-level obstruction, is to start running the second they become disturbed. It's laughable to watch a newcomer to this sport try to run them down. Give 'em a few sprints, and they throw in the towel—wisely.

It is both exasperating and intriguing to observe how the birds often half-run, half-fly. On many occasions I have pursued a group, catching glimpses of them zipping along under the brush. Then suddenly one or a half dozen arise, wings spread and barely skimming low bushes. You fling up your gun, but by then the quail are down again. Commonly several or a single will simply flutter up and over a single brush clump, as if the brief wing action was only

Blue quail flushes straight up above a hunter. More often, birds flush briefly, hop over a bush or two, and land running again.

an assist to running speed, or the brush was too much in the way. The shooting under such circumstances is certainly sporty, but you may not gather many birds.

The first lesson one must learn is that once a covey is spotted you have to get among them quickly. Often this will put them into the air. If they get a running head start, few hunters can smash through the spiny cover, keeping at least a glancing lookout for snakes, swiftly enough to put the birds up. I've seen determined hunters chase a bunch of blues literally a quarter mile or more, never getting a shot.

The Achilles heel of the blue quail is its need for companionship and its talkative nature. Years back, when I first experienced this hunting, Whit Whitenton, then game warden in Laredo, showed me how to get blues to talk back to me. Anywhere in blue quail country, if you stand still and just listen, it won't be long before you hear one or more, assuming quail are in the vicinity. The cocks crow in a reedy, delightfully happy call. The birds make a variety of sounds, but the basic call—used to find or keep track of each other, and also uttered when they're disturbed—is a two-syllable, reedy-timbred utterance that might be phonetically spelled: *kip-kerrrrrr, kip-kerrrrrr,* or *check-churrrr, check-churrrr.* The first syllable is short, abrupt, and accented, the second also somewhat accented but drawn out.

Whit explained to me that a blue quail cannot resist answering this call. He showed me how to place my palm to my lips and turn my hand from side to side, meanwhile making a pair of kissing sounds against the palm. Admittedly this is no perfect imitation, but it works. When blues have run off, you can stand still and usually get replies, which give away their location. I've hunted with a companion and used this trick—when one of us would stand and call

while the other tried to sneak slowly into range of an answering quail and put it up.

The Burnham Brothers, known for their animal and bird calls, learned to make a fair imitation of the sound by biting down hard on the tip of a predator call and more or less saying the syllables into it. They also created a fair imitation by using one of their short-range predator calls—two strips of plastic material with a rubber band sandwiched between.

Few blues will actually come to the call, as valley and Gambel's sometimes will. The idea is to locate them by getting replies. One time Winston Burnham and I made a sneak on a big covey of blues among which several were talking and crowing. He kept talking back to them, and we got so close that we could peek over a bush and see them snugly bunched and unaware.

During midday it is rather common to see a blue quail perched atop a bush or cactus. When you spot one, you can bet a covey is down below. Hunters cruising ranch trails in a vehicle often pass on by, tumble out, and make a fast rush on the area. That frequently works.

Much has been written—mostly by scribes who have no idea whether or not it is true—about how blue quail don't need water. This is nonsense. I can't say positively that *some* blues *sometimes* do not live at least temporarily in waterless situations. But I can say positively that throughout their range, if you know where the waterholes are, you can pinpoint practically every covey of blues. Year after year, covey after covey will be based within a reasonable distance of a waterhole. Many times I have hunted these quail by driving with friends from one cattle tank or windmill to another. You may not find birds right at the water, but they'll be somewhere within a quarter mile or so of it.

A friend with whom I've hunted blues

When you see a blue quail perched atop a bush like this, chances are the rest of the covey is below it on the ground. The percher is a lookout.

many times taught me years ago to keep an eye peeled for tracks wherever there is soft earth or dust enough to print them. I recall a cattle tank where three of us stopped a couple of years ago to put water in a vehicle radiator. In a narrow, sandy draw leading toward it I happened to notice a profusion of quail tracks. Actually we were mule deer hunting, but quail season was open and we had cased shotguns. We unlimbered them and spread out, making a wide circle around the water source. Blues were shortly calling, and we flushed them several times back and forth from one slope and hunter to another, winding up with nine in a dramatic flurry of action.

In the fall blue quail, like several other of the western quails, commonly gather in large packs of more than one covey. The better the year for quail abundance, the larger the groups. One season a group of us, making waterhole rounds, flushed groups that we estimated contained as many as 70 birds. Those are dramatic

sights. Often these large packs stick together better than smaller ones, fly more and run less.

The way to get at them is first to mark down places along ranch trails on which coveys are based. Then leave the vehicle well back, remain quiet, and converge on each area. Often it's surprising what marvelous wingshooting results. But be warned: once the birds have been shot into and have flown off in a group—not scattered—don't be tempted to follow. You're in for a chase if you do, with probably little to show for it but your tongue and rear dragging.

Perhaps the very best time for hunting blues and assuring wingshooting is late in the day, right up until the end of available shooting light. Like all quail, the birds forage diligently during the last hours of daylight to fill crops and tide them over the long night. They gather in and along edges of ranch roads and trails at that time, usually near the waterholes. As light lowers they aren't as inclined to run, partly, I presume, because they are uneasy about becoming scattered and separated with dark coming on.

At this time of day a whole covey may swirl up before the guns, if hunters quietly approach previously noted areas that coveys are using. Further, they usually don't fly far, and they alight together and often do not run. If you don't approach the disturbed birds too quickly after a flush and shooting, sometimes you can get the whole group up again.

In the overall approach, you have to make up blue quail hunting as you go along. There isn't the stipulated, well-entrenched routine to it that occurs with bobwhites. In my view, this uncertainty adds to the sportiness rather than detracting from it. If at times you become so exasperated at 'em that you pot a few as if you were hunting rabbits, well, don't let your

A male chestnut-bellied blue quail. This handsome subspecies is found only in a few counties of southern Texas and a modest range in northern Mexico.

conscience keep you awake that night. You've had lots of company since early man first started hunting blue quail.

Writing that, I think with amusement of hunting one year in northern Mexico. A Mexican cowboy on a ranch south of Reynosa drove me around in a battered pickup. It was plain after a couple of hours that he was disgusted with me. He'd try to sneak me up where I could pot-shoot a bundle, but I kept trying to get them into the air. By noon I had gathered only three birds, a bad day indeed.

We got into some shade to eat lunch, each of us using what little we knew of the other's language to make some sort of conversation. After we'd eaten he indicated that perhaps I'd like to rest, and asked by signs and a few scattered words if I minded if he tried a little hunt with my gun. I knew very well what he had in mind, and to salve his pride I told him to go ahead.

Presently I heard him shoot. Once. After a while a second shot. Finally he came in. With a wide and prideful grin he handed me the two broken empty hulls and counted out *ten* blues from his stuffed pockets. In broken English and with signs, he indicated his sneaking stalks and explained, "This is how you hunt quail." Didn't I know? He held up fingers to represent quail heads sticking up, and then made a small circle with thumb and fingers. Then in a mixture of Spanish and English: "Under bush. Six once, four once. Heads all together. One shot each."

How could I quarrel with his success, especially when in his view I had shown him how stupid a *gringo* could be? Frankly, that evening when we broiled all the birds over mesquite coals, each with a tiny wild hot pepper stuffed into the body cavity, I was quite sure there was nothing to quarrel about anyway.

10

The Southwest's Sand and Sunshine Quail

The year had been a dry one in southeastern Arizona. By quail season there wasn't even a minuscule tinge of green anywhere on the desert, and the country Holton McQuade and I were hunting out east of Tucson was curled up and burned crisp. But there were quail. Lots of them. That was the year of my introduction to that handsome, sporty, and tough black-plumed dandy, the desert, or Gambel's quail.

It was a far different day and time. You could drive then from the Santa Rita Hotel in the middle of downtown Tucson out east to the rodeo grounds without meeting more than maybe 20 vehicles. And when you passed the rodeo grounds, that was all. You were in the country. The city and all its environs counted less than 30,000 souls, Bob Taylor and crew were shooting one of the endless gaggle of Billy the Kid movies there, and Tom Mix had his last drink one morning that season in the Santa Rita's Cactus bar. Those random notes date the time at 45 or more years ago.

McQuade and I, both down from the Hollywood ratrace and eager to get the studio pallor off us, were spending every spare minute out on the desert, walking up quail. I recall vividly the sight and sound of my first bunch of Gambel's. These are incessantly talkative birds, more vocal, I suspect, than any other of the quail species of North America. A group of eight came walking along a fence line, pecking at some unseen scant weed-seed forage as they traveled. A cock paused, reared its head, and crowed lustily, the sound—to me at least—a reedy and almost melodic *chu-chaaa-chu-chaaa-chu-chaaa*, the accent each time on the *chaaa*. Meanwhile all the rest were gossiping away, *quoit-quoit*, *quoit-quoit*, in a low and contented cacophony.

The Gambel's quail. Its jaunty black plume is one of its identifying tags, although the valley or California quail, a close relative, also wears one.

I was so mesmerized by the dapper appearance of the birds, each with its jaunty topknot plume bobbing, that shooting hadn't occurred to me. McQuade said from my left, "Well, aren't you going to pot 'em?"

To me "pot" meant ground-sluicing the wad of them. I'd never hunted any of the western running quails at that time, and I must have looked aghast. McQuade chuckled, muttered, then yelled, "Okay, then. Come on, Big Sport!" and broke into a run right at them.

I followed. The birds were so close and so startled, and the surroundings so utterly bereft of cover, that they did indeed burst into flight. We were both shooting. Somehow these little blighters didn't fly straight, buzzing off like a bobwhite. They sideslipped and scattered, barely skimming what few weeds and bushes were present. I managed with three fast shots to put down one bird, and McQuade did likewise.

We grabbed up quail and broke into a run again as we saw the birds come to ground. I had never seen a quail switch from wings to feet so deftly and seemingly without a bit of slowdown. We ran all-out, but the birds—which as I was to learn later run at a top speed of about 15 miles an hour—sizzled off across the barren expanse, leaving us at last with tongues hanging out, gasping for breath, knees quaking and not another shot fired.

This I suppose should have been enough to discourage me about hunting desert quail. Contrarily, it simply whetted my interest, and for some weeks McQuade and I chased Gambel's quail up and down the desert around Tucson. I came to love the exasperating little devils that winter, and have seized every opportunity since to suffer over them in various cactus and thornbrush patches scattered across Arizona and New Mexico.

The Gambel's quail—named after the naturalist who gave it its first scientific name and species status—is not a bird with a large range. It is primarily a creature of the southwestern deserts, and it is without question the toughest quail on the continent, so far as making do with practically nothing is concerned. On a number of occasions I have seen Gambel's apparently happy and healthy, living in desert so barren you'd wonder why anybody ever fought over it.

To be sure, when the desert erupts after an unusual spring watering, so do the desert quail. But when the jackrabbits starve and practically everything else dies and there's nothing in sight but a few hummocks of dwarf mesquite with thorns an inch long and thick as an ice pick, the

Gambel's will be there, tenaciously hanging on though they may not be abundant. Given an occasional drink and a meager ration of mesquite beans, they can make it somehow.

I remember with amusement that Mc-Quade, who hailed from desert country, called Gambel's "sand and sunshine quail." "When things get rough," he said, "they eat the sand and drink the sunshine and crow all the louder." He claimed an Indian told him this. Having heard it from McQuade, I never believed it, for he was employed as an actor in cowboy and Indian B movies and given to romantic exaggeration. But it does make a nice little legend.

The eastward limit of Gambel's quail range begins along the Rio Grande River in extreme western Texas. Presently the bird is legal game there, but few Texans know it exists. Gambel's quail are especially abundant in southwestern New Mexico and are found sparsely along the Rio Grande and northward in that state. Most of Arizona except the northeast quarter has Gambel's, with the heaviest concentrations in the southeast and on across the south to Yuma. The range reaches into southeastern California, the lower triangle of Nevada, parts of southern Utah, and scantily in pockets of western Colorado. At least one far-away transplant was successfully established some years ago in Idaho.

This is a bird of the southwestern desert floor and foothills. In addition to open desert, it dearly loves the densely tangled thornbrush and cholla patches, where it is practically impossible for a man to hunt. This bird is astonishingly intelligent about finding places of safety. I have hunted it on several occasions with a dog. However, a bobwhite dog trying to handle desert quail would be a nervous wreck in short order. Curiously, when the desert has received

In southwestern New Mexico, a pointer stiffens out and a hunter goes on alert. Gambel's quail are great runners, but the singles lie snug.

substantial moisture and explodes in grass, the running tactics of the bird are inhibited. Whole coveys then often sit tight, and scattered singles invariably do.

When the desert floor lacks dense grass, however, it's a different story. Then the birds are really going to race away afoot. Old hands at this hunting can tell, when an experienced dog or sprinting hunters manage to get a covey airborne, how good the singles shooting will be. If the covey stays bunched in flight and comes to ground that way, the flight is just a minor interruption of the running. If the birds disperse widely, then almost every covey member will instantly find a hiding place and lie snug.

Under such conditions, you hope for sparse cover, which means fewer hiding places. I recall a hunt a few seasons ago in southwestern New Mexico, in terrain so barren I couldn't believe quail could live in it. A friend I was with had a pointer brought up on desert quail. The dog ranged widely, and when it managed—or we did by running—to get birds airborne and scattered, the pointer knew precisely where to look for singles. Any hummock of dwarf mesquite, any bush, any spot that wasn't totally vegetationless was a possible hide.

That dog was marvelously staunch and patient. He realized that with his wide casting he would find birds far from us, and so he'd stiffen out on point and wait for us to move in, apparently realizing we could distantly see him. You soon learn, too, that though desert quail love to run, when they do squat you often have to kick a bush clump apart to move one or more birds out. They also love to let you kick and stomp, and then, as you mutter and pass on, explode behind you, heading back where they came from.

One native I hunted with kept a mental list of every water source, large or small, in his hunting area. Because these are arid-country birds, they are tied to watering places, especially during the dry seasons. Years ago Arizona increased desert quail populations by building "guzzlers"—partly covered underground pits with a concrete apron around them—to catch rainwater. Even though the birds need water, you don't always find them within short distances of it. Desert quail commonly fly rather long distances from a favored feeding place to water, and to roost, much as doves do. Unlike bobwhites, they roost as a rule in bushes, not on the ground.

During cyclic peaks, quail will be everywhere. You don't have to do much searching. When they're less abundant, or in particularly barren expanses, old hands at hunting them look first for tracks, just as blue-quail hunters sometimes do. Groups of birds habitually follow such natural travelways as dry, sandy washes. A welter of quail tracks printed in one means birds are living somewhere in the general vicinity. Any abandoned buildings where at one time there may have been—or still is—a water source usually is stippled with quail tracks in dusty or sandy places. Obvious waterholes are also good places to look for tracks. Some hunters with dogs check likely spots for tracks before ever putting a dog down. It saves time and often a lot of useless tramping.

Like all quail, the desert birds feed early and late, and get under cover during the day. Because the desert even during quail season may be hot during midday, dogs and men dislike hunting then. Often it's just as well. I've watched Gambel's coveys heading for cover as soon as the sun moves up the sky, and if there is any dense tangle, that's where they'll be. Sure, you can work your way into and through it. But these smart

Dog retrieves a Gambel's quail. Many hunters walk up these quail, without a dog, because of the thorns and also the possibility of snakes.

little characters give you little chance for shots in such havens. They hop up and fly a few feet barely off the ground, alight running, and disappear. Or they go out the other side of tall bushes as you approach.

Along the Gila River in New Mexico one season, two of us fought the catclaw and other thorns, with quail constantly all around us. When they're alarmed and running they often utter a *quirrrt-quirrrt* call, not especially loud, but sharp. This leads you on, unless you know better. Except in the thinnest of cover, both man and dog are better off to hunt from sunrise until perhaps 9 a.m., and then lie up as the quail do, in the shade, until midafternoon. Even so,

the talkative quail bait you into impossible situations, for they visit when resting and dusting as much as while feeding.

A few years ago I got hold of a quail call made to imitate the California or valley quail. Gambel's and valley quail are close relatives, both great talkers, and some of their language is rather similar. Practicing slight changes, I used it quite successfully on Gambel's quail. Valley and desert quail, incidentally, might be misidentified by the casual observer. The Gambel's is mostly blue-gray above. The top of the head is a rich rust color bordered with white. The throat and face are black, also bordered with white. Breast and lower belly are yellowish-tan, with a big black spot in the middle of the belly. The plume, forward-curving and black, appears at a distance to be a single feather but actually contains five to seven. Along the bird's sides and wing edges there are white streaks over a rusty background. All told, the color pattern, though rather somber overall, is stunning. The California quail has many of the same color characteristics, with the chief difference a darker and partially scale-effect breast and belly, and the neck nape also scale-patterned.

The main call of the California quail, which they toss back and forth as they spread out and feed or keep in touch, might be phonetically spelled *cha-qui-ta*, *cha-qui-ta*, *cha-qui-ta*, the second syllable heavily accented. The series of three is most common. The Gambel's adds another syllable, *cha-qui-ta-ta*, with second and third syllables both accented, the third most heavily. At least this is the way these calls sound to me.

Any desert quail hunter learns to be ever alert and listening for the sound of calling quail. Get a call if you can—mine was made by Lohman Manufacturing Company, Neosho, Missouri—because desert quail are so talkative they are easy to call. An artist friend of mine in Arizona has called undisturbed desert quail out of the brush on numerous occasions, and right up within a few yards of where he sat sketching. When hunting dogless, after a covey has been scattered, if you let the birds settle down a few minutes (while you get your breath!), they can be induced readily to answer a call.

Because the quail season in most states is fairly long, big-game hunters in desert quail states can sometimes arrange a sideline hunt. The heaviest concentrations of these quail are found in desert foothill country and along stream courses in southern New Mexico and Arizona. From the southwestern counties of New Mexico clear west to the Colorado River, excellent hunting can be had. It is advisable to check with game department personnel about how the population looks for any given year. Because of the birds' arid environment, populations are generally controlled by the amounts of rainfall, which determine how much of the necessary food grows in a given year.

Yuma County in Arizona is a good bet, and so are parts of Mohave County, plus all of the Colorado River country on the California side of the line. In Nevada, Clark County is probably best, down in the southern triangle, with portions of neighboring counties fair. Southern Utah has a modest Gambel's population. Transplant areas in Idaho are best checked with the game department. In Colorado, desert quail are by no means abundant, but good hunting can be found at times along U.S. 50 and vicinity—Grand Junction, Delta, Montrose.

In foothill country, hunting Gambel's quail can be an exhausting experience. Whether birds flush or run, they'll immediately take to any available hills when disturbed. I recall watching Bill Huey, who was later to become director of the Game and Fish Department in New Mexico, making a fast, panting race up a series of low ridges far down in the Animas Mountains foothills in the extreme southwestern corner of the state. We'd already walked, and run, maybe a dozen miles that day. Now we had spotted a quail perched atop a bush. This is a common habit of both blues and Gambel's quail. What the tyro may not realize is that the one in the bush is presumably a lookout. The covey is usually down below in the shade.

We raced to get on opposite sides of the

bush, but long before we were in position we heard that sharp *quirrrt, quirrrt* as the sentinel hopped down. The birds were running—uphill, of course. Our strategy had already been planned. Bill swung left to sprint for the head of a draw in the hope of getting around them. He swung back in due time to head up the ridge, then headed right again, hoping he'd cut them off. The idea was to stop the run, confuse the birds, and put them up. Meanwhile, I was laboring at full pant straight up the slope behind the birds, which I could glimpse as they darted through low scrub far ahead of me.

Suddenly they flushed. Much too far for me to shoot, they split and scattered going around Bill, and he put two down. He didn't shoot again. Desert quail match the terrain so well they're hard to find without a dog. Searching, he picked up the last bird as I came wheezing up. I was motioning, unable to talk. The birds had scattered out, I thought, and come down just over the ridge. We took off again.

In open terrain such as we were hunting, desert quail can see you from long distances. What these spiteful little critters had done was to converge and alight fairly well bunched just over the ridge top. They of course ran immediately. But we didn't know that. We made the ridge top, paused to bend double, blowing hard, winded.

This scene is in the desolate, arid region south of Lordsburg in southwestern New Mexico. This area and southeastern Arizona are among the chief ranges of the Gambel's quail.

And of course the quail, seeing us plainly, all arose in a swirl of wings two shotgun ranges downhill. They sailed straight across the next and intervening canyon and scaled down on the far slope. We flopped down, got enough breath back to talk, and decided that now, by Gad, we had them. They were scattered.

Before we got across the canyon birds were talking again, trying to rally. We crept up that slope, kicking grass clumps and single bushes. Two quail got up behind us and cut wide around. As we whirled to try to get a shot, we heard wings again. A half dozen bombed up from places they couldn't possibly have hidden, it seemed—behind and almost right under our feet. They skimmed that ridge top and flipped over it, followed but untouched by a clatter of shots.

I said, "I damm well better not see one on the ground within range!"

"Look there!" Bill yelped. Two were running within easy range, just about to go over the ridgetop.

It is true that many quail hunters routinely ground-shoot desert quail. I swear I'd have done it to those two, only they were too quick for me, racing over the ridge and taking wing immediately, sailing far out of range and sight.

Way off there behind us, several ridges and canyons removed, our pickup sat waiting. I wasn't sure I could make it back. The siren song of the Gambel's quail had led me on and on, to utter exhaustion. I said to Bill, "To think that years ago I had never heard of desert quail and was a perfectly contented bobwhite hunter. A man has to be balmy to pretend he likes this."

We started back, the sun lowering behind us—just the time for birds to be out foraging and moving. Nuts to them. We took an angled shortcut, wearily slogging. Suddenly a slope we'd not been on was alive with rising quail. As if motivated by some quirk sympathy for two tail-dragging, frustrated hunters, the birds fanned out, scattering, and unbelievably came down again within 50 yards.

We hurried now, adrenaline up, exhaustion forgotten. We circled them. Up went one—BANG—up went two—BANG, BANG—now the third. Three steps, and No. 4 got up. We circled wider, putting up more singles, shooting steadily, the excitement crackling.

"They're not supposed to do this," Bill said—BANG—BANG—"Down two—mark 'em!"

We were picking up quail and poking them into game pockets as we shucked in more shells and kicked up more quail. Finally it was over. Again we fell on the ground, chuckling in disbelief, gasping for breath, every muscle aching, but not even conscious of that. Then presently we were striding back toward the distant pickup. Odd how you regain strength fast when there's been successful action.

I tossed birds from my hunting coat onto the pickup hood and was counting to see how close we'd come to pulling a limit out of a debacle situation. Bill, back at the pickup bed, was saying, "First things first. This is a matter of survival." He was putting ice and dollops from a bottle of my very special Texas red whiskey into a pair of coffee cups.

I paused in my count to accept my cup and sip it as the sun slipped lower. "Maybe you don't have to be balmy," I mused, feeling the aches already starting. "One thing's sure—you hunt these birds, and you know you've been hunting."

"Yeah," Bill said. "For a week afterward!"

11

Quail of the Far-West
Valleys and Uplands

The California quail, *Lophortyx californicus*, is that state's official bird. Some hunters call it by the state name, but probably more use the name *valley* quail. This is the official common name for this species, from which other subspecies are offshoot races. This quail has a rather narrow but extensive range along the Pacific Coast, from the Mexican border to the fringes of southern British Columbia. Several other subspecies—examples are the Coast, Inyo, and Great Basin races—range farther inland and on down throughout Baja.

In general the "valley" name is no misnomer. Valley quail are birds that gravitate whenever possible to low-country gullies, washes, canyons; the interior farming valleys, especially in California; and along far-west stream courses. As late as the 1940s some hunters and even ornithologists thought the several races of these birds were

different species. They also often spoke of this quail, confusingly, as a "partridge."

The tendency to separate into species the quail from different far-west areas had some logic. "Valley" quail are by no means always found in valleys. Several of the other races—of which there are more than half a dozen, some of them darker or lighter colored—dwell in barren foothills of eastern Oregon and Washington, in western Nevada, along the western course of the Snake River in Idaho, and even as far inland as central Utah, in areas that might properly be called uplands. Many of these inland populations were not native, but rather established by transplant. Nevertheless, in modern usage all the subspecies of *californicus* are usually lumped together by hunters as "valley quail."

By and large, these quail don't colonize the stark, baking desert that appeals to the

95

The valley, or California, quail is the top game bird of the Far West. It looks quite similar to the Gambel's quail, except for the scale effect of feather markings on nape and breast. *Erwin A. Bauer photo.*

Gambel's quail, even though the ranges do overlap a bit in the Southwest. The California quail can put up with the desert, and in numerous inland areas is found also in arid regions where sagebrush, greasewood, and rabbitbrush are the main vegetative cover. Conversely, in farming country of California, and on up the coast where crop forage may be lush and lots of brush and moisture and live streams are available much of the year, the birds often establish their highest populations. They are populous both along the coast and in interior valleys. This bird is the No. 1 game bird of much of the Far West.

I remember Ted Trueblood telling me of hunting valley quail under conditions very similar to those I'd found where Gambel's quail were the quarry—dust-dry, nearly treeless foothills covered with arid range vegetation. My first experiences with them were along the western slope of the coastal

mountains where blacktail deer popped out of the brush intermittently while we scoured it for quail.

This was rather humid country, quite different from places I'd hunted the closely related Gambel's. But there was nothing different about the speed of the quail. California quail run as readily, as fast, and as far as any Gambel's ever did. Yet they can do a sudden flip-flop and be underfoot, with singles or several squirting out from under every bush in front of, beside, and behind you, or lying amazingly tight before a pointing dog.

On one hunt a good many years ago, the landowner who had invited me had an excellent old pointer, which he'd taught to stay at heel during the beginning of the hunt. This puzzled me. We were in scattered cover of low brush. As we walked, some yards apart, moving toward a series of low ridges, we could see quail ahead of us, running. I thought perhaps the dog should be out there trying to head them and pin some of them down.

Birds were abundant. As we glimpsed the running ones, they kept gathering more, alerting other coveys by their movement. This is typical of valley quail, and I had experienced the same phenomenon to some extent with their close relative, the Gambel's. Presently my host motioned for us to circle wide to the left, then up the first low ridge to its top, where we moved back to our right.

I assumed this maneuver was to cut off the running quail. Many of them, however, had won the race and were going over the ridge as we moved along it. Now the dog, as if knowing exactly what was going on and used to this routine, moved out in front of its owner and began working slowly back down in the direction from which we had come. Within a few yards the pointer swung sharply left and froze, one front foot raised, tail rigid. The owner motioned me in. I was standing practically on top of the quail, in cover so skimpy it seemed impossible that a bird could hide, when it burst up almost into my face.

Here was a fast lesson in valley quail hunting. The bird didn't want to go back downhill. It intended to follow the others it knew had run on. Over my head it went. I whirled, shot, and missed. By then it was over the ridge and out of view.

We worked back down, the dog swinging wide to left and right, pointing every few yards. This was another valley quail lesson, but reminiscent also of the sometimes behavior of the Gambel's. Invariably when valley quail run, gathering others enroute, a bird here and there drops out of the race, preferring to hide and let disturbance pass. If the cover is thick, some never are found, especially if the terrain is dusty and dry and the vegetation heavy with its own scent—sage and rabbitbrush. Even the best of dogs can't separate out and locate the quail scent.

These birds are uncanny in their ability, as singles or pairs, to lie snug in the smallest tuft of grass or scrub or even beside a small rock or dirt clod. Without a dog, you must work very slowly, covering every inch of ground. When valley quail run, their speed is astonishing. When they stick tight, their persistence is just as much so.

We dropped six birds on our sweep back down. This was as slick a scheme for hunting valley quail as I've seen. I try not to recall how many birds we missed. One of the miss-causing problems this species presents to the gunner is its flight pattern

Hull flies as a valley quail folds. This bird inhabits a wide variety of cover from desert to foothills and river courses to farmlands.

after flushing. Seldom do valley quail rise and zoom off on an upward slant before beginning their glide. In my experience at least, almost every flushed bird will skim the cover. After the initial flush, it rises only to modest altitude, then immediately begins descending. By the time you get on one with your gun, it is lower than the point from which it started. To the average gunner this is most disconcerting, doubly so if the birds happen to fly down a slope or canyon edge.

Overall, hunting valley quail is much like hunting the Gambel's, except that much of the terrain and cover is moderately more congenial to both bird and hunter. As I've mentioned, these quail are closely related, and indeed look so much alike that the inexperienced observer might err in identification. Actually, close observation shows that each bird has most distinctive feather patterns and colors.

Both sport a forward-curved black plume atop the head. That of the male is larger and longer than the female's. Both male birds have a red-brown crown, and a black face outlined with white markings. Both have flanks that are gray and brown with smart white slashes. Both have a gray-blue throat and upper breast.

Here the similarities end. The valley quail is a darker bird overall. Its belly has scale-like feathers, whitish and with gray-blue scalloped edging, reminiscent of the scaled or blue quail. This scale effect also appears down the back of the neck. On the belly a large brownish area overlies the scaled feathers. The Gambel's lacks the scaling, and its lower breast and belly are pale yellowish with a centered large black spot. Females of both are more subdued in color tones.

Throughout the range of the valley quail, favored habitats include mixed brush and grass lands, and the streamside fringes of willows and other moisture-loving shrubs. If there are gullies and rocky canyons, the birds utilize these, too. On farms, wherever pastureland is mixed with crop and fallow fields, these quail find the combination ideal. Often this is the favorite country for the hunter, too, for the birds are sometimes easier to pin down here.

One fall at the end of the 1930s I hunted several times in the best valley quail country of this sort I've ever seen. It was in a location that today's hunters would find unbelievable – partway between Hollywood and Santa Monica, California. At that time green farming country covered portions of this area, even though today that's difficult to imagine. I was working in the movie business. The uncle of a co-worker friend owned a farm down toward the coast. It was partly lightly grazed pasture, partly cropland, with small untilled patches. There was a small creek running across it, and several irrigation diversions. Quail simply teemed, and were seldom hunted.

Had this been my only experience with valley quail, I'd have thought them the easiest of game birds. We didn't have a dog. We'd walk the fields, flushing some birds and sending others running ahead. We killed a fair number in the fields. They were a bit naive, and I confess we didn't mind that.

Our real sport hunting occurred, however, whenever we could get a covey or two of quail flying or running to the edges of the creek or an irrigation ditch. Here grass and other vegetation were dense. The birds couldn't run in it. We'd watch down a flying covey, or try to spot a covey running across a harvested field to hide along the water course. Then we'd move in. This was the fastest valley quail shooting I've ever experienced. We'd move slowly, one on either side of the water, kicking the grass and weeds. The country was flat, and shots as birds flushed were wide open. On several occasions we killed a dozen or more birds and missed as many more on a single sweep along a quarter-mile of waterway.

The last time I saw that country, it was mostly concrete. I thought, passing through it, that it was a wonder the valley quail hadn't somehow made do with it. Although their range, by bobwhite standards, is extremely restricted, within it these birds are able to sustain themselves in such a variety of terrain and cover that it's impossible to tell a hunter what is really typical.

Far south, in Mexico, valley quail are distinctly desert birds, living among prickly pear and cholla and rocks, often in seemingly waterless range. The annual fires driven by the Santa Ana winds that burn brush in California and are so destructive also wipe out prime habitat of thousands of valley quail. In some places farther north, they're found in humid lowlands and even under swampy conditions. Water sources always draw them, yet in good years they swarm across the lava-rock badlands in northern California, too, and live happily in short sage and rabbitbrush on open hillsides there and elsewhere.

In central inland valleys they consort where live oaks and varied other oaks are scattered among golden grasslands. They have even adapted to city fringes throughout their range, and often are seen in parks. Years ago the expanding vineyards of wine makers wiped out much original habitat, but valley quail then adapted to living among the vines.

Although the valley quail is a most adaptable bird, it seems unable to colonize or establish itself after transplant outside the length of the western coast and its inland

The mountain quail is the largest of our native quail. The striking long and slender head plume is its tag. An extremely sporty bird, it lacks for attention because of its steep habitat. *Oregon Department of Fish & Wildlife photo.*

fringes. Even there it is not found in the authentic uplands. Fortunately there is a relative—largest of our native quail at up to 10 ounces in weight, as compared to six or seven for the valley quail—that takes over. This is the mountain quail. Its range covers territory almost identical to that of the valley quail—excepting most of Baja—but it is higher, in the canyons, the burns, and the brushy clearings of the forested mountains.

Mountain quail are occasionally found up at 8,000 or more feet. Most, however, live during summer and early fall no higher than 5,000 to 6,000. Some nest and live within the vertical range of the valley quail, as low as 2,500 or less. The higher-altitude birds make vertical late fall migrations as the snow line creeps down the slopes.

Some cover long distances. The birds *walk* down the slopes, moving lower day by day, feeding along.

Like the valley quail, mountain quail are found in a variety of terrain types. In parts of their range they stick to the rocky canyons that have streams in the bottom. Some of these have hemming slopes covered with sage and other arid-country vegetation. Wherever I've seen them, my impression is that the mountain quail always are in steeply sloped country, some so steep a hunter and his dog have difficulty in it. Further, when disturbed they invariably run uphill. Unless you experience it, it's difficult to imagine what hunting mountain quail on a 45 degree mountainside is like.

Although brush cover of numerous varieties, including streamside willows and alders, is utilized by mountain quail, in some of their very best range they live along the edges of clearings surrounded by conifers. One of the best hunts I ever had for them as a young fellow was in Oregon, working a newly sprouted burn. Logged expanses on a steep slope, where stumps are intermingled with scattered young conifers and several brushy draws cut the slope face, are perfect places to look for mountain quail.

An Oregon friend introduced me to just such an area one fall years ago. He was partial to a slow-working flushing dog rather than a pointer. He claimed pointing dogs would try to run uphill to pin down

The mountain quail's terrain may be on conifer-clad mountainsides or along streams in rugged settings.

running quail, and in the really steep places couldn't move fast enough. His dog, a carefully trained springer, moved very slowly and quietly, and handled mountain quail beautifully, often pinning down a whole covey of 10 or 12 birds. She also was a diligent finder and retriever of downed birds. This is important in mountain quail hunting. Cover is so often dense, even if it's only grass or sage, that losing dead or crippled birds is all too common among dogless hunters.

My friend had a rule on these covey flushes. If the birds flew off in a group, we'd make one follow. If they went every which way, up slope and down, we left them. The singles sit tight, but when they're scattered on a steep slope, the work of finding them, even with a dog, is just too much. We'd move on, and often as not come back across the slope later, after the covey had gotten back together.

One of the interesting habits of mountain quail is that they're not only masters at hiding in seemingly barren areas. Among young second-growth conifers in an area cut some years earlier, flushed birds often alight in the trees. Some occasionally roost in the edges of large conifers surrounding a mountain meadow or burn.

It amuses me to remember that during the hunt with the Oregon gentleman and his springer, the dog was acting birdy in a patch of grass within a cut-over expanse where the scattered young conifers averaged three times my height. I was standing so that my left elbow touched a branch of one, watching the dog work. Suddenly there was a roar of wings within inches of my left ear. I jumped as if prodded by an electric jolt. A quail had been perched within inches in the branches beside me. I was so startled I forgot to shoot.

Mountain quail are stunningly hand-

some birds. The most conspicuous attribute is the narrow black plume thrusting straight up from the crown of the head. It is comprised of two feathers that in some males may be over 2½ inches long. This plume rises from a low, inconspicuous, ruffled crest of blue-gray feathers. The neck and breast are the same blue-gray hue. The throat is chestnut outlined in white; the lower belly is chestnut, with the flanks white-barred with chestnut; and the back is brownish. There are at least a half dozen slightly differing subspecies throughout the range, but everywhere they're simply called mountain quail and no race distinction is made.

It is never easy to pinpoint concentrations of mountain quail. In California all mountain ranges, inland and coastal, have them in varied abundance. Some of the best hunting is along the western slope of the Sierras and the eastern slope of the coastal ranges from northeast of San Francisco to Oregon. In that state the lower brushy slopes of all mountains—coastal, central, and eastern—have varying populations. In Washington mountain quail are native to the coastal mountains, but are not especially plentiful. They were established by transplant in the mountains of eastern Washington and also on southern Vancouver Island, British Columbia.

They are present in limited numbers in western Nevada, at middle altitudes and in the Sierra foothills, and in isolated pockets in Idaho. Transplants have been made to Utah, and more recently to the Uncompahgre Plateau in Colorado. In the south, the range reaches into northern Baja.

Over much of the territory, upland-game biologists from the coastal states have told me, mountain quail are greatly underhunted. This is undoubtedly because of the difficulties hunters face over much of their habitat. The hunting is plain hard work. On coastal slopes, it's often pursued in rain, which makes the steep going also slippery. In my experience at least, the birds are invariably exasperating, one bunch easily manageable with or without a dog, the next just impossible. A look at a recent upland-game harvest report from Oregon illustrates the popularity—and probably the comparative ease of hunter success—of several game birds. Kills in round figures for the season were as follows: pheasants, 213,000; chukars, 142,000; valley quail, 125,000; mountain quail (with no shortage of birds) 73,000. Knowing how tough chukars can be, I'd say the mountain quail kill, at about half that, speaks for itself!

What I remember with most pleasure about the mountain quail, in addition to the thrill of successful shots, is the clear, liquid, single-note whistle of the cocks. I won't attempt a phonetic spelling, but any hunter in mountain quail country will know the sound when he hears it. On a still day where a slope overlooks a valley or a canyon cuts sharply down to a gurgling stream, the whistle, repeated every few seconds for several minutes, can be heard from half a mile away.

Perhaps there *is* something I remember with more pleasure than I do the whistle of the mountain quail: its taste. Broiled and served with no condiments except salt and pepper, these white-meated birds are superb. After having eaten all of the nation's quail species, I'd rate the delicate flavor of the mountain quail almost a match with that of the Mearns—and that's an extraordinary compliment indeed. Interestingly, in this age when many other upland species are too severely pressured, this unique and beautiful bird is one that can accept heavier utilization. Upland bird-hunting enthusiasts who'd like to sample something different should do something about that.

12

The "Fool" Quail That Makes You Feel Like One

One of the most amusing hunting incidents I've ever experienced occurred on a bright winter morning in the foothill country of southeastern Arizona. There were three of us: one a local with a fine little slow-working Brittany, myself, and another hunter down from Texas, hunting Mearns quail.

The surroundings were typical habitat of this quail, the grass and oak and scattered juniper zone well up above the desert floor. My Texas companion had managed, more by luck than by expertness, to collect a quail first thing. He had admired it, then stuffed it into his game pocket. Now, 20 minutes later, the meticulous Brittany began moving very slowly and deliberately, a few feet ahead of us.

We were spaced in a line only a few feet apart, the Texan in the middle. We stopped, watching the dog, which turned now to face us and took a tentative step toward the Texan. Then another, and another—slow motion, poker stiff. The dog finally came to a stop, trembling, her head and nose literally only a foot from the Texan's boots. The ground cover was short yellow grass. There wasn't a bush or tree for yards in any direction.

Out of the silence the Texan murmured, "Crazy fool dog! She's pointing the one in my pocket!"

The native who owned her snorted, resenting this. He said, "Move your feet around, and we'll see."

The Texan scuffed at the grass. He had on a cap with a prominent bill. The quail exploded from nowhere, in the narrow space between him and the dog. It had only one way to go—up. One wing actually brushed the hunter's cap visor. He threw up his arms and stumbled backward, letting out a yelp and coming down hard on his seat.

The local and I were jackknifed in laughter, and the poor Brittany looked at all of us in disgust because no one had tried to shoot the quail. The local said, "Charge it with assault, Tex. You might win a bundle!"

The Texan had come with me reluctantly. He had read, as have many others, that the Mearns is the most naive of birds, hardly deserving classification as "game." But then, for many years writers have been telling all sorts of untruths and inaccuracies and repeating hearsay about the Mearns quail, and more such nonsense has been spread by some naturalists, copying from other naturalists, probably none of them having had much personal experience with this bird.

That ought to give me the right, as one who has hunted all of the nation's quail species, to give an opinion. It is simply that the Mearns is not only the sportiest quail of all, but just possibly should rate, quality by quality, far out in front of all other game birds.

This quail is drastically different from all others, in appearance and in habits. It is a comically dumpy-looking bird, the illusion caused by its very short tail and its arched back. Mearns quail always remind me somehow of guinea hens—miniatures of them. They even appear smaller than they are, again probably because of the short tail. I've read in several references that they are the smallest of our native quail, weighing only three or four ounces. This is patently inaccurate. Steve Gallizioli, who worked with the Arizona game department and who has hunted them for years, claims that adults are a third heavier than Gambel's quail. One Tucson native with whom I hunted told me that birds he'd weighed

Male Mearns quail at right, female at left. The sexes look quite different. This bird is sometimes called "harlequin quail" because of the clown-like mask of the male.

Male Mearns quail in grass. The preferred habitat of these quail is the grassy highlands at altitudes of 4,000 to 6,000 feet.

average seven ounces. I've never weighed either, but Gambel's are claimed to go about six to seven ounces. I've killed both species during an Arizona hunt, had both in hand at once, and I'm inclined to believe that the Mearns, though deceptive to look at, weighs at least as much as the Gambel's or slightly more.

Among other quail species, males and females look generally similar, the females being less colorful. Male and female Mearns are strikingly different. The male has a pale brownish crest, but it is seldom raised. The face is striped with black and white in a pattern reminiscent of a mask, which gave rise to a name often used, especially in books, the "harlequin" quail. The back is streaked and speckled with brownish and black, and some feathers are edged in near-white. The breast is deep chestnut, the lower belly jet black. The sides and flanks are grayish-black stippled with scores of large white dots. What a dapper bird!

In my office I have a mounted pair. As they pose together, you would hardly guess that the female is of the same species, except for her shape. The overall impression is of a pale pinkish-buff bird with pale brown markings. The facial mask is barely suggested. The upper parts, back and wings, are paler than those of the male, and the breast and belly are pale brownish-buff, with scattered black flecks.

Distinctive markings are not the only unusual physical attribute of this quail. When you get one in hand, you immediately notice the heavy beak, the unusually stout legs, and the large, strong feet, the toes having extra-long claws. The feet, long claws, and strong legs are purposefully designed. So is the powerfully bowed back. Much of the year the diet of the Mearns is predominantly small tubers, those of sedge grasses and oxalis being favorites. The birds must dig for these.

In fact, hunters who know Mearns quail habits keep diligent lookout for patches of pockmarked ground where the birds have been feeding. These signs are usually in expanses of short, open grass. Once you spot such a place, you know quail are in the vicinity. I've seen patches where a covey had been working, leaving little pockets possibly two inches across and two or more deep. Scores of these diggings covered the area.

Although Mearns quail are not hunted in Texas and are not abundant there, once while mule deer hunting north of Alpine in the Trans-Pecos region I drove my 4WD along a mesa trail and came upon a covey of Mearns at their foraging. The earth was hard, but their strong toenails made the dirt fly. Then the stout, short beak would whack down into the little excavation and give a twist, and up would come a tuber.

During my first Mearns hunt in Arizona—the only state where this quail is presently hunted—I had a comical experience with Mearns food. Seymour Levy, who lived in Tucson and was something of an expert on these quail, showed me in his palm a scattering of small, dry tubers, samples of the mainstay of the Mearns diet.

"Try a couple," he said. "They're good."

I did. Not bad, a nutty, crisp flavor. "Did you dig these just to show me?" I asked.

"No," he replied. "I took them out of the crops of some quail I shot last week."

I recall hunting dogless in the uplands southeast from Tucson one midday. Because Mearns quail lie so tight, hunting dogless is always tough going. I came upon an area of short grass, in an open valley with only a scattering of small gray oaks in it. A few angular stalks of up-country cholla and a bush or two were the only other features of the small meadow. I stood looking down at the pocked ground where a covey had dug for tubers. The little holes looked fresh. There were small patches of snow in protected places where ground contours had protected it from melting after a flurry two days previously.

Suddenly I thought I could see quail tracks showing distinctly in a nearby snow patch. After a long look, I realized they were pointed *toward* me. I took a step forward, gun still under my arm, to peer more closely at the tracks. The whole flat seemed to explode around me in a blizzard of noisy wings. It just wasn't possible that I would not have seen the hiding quail. It was difficult to believe I'd been standing in the middle of them. I recovered enough to shoot—harmlessly. I had been walking until I was utterly frazzled. This had been my only chance. Talk about total frustration—and a lesson in the value of hunting these birds with a dog!

Years ago, when Arizona researchers first suggested putting the Mearns on the game list, there was much controversy. Some said the quail were so scarce they'd be wiped out. After all, they had been on the original rare and endangered list. Presumably that error had been made because they were so seldom seen or heard, even by those who purposely sought them.

It's not surprising that so little is known of the Mearns quail among U.S. gunners, and that so many fallacies concerning it have been encouraged. Its range within the U.S. is the smallest of any of our quail. The far-west Big Bend country of Texas has a scant few. Their official range covers the southwestern quarter of New Mexico and the Rio Grande valley well up into the state. They're not common anywhere in it. The foothills of individual mountain ranges of southeastern Arizona are where most of them are in the U.S. Even here, some people who've literally lived among them have never seen one.

These are not authentic desert dwellers by any means. They inhabit the grassy uplands. Where I've hunted them, we operated in prime habitat at 5,000 to 6,000 feet. I've been told they occasionally range higher, to 9,000 feet. The ridges, mesas, and benches at the middle altitudes in southeastern Arizona are the classic oak and juniper and grass zone, with pines clothing higher background peaks. Mearns quail of one subspecies or another range far down through Mexico, and are sometimes present there in brushy regions and forest fringes where pine, especially pinyon, and oak intermingle in broken, rocky country.

The Arizona range is delightful country. This is the home of the small and sporty Coues or Arizona whitetail deer. Occasionally several are jumped by quail hunters. Seldom do you see other hunters. Although the Mearns has been hunted in Arizona for 20 or more years, it still gets only modest attention. There may be logical reasons. Hunters after deer or javelina in the quail country seldom see quail. The birds lie too snug and let them pass. Sportsmen

who are in the range for one reason or another at any time of year, in fact, seldom see these secretive quail, and never hear them, or recognize their few low sounds if they do. The Mearns is the quietest, most retiring of the quail tribe, and it much prefers to freeze rather than flush when disturbance occurs.

Further, many have claimed they are such fool birds that hunting them couldn't possibly be sport. The Mearns had been dubbed "fool quail" for years. Supposedly it was so trusting and naive that it had no fear of man. The Arizona hunting license back in the 1930s and 40s, so I was once told by an old man in Bisbee, used to have a warning on it that there was no open season on "fool, or Mearns, quail." The late Jack O'Connor, renowned outdoor writer, once wrote that while he was hunting deer in Texas' Big Bend country, a flock of Mearns fed all around him on fallen pinyon nuts

Hunters work typical Mearns quail country in the uplands. The quail feed chiefly on small tubers, which they scratch up with their extra-long toenails.

while he sat resting. A cock began picking pinyon nuts beside his boot, he related, and he reached out and picked it up.

Undoubtedly there was truth to the tales of fool quail, in both the U.S. and Mexico. Many bird species that have never been hunted and live in remote or isolated wilderness are naive. Ruffed grouse in early times were called "fool hens" in the Colonies. I've encountered ruffed grouse in the bush in Canada that wouldn't get out of the trail but sputtered and fussed while I walked around.

Whatever the truth about the Mearns, the "fool quail" designation waned swiftly in Arizona beginning with the first experimental season, of only two days, in 1960. Few birds were killed. From then on, as hunting continued up to the present, the fool quail was no longer called that, but many a hunter, sampling it for the first time, has left the foothills feeling like one.

Those who would like to experience this unique shooting must make plans for late in the year or early in the next, because of the birds' habits. Desert quail, and bobwhites, may be nesting in some areas as early as April and May. The Mearns doesn't nest until August. The young are therefore only partly grown by early fall. This habit is related to the timing of rains in their bailiwick. At lower altitudes, winter rains set the stage for the early nesting of Gambel's and scaled quail. The moisture and heightened humidity influence and enhance nesting success. In the higher Mearns range, summer rains are the important factor. The season is therefore set late, usually in December and January and to about the middle of February.

"A prospective hunter should keep track of the southeastern Arizona weather in summer," a state game biologist told me. "If we have lots of summer rain in the foot-

hills, it's almost a sure bet the Mearns population will be high. If it's dry, birds will be few."

I was fortunate to have a hunt during one of those peak years. I had driven from my Texas home to Tucson in late January. The coveys had been combed over some, but by no means had been appreciably thinned. To our great pleasure, we had no competition—we never encountered another hunter in the hills. I had two friends with me, and we hunted with two residents, each of whom had a dog, one a pointer, the other a Brittany.

"Let's meet around nine," one of our hosts suggested. "Hunting will be better after the sun is well up."

That suited me fine. I've always despised rousting out before dawn. This is one appealing part of a Mearns quail hunt. The birds are not eager to leave their roosting places on the ground. Further, dogs have a tough time locating them until they've moved around, feeding. Some hunters prefer to start after the feeding period, when scent may be tracked over each covey's domain and the coveys are bunched up again. Some don't hunt until midafternoon, when feeding has begun again. The period from then until waning light ordinarily offers the most action.

We had barely gotten under way when one of the local hunters found a freshly scratched area. He said, "Look alert now. Mearns aren't wide-ranging birds. If food is plentiful, they'll be at the same feeding stands every day, and when you find good sign, they'll invariably be within at most a circle of 200 yards, more often half that."

His estimate, it turned out, was long. The pointer set up in a patch of grass studded with several oaks not 50 yards ahead. We moved in. This once the birds acted exactly as quail should. As we came in,

Shot quail falls on a patch of snow. The season usually runs quite late, because these birds hatch late in summer and do not mature until well into fall or winter.

they swirled noisily up, swarming toward and through and quickly screened by the oaks. Two were not quick enough. We all were shooting. No one was sure who dropped the birds. In the ensuing quiet a bird got up, I swear, precisely behind me. My impression as I wheeled around was that I must have stepped over it. But now it was above the open grass, and I threw a load of 7½s after it from a modified barrel. Down it came.

Experienced hunters like to insist that every flushed Mearns quail will put an oak or juniper between it and your gun. Well, maybe they try. And maybe they simply fly. They don't all manage a screen. That day we crossed an open valley of grass, not a bush or a tree in all of it. Grass is the key to finding Mearns quail. If it's too short they may shun it, but much of the region where we were had tall, yellowed grass that was just right, except that it hid jillions of rocks over which we stumbled incessantly, wearing leg muscles to a constant ache.

It was getting late in the afternoon, and I was wondering if I could possibly drag back to the vehicle. Then both dogs stiffened out, and miraculously all my pains disappeared. A covey of 10 birds swirled aloft in typical high-decibel Mearns fashion. They were limned against a bright sky and a far-off mountain with snow on it. When the shooting was over, the dogs patiently and proudly gathered six quail.

This was my last afternoon of this trip. What a perfect ending for it. But no, not yet. I had my eye yearningly glued to the distant vehicles, parked on a ridgetop, when in the same flat the weary dogs set up again. Once more the flush was wide open, and once more birds fell, four of them, all handsome little cocks.

Only one Mearns quail experience can tie that kind of shooting. That's sitting down at table after the hunt, with the gathered quarry the main course. I said in writing of the deliciousness of the mountain quail that I'd rate it *almost* a match for the Mearns, and that this is an extraordinary compliment. True!

If you skin one of these "fool" quail, hold the bird up to the light, and look at the breast, you'll notice that the flesh has a translucent appearance. Whether this is from their diet or from their gene arrangement, no one seems certain. However, if you have eaten all the other quail species, there's no doubt whatever that you'll pronounce this the most delicate and delicious of all.

Part III

THE GROUSE AND PARTRIDGE

There is a tilt toward North America when one tallies the number and location of grouse varieties. We have slightly more than half of the world's species—10 all told, and those are divided into numerous subspecies or races. The term "grouse" does not include the quail, although many hunters think of all these birds as belonging to the same family. They don't.

Quail belong to the family *Phasianidae*, which also contains the pheasant and the partridge. These birds—of enormous variety, over 160 species worldwide—are predominantly native to Europe, Asia, and the Orient. No true partridge or pheasant was indigenous to North America. The grouse are members of the family *Tetraonidae*. American hunters are blessed with a rich assortment of them. Most of the species are native to Alaska, Canada, and the northern half of the United States. Only one, the prairie chicken, was originally native in one subspecies or another clear down to the Gulf of Mexico and the Mexican border.

The statement that no partridge were native to this country may seem confusing to some hunters. The word "partridge" has been widely misused. In the East the ruffed grouse is commonly called "partridge," and in the South the bobwhite in early times was spoken of as a "partridge." Several western quail species were called partridge even up to midcentury. From the nonscientific view, it is in fact perplexing to define which is which. One unscientific difference is that quail in general are smaller than most partridge.

Regardless, it is easy for American sportsmen to keep the two separated. The partridge now present on this continent are foreigners, although both of them, the chukar and the Hungarian partridge, called simply "Hun" by most sportsmen, have been so long and well established that, like the pheasant, they have become quasinatives.

The delights of hunting grouse and partridge are emphasized by the fact that these birds in total blanket a vast area of the continent, and have fitted themselves species by species into practically every habitat type. If you make a point of trying to experience hunting for each species, you will traverse much of the United States and Canada, and flush birds from crop fields to remote forests, from treeless prairies to the fringes of suburbia, from brushlands to rocky badlands.

Of all these birds, the ruffed grouse has always been the most publicized since days of early settlement in the East. In fact, a kind of mystique has built up around it. To this day, when grouse hunting is mentioned, it is commonly assumed that the ruffed grouse is the target. As with the southern quail elitist who pretends that "bobwhite" and "quail" are synonymous, his counterpart in the eastern ruffed grouse woods presumes that "grouse" refers to ruffed grouse. Is it possible, he might inquire, that there are *other* grouse?

No doubt the ruffed grouse deserves the adulation its enthusiasts offer. It didn't always. When the Colonists arrived, ruffed grouse were such gentle, naive birds that often one could be killed with a stick. Some of them still today, over their enormous range across Canada and Alaska and down through much of the Rockies and Pacific Coast ranges, live in such remote wilderness that they act the same way. They've never been introduced to man and the gun. The others have certainly learned wariness.

Ruffed grouse, as most hunters envision them, are "eastern birds." They are heavily hunted from New England down through the eastern mountain chains to northern Georgia, and throughout the Great Lakes region and the eastern half of southern Canada. Westward, ruffed grouse are often incidentals. A few hunters in the Rockies states discover pockets of ruffed grouse abundance and annually pursue them along mountain stream courses and in foothill thickets. But these are specialist hunters, whereas in the East and the northern Great Lakes the ruffed grouse is THE important game bird.

Other forest and forest-edge grouse include the spruce grouse of Canada and the mountains of the western U.S., a bird so naive it is invariably called "fool hen." Little sport hunting is attempted for it, although it is pot-hunted by natives over much of Canada, where it is most abundant.

In the western mountain forests, the big blue grouse—cocks may weigh as much as four pounds—is also at times a rather tame bird, but it has a split personality. Under proper circumstances, it can turn into a dynamic game bird, as hard to hit as any target imaginable as it explodes at close range and sizzles down a mountainside. This, too, is a specialist's bird, partly because of the rugged terrain and high forests it inhabits.

The ptarmigan—willow, rock, and white-tailed varieties—are handsome creatures, and would unquestionably be immensely popular with American gunners, except that they dwell in places too remote and discomforting to draw more than a meager scattering of attention. In general they are all but unknown to sportsmen. They range, one species or another, throughout the Arctic, Alaska, and much of Canada. But even the willow ptarmigan, which is seen occasionally in southern Canada, is seldom found in great enough abundance there to entice hunters from the states.

The chunky and appealing little white-tailed ptarmigan, smallest of the family, which turns totally white in winter except for eyes and bill, does offer a small oasis of population and hunting in Colorado. In scattered timberline locations these birds are fairly abundant. Few hunters ever learn that from experience. Getting to the hunting ground is discouraging even to contemplate. Finding the birds, once there, often becomes a long, gasping, and exhausting task. Anyone planning a Colorado ptarmigan hunt should first contact the Colorado game department to pinpoint areas where the birds are known, then perhaps track down a local warden or biologist who is familiar with a specific high-country range. I must admit I've never killed one.

During settlement, the open-country grouse were the most abundant of all American grouse species. In places and at certain historical times, they were unbelievably so. The prairie chicken, in one race or another, was spread over a vast midcontinent area, and its close relative, the heath hen, long extinct, was abundant from lower New England down to the mid-Atlantic coastal states.

Prairie chickens are birds that require large areas of unbroken grasslands. When farmers came into their range, tilled lands intermingled with virgin sod enhanced their colonizing and propagation abilities. The birds exploded in numbers estimated in millions. Market hunting and a growing imbalance between the amount of tilled land and unbroken grasslands eventually all but did them in. Today prairie chickens, the lesser and greater varieties, are still hunted in restricted areas of a few mid-U.S. states from South Dakota to eastern New Mexico and western Texas. Although the birds are reasonably abundant in a few places within this range, most hunts are token affairs, and some may be closed down at any time.

The sharp-tailed grouse has done better than the prairie chicken, even though the two originally shared portions of the same habitat, and in a few places still do. The sharptail is more adaptable. Further, its favorite ranges include grassy prairies, especially the portions of them merging into open woodlands, and large brushy expanses of cleared lands. Some of the country in the prairie provinces of Canada, where scrub poplar in thin stands intermingles with grass and brush, is classic sharptail habitat.

The brush and open woodlands favored by the sharptail—and the fact that its prime original range did not reach very far south (Colorado was the limit)—kept this bird to some extent away from the mass westward migration of human settlement. For example, where I hunted sharptails in Michigan's Upper Peninsula years ago—and they were then abundant—there were vast wild-hay meadows with strips of poplar and jackpine intermingled. The birds thrived in such country, until clearing and the push of settlement eliminated them.

There is still fine sharptail shooting to be had in parts of the Dakotas and Montana, for example, and on into enormous reaches of interior Canada. There is token hunting elsewhere. The range of abundance of the sharptail has diminished drastically, but as long as the regions where it is plentiful remain unappealing for farm usage and heavier settlement, the birds will probably be available to hunters.

The one other American open-country grouse, the largest of our native tribe, is the sage grouse. It also holds forth in some of its original range nowadays in surprisingly high numbers. It is, however, undoubtedly in serious trouble, its range annually shrinking. This highly specialized bird is totally dependent upon sage. It nests in sage-covered hills and flats, feeds on the leaves, and apparently cannot adapt to sageless expanses. Spraying of sage over enormous areas, in order to kill it out and allow grass to grow, has totally extirpated sage grouse in great chunks of their range.

The bright side is that there is much excellent sage grouse hunting left. Several western states still have open seasons. The eastern half of Montana, much of Wyoming's sage country, and northwestern Colorado presently offer the best shooting.

While some of our grouse species have been severely diminished, the two imported partridge have achieved rather astonishingly successful colonizations. The larger of the two at about 1¾ pounds maximum, the chukar partridge, has become an important game bird in portions of a number of western states—all the Pacific Coastal states plus Idaho, Montana, Wyoming, Nevada, Utah, Colorado. It is being tested in several other states.

The American chukar, named for the crowing sound of the male, is an undecipherable mixture of several subspecies. Introductions, beginning early in this century, were from various places in Asia and elsewhere. Some were unsuccessful, chiefly in the East and Midwest. Birds from the foothills of the Himalaya Mountains were among the first to establish themselves here. Practically all of the successful introductions of various subspecies have been in fairly high and distinctly dry regions.

The bird has caught on invariably in western foothills, where rocky outcrops and talus slopes offer, among various seeds and other forage, a favorite food, cheatgrass seeds. Chukars have also done well under desert conditions. They are hardy birds, able to contend with severe winters. They are also exceedingly sporty, sometimes running exasperatingly but at other times sitting snug for a pointing dog.

The remarkable and important attribute of the chukar in the scheme of modern game management is that it successfully fills niches in western terrain, where it competes very little with any native game bird. Thus it adds immensely, wherever it has become established, to opportunities for gunners. In several western states the chukar has in recent years moved into second place among upland birds in annual harvest surveys. In Nevada, where it had one of its early successes back in the mid-1930s, it swiftly moved up to become most popular and most numerous of that state's several upland birds.

The Hungarian, or gray, partridge has a somewhat different history. It has been immensely successful in a number of states and the Canadian prairie provinces, but it is such a perplexing and often frustrating bird to hunt that over much of its North American range it is far underhunted. In western Iowa, for example, where it is abundant, I once begged several native hunters to go after Huns with me. They just laughed.

"Why go through that," one said, "when we can hunt pheasants and be fairly certain of much more weight in the game vest?"

The Hun is a handsome little game bird weighing at most a little less than a pound. The best of the hunting available nowadays is in eastern Alberta, on across southern Saskatchewan and Manitoba, and southward into eastern Montana, the Dakotas, western Minnesota, and Iowa. Other excellent populations are in eastern Washington and Oregon, southern Idaho, and northern Nevada. There are modest populations in several midwestern states and in southeastern Ontario.

Like the introduced pheasant, the Hun is chiefly a bird of the grain fields and their weed and grassland fringes. This places it always where it is easily accessible to sportsmen. Because the Hun receives such modest attention, it offers an exceptional opportunity to those who've been passing it by, or are looking for new upland experiences. However, they must be willing to work at solving the riddles of the Hun's exasperating habits and, above all, be persistent.

Overall, the immense appeal of grouse and partridge hunting in America is, in my view and after long experience, based chiefly on the exciting variety both of birds and of terrain. The wingshooting menu this tribe serves up includes entrées for all gunning tastes.

13

The Most Revered "Pahtridge"

In northern Michigan, where I enjoyed over a period of years what I considered the finest ruffed grouse hunting to be found anywhere, few natives ever spoke of the bird by its proper name. They were called "pats," and everyone knew what you meant when you said you were going "pat" hunting. In this midcountry region, use of the rather undistinctive nickname was nevertheless a colloquialism that indicated to any close listener and translator of local idiom the love natives had for this bird.

In New England, where I had also hunted "pats," no sportsman would have condoned the word. Most hunters there, amusingly, have always spoken of the birds as grouse, without qualification. This is like saying that though there are numerous species of grouse, the only one with the class to deserve the name is the ruffed grouse, so obviously you don't need the qualifier.

The super-elite of eastern grouse hunters, however, would not deign to use even that term. To them the ruffed grouse is a "partridge," giving it an aura of aristocratic Old-Worldliness. Only they don't pronounce the word that way. In that unexplainable southern twist New Englanders give to certain words, they pronounce it "pahtridge." A gentleman I shot with there once spoke of it in a letter to me as "A most revered bird, indeed."

I was musing about this one early morning some years ago as three of us drove along a forest road in northern Michigan, parked, and piled out. My musings were not to last long. This was one of those delightful hunters' mornings that open with a burst of excitement that stays bright for years.

We moved quickly down along a wild river course. Frost was stiff on the grass. A

The forest-dwelling ruffed grouse is an elite member of the upland game bird tribe, with all the "game" qualities any gunner could desire. *Pennsylvania Game Commission photo.*

jay, sighting us and irked at our disturbance, cut into the stillness of the deep woods with insistent ridicule.

We'd walked only a few steps, and paused to load our guns, when Andy Loizos, a southpaw who shot a pump so fast you'd swear it was an automatic, said, "Look—blackhaw bushes!" In that region, such a statement had significance to any ruffed grouse hunter who knew his business.

As Andy spoke, one dog raced ahead into the patch of tall blackhaw bushes, tail straight and quivering. There was a mad scramble to load. The dog never had time to set up. Two birds flushed vertically through the blackhaws and then curved high to the left, over the river. Andy's gun slashed the quiet of the river bottom twice,

in measured rhythm. Both birds crumpled clean and splashed into the water's edge.

I, on high ground to the right, caught a glimpse of the dog racing on through the thick patch. More birds—running, I thought. And then they were up, almost before Andy's shots had died. Two came out of the far end of the thicket like rocket bursts, one tailing the other by perhaps 20 feet, flying low. I had a glimpse of Andy and my brother Bernard swinging their guns. Mine was already up and marking. Its first blast cut the lead bird down clean; I racked in another shell, fired, and saw the tail bird come down too.

Quicker than it can be told, Andy and I had each chalked up one of those rare experiences in "partridge" gunning: a double. Astonishment left a momentary silence.

Though no one knew it then, we were to witness a shooting exhibition far more startling before the day was done. Somewhere behind me I heard my brother say, "That calls for coffee, while you deadeyes tell how you did it."

It was a standing joke, the way Bernard was always breaking out his two-gallon coffeepot on trips like this. Nevertheless, these pauses were useful. During coffee stops much solid grouse wisdom was poured out in our discussions, along with the steaming brown liquid.

We'd had a loose group of a half dozen dedicated grouse hunters together for several years. It included several locals besides ourselves. Several of the group hunted prac-

tically every day of the season. We were proud of the fact that among us a great deal of ruffed grouse lore was pooled. We knew most of the time where the birds would be, when they'd be there, and what to do about it. Unfortunately, much of this knowledge we shared is not commonly known among average grouse hunters.

For example, there has probably been more nonsense written and mouthed about the ruffed grouse and how to hunt it successfully than about all other game birds combined. The bird is usually depicted as a crafty character with sixth and seventh senses, credited with all manner of shrewd schemes to outwit hunters. Actually, nothing could be farther from the truth. The

Ruffed grouse are most abundant in New England and the Great Lakes region, but also dwell in western mountains. *Pennsylvania Game Commission photo.*

quicker the grouse enthusiast learns it, the more successful he'll be.

In reality, this wonderful game bird is simple, direct, and elemental, in both its reactions and its daily routine. It isn't even especially brilliant as birds go—not that the fact makes me think less of it. The legends have grown up about the ruffed grouse mostly because of its habitat. Since we can't observe the birds readily in their deep-woods living quarters, which seem to be complicated diggings to the eye of the hunter, their movements and intentions take on a mystery that is 90 percent imagined by the gunner in order to excuse his own shortcomings.

"They'll always put an obstacle between the gun and themselves."

"Catch them on the edge of the thick stuff, and they'll dive into it, not giving you a shot."

"They'll fly right at you to keep you from getting a chance at 'em."

Every grouse hunter knows the tales. And they're all true. But the bird doesn't plan all that. When it flies through woods, obviously there will always be trees in the way. When it dives into the thick stuff, it simply proves what any hunter should already know: that Old Ruff is most uneasy about open spaces, and that this is a deep-woods species right down to its pinfeathers. It likes the edges, but mistrusts blue sky and long vistas. When it flies at you, that's your fault. The bird has kept its beloved cover handy, and is getting to it in the quickest way. You simply approached from the wrong direction.

Once you thoroughly understand the grouse's instincts, the next step is to wonder what it does all day long in its "mysterious" deep-woods bailiwick. No species of wildlife is ever at any given location without a very good and very simple reason. If you remember that, you soon know where grouse *won't* be. That saves time and averts empty game pockets.

I recall how one of our group, who had spent a lifetime in the places where grouse hang out, described the day of a grouse during one of Bernard's many coffee breaks. Here's the way his outline went:

Invariably ruffed grouse will roost in an evergreen thicket, if it is available. If the dawn is cold or wet, they'll be late getting to breakfast. But when they do go out, they'll simply drop down and walk to the table. Or, at best, they'll fly no more than a few rods. This holds when food is plentiful. Of course, the birds can't always find food and roosting sites close together, and then they must fly some distance for their meals. But that's the exception.

At breakfast they dawdle. They're heavy feeders, and that takes time. After breakfast, they have a drink. If the day is pleasant, by 11 a.m. they're on a reasonably open southeast exposure close to thick cover, sunning and taking dust baths. If it's nasty, back they go to the thickets. They're feeding again from late afternoon until dusk. Then it's time for a drink, and back to roost. During the whole day, unless unduly alarmed, they will have walked much farther than they've flown.

What could be simpler? But all this presupposes that food, water, and roost will be fairly close together. Old Ruff despises hard work. So don't bother to look for birds unless you know there is water within half a mile. That is the first rule: water. If the water is there, plus adequate cover, the grouse will look for proper feed. If it's lacking, they'll pass right on by.

As one of our group pointed out during a hunt: "Most hunters just go out in the woods anywhere and start looking for birds. That's a big place, and to the careless observer it all looks pretty much alike. But it isn't. The birds are the last thing to look for. You have to find the *place* first, and be able to recognize it when you do."

On that occasion I remember mentioning a nearby beaver pond. "There's high ground around it, with scrub pine, birch, and poplar, and some fairly open cover thick with clover. It's 9:30, which ought to be just right."

I was especially anxious to try that clover patch. I had sent a party of hunters out there a couple of days previously. They had come back disappointed. Not a bird around, they said. But on questioning them, I discovered they'd not tried it until early afternoon. I surmised that the birds had fed on the clover, which they dearly love, and had moved out until next mealtime.

We edged into the clover patch tensely, keeping watch to see that we didn't have a big tree in a direct line ahead. We hadn't gone 10 paces when a brown form skipped along the ground, ducked around a pine, and was up with a roar of wings. I heard a gun crack and someone mutter. Then another gun spoke, and one of the boys yelled, "Got him!" Before we finished in the clover, we put up 14 birds and accounted for three. The others, in the thin cover, flushed too wild for shooting. The important point, however, was the satisfaction of having known exactly *where* and *when*.

That clover patch intrigued me. I kept thinking all the time I was in it of a deep trout pool in a stream. Unless you know their ways, you can fish a lot of water where trout aren't, and be thinking all the time that they're there but aren't hitting. Somehow the deep-woods habitat of the ruffed grouse seems to me exactly comparable. It is a great stream of forest with "grouse pools." I had watched two hunters,

earlier in the season, skirt that clover patch at feeding time. They went crashing through thick surrounding woods where no bird would be at that time of day unless it had been flushed into hiding. They passed right by the small oasis which held birds.

If you get so you think of grouse country not as a great stretch of forest in which birds may be anywhere, but as a stretch dotted with small oases that offer perfect living conditions for grouse, you're on the right track. Next, if you know what those oases must have—the water, feed, dusting, and roosting places—to make them suitable, you're well on your way, for this partridge is no wanderer. A ruffed grouse is a

Most ruffed grouse average 1½ to 1¾ pounds. This old cock was an extra large specimen. These birds have white meat and a large breast and are among the finest of upland game birds on the table.

sedentary little chap when left alone. Add to that a knowledge of its daily schedule, and you can't miss—finding birds, that is!

The windup of the clover patch called, naturally, for another coffee session. This time we shared it with a stranger who insisted, in return for our hospitality, that we come and have a whirl across his private land. It proved to be a waste of good time, but the incident is worth telling because it illustrates the relationship between a grouse's chow line and the fatness of a gunner's game pocket.

We piled into the cars and followed the hospitable gentleman to his cabin site. It lay along a winding river branch bordered by swamp alders. Flanking the swamp were steep, rather open hillsides, covered on top with maple and beech. We cased the territory with a quick appraisal, and I'd bet we all thought the same thing. By then our host was beckoning us uphill.

"The hardwoods up there," he said, "will be full of birds."

Reluctantly we trailed along behind him. This was a fall when grouse food in the Great Lakes area was plentiful. Natives said that not in years had the wild-fruit crops of all kinds been so lush. A hard winter ahead, that's what they said it meant.

Now, grouse love beechnuts and acorns. Nevertheless, when soft food is abundant, they'll take that first. It's easier to eat, and they seem to know the mast will keep. We had already made a check of beech groves. The crop of nuts was not large.

In the soft-food line, however, wild pin cherries and choke cherries were literally everywhere, the trees loaded. Snowberry bushes were burdened with the soft, white fruit that turns pale blue as it overripens. You could spot the bushes at a great distance because of their red leaves. High-bush cranberries were loaded with shiny, mushy,

red fruit, and in the few places where blackhaw grew, the wizened, midnight-blue fruit weighted the branches.

Not so on the hills. After we had tramped them silently for a time, our host stopped and scratched his head. "Can't understand it," he said. "I was sure there'd be birds here."

"Nothing for 'em to eat," Bernard said bluntly. He turned and pointed toward the stream bottom, looking at his watch as he did so. "It's 3:30. There are wild cherry trees just off the edge of the evergreens down there, and I'll bet there's clover growing in the shade. The birds will just be coming out of the thickets right now. Some will already be under the cherries. Some will be right on the edge of the swamp." He didn't wait for agreement. He started down. We didn't need to be coaxed.

He walked straight to a wild cherry, swung on a bird that zoomed up in frantic flight toward the thick stuff, and dropped it. We moved into a line close to the edge of the evergreens and forged ahead. It was fast, wild shooting. Two birds were up on the very edge, diving headlong. A clatter of shots, all misses. Four more grouse burst from under an old down tree, and one of them fell clean. The march never slowed. The excitement was electric. The fellow who had brought us here trotted along, gaping in astonishment.

Then a lone bird exploded right behind Andy as he rushed to get up on a point the dogs had made far ahead. It scared him half witless, but he recovered to do some pretty shooting. As he jumped at the flush, he was already wheeling around—the wrong way, away from cover. That meant he had to keep on going, making almost a full circle, with his gun swinging so fast you could hardly follow it. The bird had made the edge and swung high behind a big spruce.

But habitat wasn't going to confuse Andy. He was thinking "bird," not "trees." His gun spoke, and the blind shot laced through the spruce top. As the echo lashed back from the hills, there was a light *plunk*. The bird, falling unseen, was down clean.

We finished out the sweep and came to our host's line fence. We gave the collected birds to the gentleman and went back to our vehicle. We'd laze around a bit, and be back in the blackhaw patches on the big river by 5 p.m. From then on until shooting light waned, the blackhaws would be the place.

During those years in northern Michigan, I learned a great deal from my hunting companions and from natives there who had for years studied the diet of the birds. That knowledge is probably the most important key to good shooting. Availability, of course, dictates what the birds will eat. Favorite forages obviously differ from location to location. Grouse foods abundant in

one area of the bird's huge range—clear across the continent—may not even be present in another.

Further, the season may dictate what is eaten. Some years acorns are abundant; some years they're scarce. Fruit of varied kinds may make a heavy crop one year, and the next the trees or bushes may be barren. Additionally, ruffed grouse are known to eat literally hundreds of different items. One scientific study lists over 500! Of those, however, only a few will be staples in any given place. Of the staples, only a few will as a rule be abundant during a given year. Thus, if you learn which foods are indigenous to your area, and check which are especially abundant during a given fall, you know precisely where to look for birds.

I remember seasons when highbush cranberries were aglow with red fruit. These bushes seldom grow in large patches, but rather are scattered as individual shrubs.

A springer spaniel fetches a grouse. Ruffed grouse are classic game for bird dogs, and lie snug for pointing breeds.

That fall we hunted dogless, walking from bush to bush. At least one out of 10 had a bird under it. Another fall three of us hunted snowberries, again bush to bush. That season much other food was scarce and perhaps one bush in five produced a bird. All these hunts impressed on me not only that food is the hottest clue to success but also that ruffed grouse, like all game birds, have distinct preferences. Finding the favorite foods in your area that are abundant during the season you're hunting is like having a map showing where the birds are.

There's another important angle. Knowing precisely where to look for birds increases your confidence in your shooting eye. You know when to get ready, when to relax. This factor, and calm but swift shooting when birds flush, are among the top secrets of regularly bagging ruffed grouse.

That late afternoon in the blackhaws along the river seemed like a reward for our diligent gathering of ruffed grouse lore. The clumps of tall shrubs grew densely. They stood tall and leafless and hazy blue with clusters of fruit. The birds were present. Their favorite dinner for that locality was spread before them, their evening drink and roosts were but a step away.

The sound of our high-tempo shooting was intermittently loud in the river bottom. The pounding of racing pulses was loud in our ears. One of us dropped a bird on the opposite side of the river, and my brother said, "I'll go pick it up. The stream's shallow here. I'll stay on that side, just in case."

"Just in case" was right! The rest of us suddenly found ourselves out of the blackhaws, and out of targets too. And as we stood there in an open grass flat watching my brother come abreast of us, we saw him step up to a blackhaw patch on his side. There was a chippering and a mad scramble

of grouse feet on dry leaves. There were assorted bursts of wing sound and of feathers slapping against the brush.

I knew he had run slam into a pack, and I knew he had his pump gun plugged to hold only three shells. The first bird to top the haws was directly in front of him. I don't remember hearing the gun, but I saw that bird drop before it had cleared the stuff by two feet. By that time several more were in the air. Why he picked the one farthest to his right, toward the river and us, I couldn't guess. It meant the longest swing. But it was fast and confusing work he was at just then, and he probably took the one his eye first recorded. The bird tumbled and splashed into an eddy on our side of the river. By that time he had his back to us. He had made a full-arc swing on a bird far back to his left!

I heard the third shot lace out—his last—and saw his third bird come down. The exhibition was such a startling thing, especially on ruffed grouse, that the rest of us never thought of shooting although the air had more than a dozen birds in it, all traveling in different directions. The whole dramatic moment had taken perhaps two or three seconds. It was worth a month of hunting. That was the only triple kill on grouse I've ever seen.

We all knew right then that the day's grand shoot was ended. Our silence was a compliment of the highest sort. We walked up as my brother gathered up his birds and stood there, looking half apologetic.

"I guess," he said, "that batch of shooting must have come out of the two-gallon coffeepot. I don't know how else to explain it."

It might have, at that. Considering the grouse-wise heads I had listened to so many times as they sat around his big jug, I wouldn't have been surprised.

14

Wild Flight

The October morning that I scalded my hand with boiling coffee, I was so mad at a certain ruffed grouse that I would have wrung the blighter's neck—except that it was already dead. I was having breakfast with a friend at his cabin in the woods, that opening morning of ruffed grouse season. I had gotten up from the table to take the coffee off the stove before it boiled over. Just as I lifted the pot, there was a shattering crash of glass behind and to my right. I jumped about a yard straight up, and the coffee went flying, scalding me. When things settled down again a few moments later, we were amazed to find a dead grouse on the floor amid a pile of broken glass.

Now, I'd like to dispose of the obvious question, "Why did the grouse fly through the window?" by saying that the early morning sun was in its eyes, or that the bright reflection in the window blinded it.

Or the question could be neatly explained by saying it saw a reflection of trees in the window and thought it was flying through an opening in the woods. A lot of explanations like that could be thought up by an imaginative gunner. In fact, most of them have been, because ours was by no means the first recorded instance of a ruffed grouse flying through a window, or doing some other crazy trick, in the fall. Unfortunately, not one of those explanations stands up. The sun in this instance wasn't even over the ridgetop, so the bird certainly was not blinded from either direction. And no grouse in its right mind—and note that phrase well—is fool enough, seeing a cabin looming up in front of it, to pick out the window, reflected trees or none, and try to fly through the supposed opening.

For many seasons I have been collecting bits and pieces of information about such

During some falls ruffed grouse fly into the sides of houses, crash through windows, hurtle into tree branches. Why they do this has perplexed hunters and scientists for years. *Pennsylvania Game Commission photo.*

crazy didoes of ruffed grouse. They constitute one of the most intriguing—and, to grouse enthusiasts, well-known—facets of grouse behavior. To my own satisfaction, at least, I have the answer. Many will not agree, especially scientists. But I'm convinced of my thesis here and have pretty good grounds, I think, to explain what causes that strange phenomenon known to grouse-country inhabitants as the "wild flight" or "crazy flight."

The first time I ever heard of the wild flight of grouse was the first fall I hunted them. I thought the native who told me about it was pulling my leg. "Some falls," he said, "you don't see a single bird acting crazy. Then in others you'll see a lot of them cutting up like a bunch of boozed-up conventioneers."

There was a tremendous crop of wild

cherries that fall, and we were doing our hunting in the cherry patches during feeding hours. The second afternoon we didn't hit it just right. After an hour or two we drove back to this hunter's house. He lived at the edge of a small village. There wasn't any grouse cover within a mile or more. The country was mostly open fields. Nonetheless, as we sat on his porch wondering where we should try next, we saw a bird come zooming across an open pasture field. It was twisting and turning crazily like a mourning dove, but the instant we saw it we knew it was a grouse. In this man's yard were three big spruce trees. The grouse came zooming along, wingtipped the top branches of one of those trees, and went into a wild spin that grounded it. The bird got up, shook itself, and walked around in circles, *cheeping* and acting dazed. Then it took off straight up, slamming itself into the branches in a most unprofessional manner. Finally it teetered on a limb and sat right there looking at us for 15 minutes or more, having difficulty keeping its balance.

"So now what do you think?" the old grouse hunter asked. "Is there or ain't there such a thing as a crazy flight among grouse?"

As my years of grouse hunting went along, I saw many more exhibitions of fantastic behavior by individual grouse. I never forgot what the old-timer had told me: that it happens some falls, and some falls it doesn't. In my observation, the man was absolutely right. The question that kept picking at me, of course, was: why?

To cite one specific instance of this odd cycle, one year in the vicinity of my home, which was then in northern Michigan in some of the best grouse country I ever expect to see, I collected an even dozen tales of incidents which had occurred that fall wherein grouse had killed themselves by flying into buildings or trees. Having seen hundreds of grouse dodge through fantastically tangled woodland mazes at full speed without difficulty, I just couldn't believe the normal accident rate would be so high. The following fall, as if to prove my point and to prove that the cycle had some definite reason, I neither observed nor heard of a single instance of a grouse knocking its brains out that way. I had long suspected that the answer lay in some variation in seasons or terrain. Certainly those two years tended to convince me further, though I have never found a scientist or a scientific reference to back me up.

Before I present this hypothesis, held by many observers in grouse country, it is necessary first to consider briefly the life history of the ruffed grouse, and what grouse experts in the wildlife-biology field term

the "fall shuffle." All birds, come nesting time in spring, choose a territory, just as man selects a place to build a home and raise his family. Man purchases his living plot nowadays. In primitive times, whenever one man happened to want another's territory, there was a battle and the winner had his homestead. Though man has progressed in his relationships with other men—at least in this respect—birds have not. Birds either bluff or battle for the living space each has chosen. It is even believed by some ornithologists that bird songs are a means of letting the other feathered gent know that he'd better keep out.

This ruffed grouse didn't need to be shot. The author picked it up dead beside his house in northern Michigan one fall after watching it fly crazily from a nearby woodland edge and crash into the wall.

Suppose now that a grouse hen has set up housekeeping. After the young grouse are hatched, the summer probably will never find them ranging over more than 40 acres or so around the nest site. Obviously something has to happen eventually to disperse them. Otherwise—ruffed grouse being nonmigratory—there would be constant inbreeding, harming the race, and the whole new family probably would try to raise young the next year in the same territory. Nature has to do something about this.

And she does. By fall, around hunting-season time, the young grouse have become sexually mature, though they will not breed until spring. They may have argued like kids during the summer, but with maturity they enter into really nasty fights. They fight not only with each other but also with other, strange grouse they meet now that they are out from under the parental wings and ranging wider. Somebody is bound to get licked or take to his heels in frustration. This whole operation, undoubtedly caused by the coming of age of young birds, is nature's mechanism to scatter and mix them to avoid inbreeding and to extend the range. It is commonly called by scientists the "fall shuffle," and it is in some ways a reverse process of the spring claim staking, with about the same results.

Tagged young ruffed grouse have been found, after this fall shuffle, some miles from their birthplaces, though normally in its life cycle this grouse does not move from a small range unless driven off by lack of food or water or by too much disturbance. Now put yourself in the place of a grouse youngster that has been set upon by his brothers and sisters and driven to seek a new home elsewhere. He just gets nicely settled a couple of miles away when he meets another grouse that perhaps has also been driven away from home. There is a battle, and our poor frustrated partridge loses and takes off again. If this happens several times, he becomes so jumpy and desperate that he is practically a mental case. He yearns for a home. He can't find one. The whole world has turned against him. In his desperation he does crazy things. He may start out on a directionless flight—and wind up brainless at the foot of a tree!

This, then, is what some scientists have termed the "crazy flight," a culmination of the fall shuffle. There's no doubt that up to a point the fall shuffle theory is completely sound. Quail go through the same ordeal. But I would stake my last buck that the so-called crazy flight in itself has little, if anything, to do with this fall shuffle directly.

One fall I was hunting in a burned-over territory grown up lushly with a species of harmless nightshade. Berries hung everywhere, and you could not walk a city block without flushing several grouse so gorged with these berries that their crops would sometimes burst when they fell to the gun. The fruit had been frosted, which apparently had made it all the more appealing. During the hunt in that territory that fall, I had no less than five odd experiences with crazy-acting grouse.

One of these birds hopped up from the ground and sat on a bare twig, staring at me and chippering. It craned its neck and bobbed its head—and literally fell off! It hit the ground and started walking around within 10 feet of me. I didn't have the heart to shoot it. Suddenly it zoomed off and slammed straight into a pine tree, falling stunned to the ground. I picked it up. The bird finally came to, and I let it go. Other incidents were comparable.

Another fall I saw three different grouse run down by cars—actually saw the birds as they were hit. These birds were walking along sand trails in the woods, and the cars in no instance were traveling fast. The drivers assumed the birds would fly. But they didn't. They acted as if they either couldn't or else didn't give a hang what happened.

We are also told that during fall the incessant dropping and rustling of leaves frays the nerves of grouse so badly they fly off on a blind bender and kill themselves. This I have heard for years and never have been able to swallow it.

It is completely incongruous that nature would fashion a species for life in the deep forest and so poorly adjust it to this habitat that each fall certain of its numbers would be driven to suicide by the habitat itself. I have spent many days in grouse country during the heaviest period of leaf fall, prior to hunting season when grouse had not been made jumpy by hunters. I have sat and watched numerous grouse feeding placidly on the ground among hardwoods when leaves were making a constant whisper and rustle as they tumbled. The birds paid no heed whatever.

One season I was out driving the day before opening, and happened to hit the time when the birds were extremely active. That afternoon I counted over 50 grouse lazing along the trail sides. Not only were they not jumpy despite the falling leaves, but they also didn't pay any attention to us or our car, unless we forced them to fly.

Another theory is that internal parasites, growing more numerous as the birds mature, drive them to distraction and cause the crazy flight. This theory interested me because parasites—such as "wireworms" that infest the body cavity—are more numerous in some seasons (usually in slowly building cycles) than others. This would account for my observation that in some falls there are no crazy-flying grouse and in

others there are many. However, I have long opened my birds carefully each fall and looked for parasites. Some years ago, when birds were knocking their brains out on every hand in my bailiwick, the parasites were almost nil. The following fall, when no crazy-flight instance was reported to me and I saw none during many days afield, I killed a season limit: 25 birds. I searched for parasites and found them in such abundance that I was alarmed. Our grouse cycle, currently up, appeared to me to be preparing for decline. Numerous parasites often are an indication of too-abundant grouse. The parasites do not necessarily cause the cycle decline, but they are quite commonly a tipoff to crowded conditions.

I reasoned, therefore, as I had done many times in past years, that the parasite hypothesis for the wild flight did not hold up. What, then, could cause wild-flight tales and incidents to flourish one season and be wholly absent the next? Long before I had pondered the parasite and falling-leaf and fall-shuffle theories, I had begun to settle on a very simple and rather curious answer.

From the fall of my first grouse hunt, I have always made it a habit to take the crops out of birds just after they are killed. This serves two purposes: it keeps breast meat from souring, and it allows the gunner to know immediately what the birds are feeding on, thus tipping him off to the best hunting spots. It didn't take many seasons of observing crop contents to point up the fact that during one season the birds might be literally gorging on soft fruits, while during the next very little fruit might be in evidence. Why? Simply because grouse will always take soft food, especially fruit, when it is available in preference to other foods. Some years, as any hunter knows, are excellent fruit years, and some

The crazy flight of ruffed grouse seems to coincide with falls when wild fruit like these chokecherries is abundant. The birds gorge on them, the fruit begins to ferment in their crops, and they become tipsy.

are very poor.

A neighbor of mine had a house that stood fairly close to some good grouse cover. He, too, long had been interested in the wild-flight phenomenon. One fall, three grouse flew against his house and killed themselves. Another fall, four grouse did likewise. But in the years between these incidents, no grouse hit his buildings. The seasons when wild-flying grouse dashed themselves to death were bountiful fruit years. Wild cherries, black haws, highbush cranberries, wild blackberries still clinging to the bushes, and thorn apples were everywhere. The seasons when no grouse blew their tops were seasons almost bereft of wild fruit.

"For a great many years," this man told me—he was past 70 and a very careful, competent observer—"I have been checking crops of grouse that have killed themselves in a wild flight. I have never yet opened such a crop without being reminded of pulling the cork out of a bottle of wine. The wild-flight season comes exactly at the time when old fruit is beginning to ferment."

The exact experience has also been mine and that of several other competent observers of my acquaintance. One season I flushed a grouse very early in the morning from its perch in a low pine. It flew with wobbly motion toward a steep ridge nearby. But it never made the grade. It slammed into the ridgetop with a flurry of flying feathers. When I picked it up and opened the crop, a mass of fruit, presumably from late-evening feeding, was in it. And brother, what a barfly odor! That grouse unquestionably was loop-wing drunk!

Someday some grouse expert is going to do a study on this subject. He is going to test alcohol content of the fermented soft fruit in crops of grouse which have gone on flying benders, and analyze their blood. Until that time, at least, I'll put my money on the theory that the wild flight is purely and simply a matter of unwitting tippling by Old Ruff. If any grouse happen to be listening, I might point out to them that, like automobiles and alcohol and guns and alcohol, wings and wine don't mix!

15

A Taste of Wingshooting from Out of History

Late in the last century a famed shotgunner with worldwide experience on scores of game-bird species was quoted as saying that if the whole world's wingshooting were distilled down to the purest essence of its drama and excitement, the result would be a hunter standing amid the vast grasslands of the interior U.S. with a blizzard of prairie chickens bursting up before him.

Not many modern hunters have experienced that incredible sight. The prairie chicken, once present in millions over an enormous expanse of the central and Great Lakes states and the plains, was diminished by ever-intensifying settlement, market hunting, and drastically changing land use from pioneer days to the present, until only remnant populations remain. Nevertheless, these grand game birds, now meticulously nurtured and managed, are still available in portions of a few states of the central plains

in huntable numbers. Any enthusiastic bird hunter should vow to savor this unique shooting at least once while it's still possible. None other quite matches its specialized surroundings and nostalgic flavor.

I was thinking about this on a bright dawn of a recent September, as native Nebraskan Virgil Laursen pulled up to a farm gate and I got out of his pickup to open it. As we drove, we'd been alertly watching the huge, freshly cut hay meadows with their mower-skirted swales of weeds and brush, checking for birds perched on haystacks that dotted the meadows, watching for coveys flying to or from feed or showing up-stretched heads in the stubble.

As I closed the gate, a chicken unexpectedly lifted with a rush of wings from grass 30 steps out, hurtled high, and rocketed off in typical prairie hen rhythm—several quick, strong wingbeats, a long, cupped-wing glide, then repeat. Instantly I was scrambling to reach and load my gun. Virgil, opposite, mimicked my awkward fumbling, and our actions were exasperatingly punctuated by flushes of more birds. At last we walked toward the spot, not hopeful now. Then a sit-tight single burst upward, and I managed to put it down.

Laursen, who annually gets a satisfying quota of this shooting, said, "That's a start."

I'd paid $48 for the license, $20 for

The prairie chicken. Once present by millions, it is down now to token hunting in several states, with fair numbers in a couple.

shells. There were several hundred bucks in the motel, meals, and the fact that I was a thousand miles from home, and with only two days to spend. This wasn't exactly bargain fare. But as I retrieved my bird, I looked at the handsome barred breast and the short, jauntily styled squared tail, and knew I was addicted. Each feather seemed suddenly overlaid in my mind's eye with the sheen of remembered other places and other prairie chicken hunts, and with the long and dramatic boom-and-bust history of these birds.

I said to Laursen, "A start? I could quit happily right now. I've already collected my money's worth."

Nowadays the Sand Hills country of Nebraska is a hub of prairie chicken abundance. My love affair with these birds began, however, in Michigan's Upper Peninsula—the barrens of jackpine, scrub poplar, and wild-hay expanses west of Seney—back in the late 1940s. Here chickens shared habitat with the more populous sharptailed grouse. This was not suitable chicken habitat. Pushed back from better range, they were making a final stand. Today they're gone from there, as from most of their original range.

The eastern prairie chicken or heath hen, once abundant in Massachusetts, Connecticut, and New Jersey, became extinct in the early '30s. The greater prairie chicken was unbelievably abundant throughout a tremendous sweep of the central and Great Lakes states, the interior plains, and at one time far up into Canada's prairie provinces. Now pockets of huntably abundant greater prairie chickens are found only in portions of South Dakota, Nebraska, Kansas, and Oklahoma. The lesser prairie chicken—slightly smaller and paler in color, a southwestern replica—is presently hunted in southwestern Kansas, western Oklahoma,

Dogs were often used on prairie chickens in their earlier days of abundance. Today only a few hunters use dogs. Here a dog is slipped at dawn to begin a morning's hunt.

Panhandle Texas, and extreme eastern New Mexico. Regulations, of course, can shut off hunting in any state any year. Attwater's prairie chicken, a subspecies of the Texas Gulf Coast and southwestern Louisiana, barely survives, endangered and fully protected.

Severe hunting pressure nudged the great prairie chicken debacle along. Tales of prodigious kills by both market and sport hunters thread prairie chicken history. Early 1800s records show birds available in New York City markets at $1 a brace. Closer to the centers of chicken population, prices were lower. In the 1870s in Chicago and Minneapolis markets, birds

cost 20 or 30 cents apiece. During that decade, Chicago meat markets passed over their counters an average of around 600,000 prairie chickens annually. In New York during holiday time, Fulton Market alone sold several thousand daily.

Thirty-odd years ago I visited an old gentleman in Grand Forks, North Dakota, who as a youngster lived with his parents in a soddy on the plains. His chore was to box-trap "yellowlegs" as a staple of the family's larder. That colloquial name distinguished the prairie chicken from the sharptailed grouse, also present and abundant. Its legs were dark. Prairie chicken is superb table fare, but settlers eating it almost daily

The lesser prairie chicken is still hunted in Kansas, Oklahoma, Texas, New Mexico. Here a New Mexico hunter swings on a flushed bird.

year round often came to think otherwise.

"I could catch all we needed in a short while any day," the old man said. "My father always claimed the reason he wanted to get to Heaven was that he was certain the other place would punish him with endless meals of prairie hen, and surely they'd not serve *that* up above."

He told how market hunters, and sports who came even in private railway cars late in the last century, would drive team and wagon across the prairie and fill the wagon box with birds in a day's shoot. It was not, however, overhunting alone that finally squeezed the prairie chicken into its present remnant range, but changes in farming practices. When the virgin sod was first broken by farm crops, the chickens, already swarming, literally erupted. Habitat was improved by the more abundant food. It is now known, however, that this species cannot tolerate less than approximately a 60:40 ratio of unbroken grasslands to crop fields. When land-use practices pushed the ratio beyond that, shrinking suitable chicken range drastically, populations plummeted.

Although there's no chance that peak days will return, chicken numbers on what's left of livable habitat remain reasonably stable, some seasons even abundant. As long as land use there doesn't drastically change, those numbers will continue. A taste of this shooting from out of history certainly beats none.

Most of the best is on private lands. Permission is not too difficult to get on much of it. There are some National Grasslands, several Public Shooting Areas in the better South Dakota range, and a few state-owned Special Use Areas in Nebraska. Game Management Areas are available in Kansas, and in Oklahoma a few state-owned Public Hunting Areas are within chicken range. Lists and locations can be obtained from game departments of those states.

In Texas and New Mexico private ownership is the rule. In Texas you may locate fee hunts by contacting chambers of commerce in the Panhandle counties that have a brief, low-limit season. In New Mexico I've had little difficulty obtaining permission simply by asking.

Nowadays only a few chicken hunters

use dogs. This shouldn't discourage visitors with steady pointing breeds. Years ago hundreds of field trial and hunting dogs transported from the East and South were annually trained on prairie chickens. Most were quail dogs.

Over the years I've made several hunts with dogs. Good ones work chickens well. A fast dog accustomed to pheasants, which are often running birds, has difficulty pinning prairie chickens. In groups, they're inclined to flush wild. Pheasants as a rule duck and run singly. Chickens stick their heads up from the grass distantly, and if you see that, you know they're going to go, dog or none.

I remember one morning years back in South Dakota when every flock was spooky. They wouldn't hold. The frustrated dog unintentionally put them up as it tried to move in gingerly. We would carefully watch their flight. Prairie chickens commonly rise extremely high and fly half a mile or more. Occasionally, however, a covey will skim off a few feet above ground. In most habitats, there'll be lines of distant trees, or a brushy swale, or an expanse of weeds and tall grass. If they're flushed from short grass or a harvested grain field, they'll usually come down, scattered, in the first substantial cover.

That morning we all ran as birds flushed, keeping the dog close. Then we slowed where the birds had dropped in, letting the dog search for singles before they regrouped. Greater prairie chickens weigh up to 2½ pounds, lessers 1¼. They're 15–18 inches long with a wingspan of 22 to 27 inches. That's a good-sized bird. Yet close-on they can disappear completely, even in short grass. Walking them up, I've had singles literally explode at my boot toes. Scattered, they lie well to a dog, and those birds did so that day. We never once managed a

covey shot. Every bird was set up by the careful, staunch pointer.

Many natives who hunt every season have general flock locations well scouted before the season. They drive farm and ranch roads and get down to walk up birds they've spotted. Laursen knew a few likely locations. We also used binoculars to check distant haystacks. Chickens like to perch on them. If you spot one, it's fairly certain more are aground nearby. You maneuver to try to get within range, a difficult business. Seldom is there "stalking cover" on the plains.

In midmorning we flushed a dozen birds right beside the farm road, in an area where Virgil had previously seen some. We watched them come down over the distant brow of a small tall-grass rise. He quickly drove us near, and we left the pickup below the crest, trotted up the rise, and eased over. Expecting they'd have moved on 50 yards or so, we were unwittingly right into them.

Up they went. We recovered with enough alacrity to let off a successful shot each. I swung on a second chicken, feeling confident as I did so that my third—and final bird for my day's limit—was as good as bagged. When I pulled, nothing happened. How can you travel a thousand miles for two days of hunting, I thought, and during the split-second moment of truth have an otherwise faultless automatic jam on an empty hull? It was the last opportunity I had that day.

If you hope to locate flocks flying to morning feed, an ingrained chicken habit, be up before daylight. I've heard them come over a known feeding field when it was still not light enough to shoot. After feeding, they fly back to resting cover. This may be a fallow field, weedy or brushy swale, dense, tall grass along a line of trees—wherever copious ground cover is available.

Some dogless, vigorous hunters claim the best shooting is from midmorning to mid-afternoon, when the birds are in resting cover. It's easy to pinpoint likely areas, especially in farmed country. Walking may be strenuous, but in heavy midday cover the chickens usually sit extremely tight. They leave such cover late in the afternoon and fly again to feed. Then, often near or at dusk, they fly back to heavy ground cover to roost, scattered out loosely, not in a group like quail.

A South Dakota chicken hobbyist once told me, "I try to locate patches where birds roost. I pick one that's fairly small, located so I can hunker in it late, with birds coming in from the east, the light at my back. If they go to roost early enough, it's often a successful trick. Their flight habits and lanes in fall are surprisingly consistent and predictable."

Indeed, those distinct flight lanes to favored feeding grounds gave rise long ago to what is often the most successful and sporty method of hunting prairie chickens. This is a kind of pass-shooting. Most

Prairie chicken shot as it flew to a feeding field in the morning. The "pinnae"—stiff neck feathers of males used in the mating display—show plainly on this bird.

sportsmen in chicken range call it "fly-in" shooting. During summer the birds feed heavily on grasshoppers and other insects. By hunting season, most insects are gone. The birds then seek grain fields—sorghum, wheat, oats, corn.

A field with abundant waste grain, especially with prominent stubble cover, attracts them. One or more coveys, or groups formed from several coveys packed up, begin to fly to and from the same field, from the same resting and roost area, sometimes each day over a period of several weeks. In New Mexico one fall I watched them come so unerringly over the identical stretch of fence at identical height time and again that biologists trapping them for transplant were able to string mist nets on long poles and catch several at dusk or dawn.

For this shooting a hunter must locate a field habitually used, and know where birds come in, so he can arrange a payoff stand within range. Writing that, I visualize a New Mexico predawn when I lay on the ground shivering in 20-degree weather in a cutover grain field south of Portales. Right here, a year earlier, I'd gone through the same suffering, had one chance—and missed. Why I'd come back defied logic. A partner beside me was probably also pondering this.

Suddenly, with barely enough shooting light, there they were! They came from our right, a big flock, precisely where they were supposed to be, wings whispering, cupped in a glide. We gaped at the sizzling approach. We leaped up. One shot each. Two birds down. The flock dissolved into low light. Across the field another gun boomed.

I said eagerly, "Let's pick 'em up."

"Wait! Down!"

The flock, spooked by the other gun, had circled back and now whooshed directly over-head. We rose and turned, grabbing a last-chance tail-on shot, and luckily put two more on the ground. That wrapped it up.

"Not even full light," my partner said happily, "and we're through for the day."

"I'm through for the season," I said. "Remember, I only had one day."

"You must be addicted," he replied. And he was right. However, that time I was only 700 miles from home.

16

A Sound to Remember

Most hunters, remembering some dramatic experience from out of their far past, launch tales of it with an animated description of the setting. I could do that, recalling my first experience many years ago with the sharp-tailed grouse. . . . I still see the enormous wild sweep of frost-tipped yellow grass shimmering in low-slanted dawn light, broken by pockets of black-green jackpine and strips of golden-leaved scrub poplar and white-barked birch. The place was the nearly roadless and meagerly inhabited expanse of Michigan's Upper Peninsula west of the withered old lumber-days settlement of Seney.

Curiously, perhaps, it is not so much the details of that wild region that I so vividly recall. It is a *sound*, a sound that sent all of us running to try to catch up with birds, scurrying and intent on flushing wild from the tall grass. Even remembering, I feel ex-

citement. At that moment I had yet to see my first sharp-tailed grouse, dead or alive. And so it was the sound of their talking at our disturbance that impressed me and shot adrenaline through my system, weakening my knees and making my breath come short from more than running.

The next 20 reference books you read will tell you the sharptail usually "cackles" *when flushing*. Not one writer I have ever read tells you the far more important fact that the sharptail begins "talking" when first disturbed in cover, and that by the time the hunter disturbance is close enough to a flock to put them up, they are already running—running and talking. Not cackling. The sound is definitely no cackle. It is a continuing series of a single syllable, uttered in a grating, harsh monotone: *kuk-kuk-kuk-kuk-kuk-kuk*. . . .

Singles from a scattered covey, which

sometimes lie as tightly as bobwhites, do indeed as a rule shower down the same series of sounds when they flush. But it is the chatter of running groups of sharptails that's important to the hunter, especially if he's walking them up, as we were that day. It tells you, "Here we are—and this is the direction we're going." In an immense sweep of range, with birds "packed up" in late fall, often several coveys together, a hunter might easily walk past his quarry if it were not for the sharptail's vocal outbursts.

We ran, and then we could see bird heads moving in the grass, way out there three shotgun ranges. The grouse swirled up in a blizzard of wings, their acceleration and steep climb astonishingly swift. We hauled up, panting and muttering, not a shot fired. The birds climbed still higher.

Later I was to observe that often sharptails intent on a long flight will travel at an amazing altitude, almost like ducks. Their strong wings, I noted, beat powerfully for a few strokes after they'd gained altitude and then, in the fashion of all the prairie grouse species, were cupped as the birds soared. As speed diminished, the wings beat again, and then came another glide, the pattern repeated over and over.

The first strip of timber was perhaps half a mile distant. The birds were aimed right at it. I was also to learn later that sharptails, used to vast spaces—especially when harassed during hunting season—don't mind a bit flying a mile before coming down. These pitched into the scrub. Once more we ran, paused to blow, and ran again. Today I'd say to hell with them, they could wait on me. Back then, my eagerness was

The sharp-tailed grouse is a compact, handsome bird. Its tail, for which it is named, tapers to a point—just the opposite of its relative, the prairie chicken, which has a squared tail.

uncontrollable. I had to get one in hand—right now.

There were five of us. We fanned out, guns ready, moving into the poplar stand. One hunter, experienced with sharptails, cautioned us to go slowly. The birds, he said, were scattered. They'd probably stay snug, easy to bypass. *Kuk-kuk-kuk-kuk.* Spang in front of me. I saw the bird running, and then it was up, the range perfect, the poplars annoyingly arranged in a vertical grid to give it protection. But I had been hunting ruffed grouse already that season and was in tune with timber! At the shot, my first sharp-tailed grouse was down in the grass and a rain of yellow poplar leaves from stray shot was sifting after it.

Remembering that first bird, I am struck by what seems now the most delightful aspect of sharptail shooting: it is still in modestly ample supply. Although the other prairie grouse—prairie chickens and sage grouse—today are hard pressed, precariously so over some of their range, the sharptail is still abundant. Not, to be sure, remotely as abundant as it was many years ago, but somehow this bird has managed to adapt, in the better portions of its natural range, to changes in land use much better than the others.

The chicken requires unbroken expanses of grass checkerboarded lightly by the plow. Unfortunately for it, very little virgin or restored tall-grass prairies are left. The sage grouse must have its beloved sage, which is systematically being destroyed. The more fortunate sharptail is a species of the distinct transition zone between prairie and forest, between flatland and foothills, a bird of intermingled grass and brush and scrub. The classic example of prime sharptail habitat occurs in the region where the bird is still most plentiful: portions of the western Dakotas, eastern Montana, and the prairie provinces of Canada.

Here brush patches and brushy stream courses plus open stands of small timber pattern the undulating, sometimes rough landscape, with expanses of grass everywhere filling the openings. In places there are burns, also stands of second-growth aspen, alder, or willow thickets, patches of wild rose. Nowadays there are in addition, of course, the endless farms. But the sharptail has taken to these, with their wheat and corn and other prime forage, almost as eagerly as did the pheasant. As long as its traditional cover of transition shrubs plus grass is present in adequate amounts, the bird does well.

The sharptail has another built-in advantage. Kin to the ptarmigan of the far-north areas and tempered by centuries of severe winters, it is far less subject to population fluctuations related to winter hardships than are the pheasants, Huns, and even the prairie chickens that in some areas meagerly share its habitat. In fact, this grouse was born to cold country and tailored for adaptation to variances of terrain that enabled it to colonize one of the most immense ranges of any of our native grouse. Originally, it was found from Quebec to interior Alaska, southward in the Great Lakes region clear into northern Illinois, and in the West far down into the fringes of New Mexico.

Present-day range has shrunk, but still is enormous. Like all grouse, the sharptail is somewhat cyclic, with periodic ups and downs. But central and eastern Alaska, in river valleys such as the Yukon, still have good populations in peak times. There's scattered abundance in the southern Yukon Territory and below Great Slave Lake in the Northwest Territories, and fair numbers in British Columbia's Peace River District, central interior, and south.

In Alberta, Saskatchewan, and Manitoba, focal points of its present-day range, the sharptail is the most numerous and popular upland game bird. Shooting is excellent. For many years, and still to some extent today, bird-dog trainers from as far away as the Deep South states have taken kennels of expensive field-trial dogs to the prairie provinces specifically for the training they can get on sharptails. The species blankets much of these three provinces, but the cream of the shooting is spread across the easily accessible southern portions.

Ontario offers some shooting, the best of it in the West and Southwest. But goose hunters going to James Bay get a chance at sharptails, too. Quebec, eastern fringe of the range, offers sharptails only along Hudson and James Bays, too far north for much more than incidental hunting.

The best hunting in the Lower 48 undoubtedly is in central and eastern Montana and the western halves of North and South Dakota, right below the prime Canadian range. The Sand Hills region of central Nebraska rates fair. Wyoming has token populations, chiefly in Sheridan and Johnson counties. There are birds in eastern Washington, a few in eastern Oregon, some in southeastern Idaho. In both Utah and Colorado, where sharptails were once abundant, there are now only token populations.

Minnesota, Wisconsin, and Michigan

Hanging sharptails out of reach of predators at an old hunting camp of the 1940s in Michigan's Upper Peninsula. Severe weather here and elsewhere in the sharptail domain doesn't cause many grouse losses. Sharptails are well equipped to brave cold weather.

once supported superbly abundant flocks. Presently Minnesota's best population is on the fringes of northwestern farm lands; Wisconsin's birds are scattered across the north but best in the northwest; Michigan's remnant is restricted to a small portion of the Upper Peninsula.

The existence of sharptails in any state or province does not necessarily mean there'll be an open season. In some instances token seasons are opened one year, closed the next. Winter and cyclic losses must be considered by game managers. In planning a hunt, the prairie provinces should be considered first, Montana, the Dakotas, and possibly Nebraska second.

The sharptail, even where abundant, never fails to let a fellow know he's been hunting. In fall it is common to find large groups, apparently the joining of several coveys. An entire bird population from a broad acreage thus may be all in one place. I recall one opening-day sharptail hunt during which three of us, with a fair to middling dog, walked from dawn until noon in excellent country without seeing a feather. Beat, we ate a spike-camp lunch, watered the foot-sore dog, tied it at camp, then wearily took off again.

Like most game birds, sharptails feed from very early in the morning until possibly 9:30 or so, depending on availability of forage. Afterward they move into brush or scrub timber and rest out the afternoon. Commonly they go to water after feeding or even in the middle of a warm day. In a few instances you can surprise them at a waterhole, if water is scarce. Ordinarily there are numerous puddles they know about that the hunter does not.

Dragging our weary tails, we abruptly found birds late in the afternoon, during their second daily feeding foray. They were talking in front, at the left, at the right, and instantly the air was full of them. We'd

been moving purposely into the breeze and with the sun behind us in case we found late-afternoon action. They had failed to hear us, and we'd waded right in among 'em.

I may as well be a liar first class as second. I've always sworn that 100 grouse were suddenly in the air in an overwhelming burst. So maybe it was 50. Maybe 30. The daily bag was three birds. Amid a wild cacophony—the frantic *kuk-kuk-kuk*ing of all those birds, the whooshing rush of wing sounds as they hurtled up past our faces, the slamming fusillade of shotguns—birds were tumbling.

Without moving a boot, each of us somehow paying close enough attention to his own targets, we by great good grace failed to break any laws in all this excitement and within perhaps five seconds we laid nine grouse on the ground. There was a deafening pause. At least eight solid hours of walking had brought us five seconds of shooting. We burst into meaningless excited yammer. Next day all of us were so stove up, lame, and foot-blistered that we could barely drag out of bed. Were nine sharptails worth all that suffering? You bet!

Because of its compact build, the open country in which it lives, and the fact that it often flushes wild, the sharptail is not an especially easy bird to put down. For some years I used a full-choke 20-gauge for it, to avoid carrying anything heavier on such long hikes. I tried to be ready with field loads of No. 7½ shot when we got into sit-tight singles. But on the long shots I used No. 6 high-base loads. Those who shoot doubles can, of course, be set for both types of shots. With today's shotgun loads designed quite differently from those of earlier years, a single-barrel gun with a modified choke is a good compromise. Variable-choke devices also help.

I recall with amusement a cool-shooting

Male sharptails weigh as much as 2½ pounds. The average is a bit smaller, with young birds about 1¾ pounds.

southpaw friend, Andy Loizos, with whom I hunted sharptails on several occasions. He had a variable-choke gadget installed, and prided himself on how fast he could switch settings. We got into a small flock that went up beautifully, in easy range. With his choke set almost wide open, Andy nevertheless missed his bird. Swiftly but calmly he swung the shotgun across his chest and snugged the choke down, never taking his eyes off that particular flying bird. Then he swung up the gun and killed it.

Sharptails fly at an estimated 35 to 40 miles per hour. They use their wings much more than do, for example, ruffed grouse flying undisturbed to feed or cover. Thus they are exceptionally powerful, the dark-meated breast muscle thick and rounded. Their acceleration is phenomenal. They don't struggle up like a rooster pheasant. They're up and going in a split second.

Although a sharptail in flight looks nowhere near as bulky as a long-tailed rooster pheasant, many fully mature birds weigh almost as much. Some references I've read claim four or five pounds for the cock pheasant, which is utter nonsense. I've personally weighed scores of them. Seldom do you find a three-pounder; about 2½ catches most of them.

Several times after hunting sharptails we weighed birds, separating cocks and hens. The sexes look quite alike, except for the air sacs on the neck of the male, inflated during the breeding display. The hen is slightly smaller. Many cocks weighed two pounds; quite a few came close to 2½. Young birds were about 1¾, as were most hens. Size and coloration—darker or paler—differ slightly among the half-dozen subspecies in different parts of the range.

I've always liked close-working dogs for sharptails. Otherwise too many flocks flush extremely wild. Dogless hunters are not especially handicapped. Nowadays on the best of the sharptail range, flocks commonly consort in corn and wheat fields and can be hunted much like pheasants. Whenever a season opens in early fall, say in early or mid September, which several usually do, hunters have advantages. One is the number of young birds. Unlike some covey uplanders, young sharptails seldom flush as a group. They often straggle up one or two at a time, giving a hunter opportunity for more than a single kill.

Additionally, if the weather is warm, especially in the focal part of the range where there's much open grass or crop fields with very specific brush and tree patches, those will be the places to hunt. One year in South Dakota, west of the Missouri, two of us opened the season on an unseasonably hot day. The birds, we knew, would feed extra early and immediately get into the shade. They don't like the heat any more than the hunter does. They'd sit tight, hating to have to fly. We did no aimless searching, but simply walked from patch to patch where there was shade, and filled our quotas. However, if the season opens with cool, calm, overcast weather, all is changed. You can bet you're in for a long hike, trying to locate scattered birds.

As fall progresses, sharptails are inclined to gather, as noted earlier, in what most natives in their territory call "packs," large groups containing several coveys. This may be a habit based to some extent on available food. It may also be a part of the covey-mixing "fall shuffle" of birds, nature's device to avoid incessant inbreeding. Packs of birds, where seasons run late, are tremendously exciting but, of course, more difficult to locate than more evenly distributed separate coveys.

When the first snows come to sharptail country, the birds exhibit a trait unlike other prairie grouse. They move to strips of timber and to the tree-lined draws, perch in trees, and eat buds, just as ruffed grouse do. They commonly fly from tree to tree, spending more time above ground than on it. I've spotted them during this time from several hundred yards, looming plump and dark against the sky in leafless aspens. Approaching them is difficult, and if you do manage a few shots, the birds, possibly feeling all too vulnerable, may fly right out of the country.

For those who relish medium-dark meat, the sharptail is truly gourmet fare. During pioneer days, when wagonloads of sharptails and prairie chickens were killed on a single hunt—sometimes for home consumption, sometimes for market—many people considered the sharptail the more delicious of the two birds. During the late 1880s both grouse were supremely abundant, commonly on the same range in the Dakotas and southern prairie provinces, where incidentally there was and still is very occasional hybridization. All were called "chickens"—in fact, in Canada today the sharptail is often confusingly called "prairie chicken" by natives—but the sharptail was designated a "pintailed chicken." Old accounts relate how some crafty hunters, splitting a day's mixed bag with a novice, would slyly take the pintails for themselves.

A morning's bag of sharptails from earlier days when they were more plentiful. The dark meat is delicious. Some early settlers on the plains considered the sharptail better table fare than the prairie chicken.

In my opinion, it's a tossup. I'd hate to demean that marvelous delicacy, the prairie chicken, by claiming the sharptail is better eating. On several occasions I've shot them both on the same range, same day. With tugging nostalgia I recall an enormous platter heaped high with grouse of both species, but with sharptails overwhelmingly predominant. Four hunters, one the landowner, were bellying up to a smooth-worn rough-plank table in his hundred-year-old farmhouse. His wife, a German lady, was responsible for the after-hunt supper that practically bowed the table legs with its prodigious quantity.

She had cooked grouse the way she cooked chicken. No farm dweller of that time ever ate pallid fryer chickens like everyone buys in stores nowadays. "Chicken" meant an enormous fat hen or a giant old rooster. The birds were cut up and parboiled. Any grouse kill, she explained, was certain to contain birds of different ages. Parboiling matched the lot for tenderness, just as it tenderized an old hen or rooster. She confided that when her family first settled there many years before, they had practically lived on grouse. By parboiling a lot of grouse, you could save what you didn't cook immediately and then fix the meat quickly as needed.

The final process was simply flouring and frying the already tender legs, backs, wings, and breasts. One of our hunters, a Catholic, remarked with a grin as we ate that he was dubious about whether or not he should be doing this, and he intended to check with his padre. Anything this good, he added, undoubtedly would require confession. It is unfortunate that so few modern hunters will probably ever partake of such a meal, or of the uniquely flavored shooting that provides it. But it is also wonderfully fortunate that those who will make the effort to trek to sharptail country and hunt diligently *can* still do so.

17

Bull Grouse of the Sagebrush

I've yet to see the term "bull grouse" used in print, but a rancher friend of mine in Montana goes bull grouse hunting every fall, and as far as I know he has never called sage grouse anything else. Another friend, in Wyoming, invariably speaks of the old outsized cocks with stiff, quill-like neck feathers as "bulls."

The usage is whimsically apt. Sage grouse are big, the largest grouse on the continent. They are as ponderous, plodding, and placid as any old range bull ambling across the western sagebrush cattle lands. When disturbed by some foreign intrusion, an old rooster may mutter gutturally deep in its throat like a mumbling bull—*quork, quork*. "Bull grouse" is indeed not a bad name for these birds.

The first ones I ever saw, many years ago, I wasn't sure I believed. My wife and I were traveling in a small trailer, and in Wyo-ming—far more frontier and less settled then than it is today—we pulled off pot-holed old U.S. highway 14–16 into the yard of an abandoned ranch outpost. An ancient building had long ago disintegrated. There wasn't a tree visible for miles in this part of the state, except for a single dead cottonwood on the slope below the building remains, its barkless base marking a tiny seep oozing out of the clay and shale.

We were in the trailer fixing lunch when I looked out and saw the birds. Five of them. They looked as big as young turkeys. They *were* as big as young turkeys. They came plodding slowly up from the seep, heads stretched erect, looking tall and unreal and ridiculous. They came straight to the trailer.

Dumb! Or were they? They walked purposefully to it, around to the thin slice of shade it threw in the high sun, and hunkered down, unconcerned and at ease. There and then my love affair with these big dumb grouse began.

Next time I consorted with them, I began to suspect I was the dumb one. Again I was in Wyoming, hunting with a native. When we least expected it, we bumbled into a pack of perhaps 50 birds. Sage grouse are noted for their fall gregariousness. Old accounts tell of massive gatherings, a thousand or more in a small area. They waited until we were into them, in knee-high sage, then up they went with a rush and clatter of stiff-feathered wings, bulky bodies lumbering into the air as the birds uttered their usual cackle of alarm at flushing, *cuk, cuk, cuk, cuk.*

There is no earthly way a hunter who can hit the ground with his hat can miss a bird that big that heaves itself into the air

that slowly. Or is there? I have to admit I fired three times, the sky simply a blizzard of huge, flapping targets, and never creased a feather. Nor was that all. We watched them fly off and finally scale down. Sage grouse once aloft rev up surprisingly fast, from flush to 40 m.p.h. in seconds. They often rise high and reach a steady speed estimated at 50-plus, and substantially faster in a tail-on blow. They also usually fly far, making a few quick wingbeats, then sailing, then repeating the process.

"Let's go after 'em!" my partner said. He, too, had drawn a blank.

We hit out at a trot, and up went several scattered birds that had sat tight. We managed to miss those, too. Half a mile later, tongues and rears dragging, we could finally see birds on a ridge. They were walking with necks thrust high, heads inter-

Male sage grouse beginning the spring mating display. The sage grouse is the largest grouse on the continent. *Oregon Department of Fish & Wildlife photo.*

The sage grouse appears to lumber up into the air on the flush, and there seems no way the hunter could miss. But the flight is deceptive.

mittently above the sage, watching. When sage grouse set out to walk fast, they can outwalk a hunter, keeping well out of range. Often they run. We finally lost that whole batch, never flushing any of them again.

It is a fact that sage grouse are not especially intelligent, as one thinks of wily old cock pheasants or ruffed grouse in that light. They are naive. They are also beautifully fitted to their highly specialized environment. They are birds strictly of the rolling sage prairies. They can be stupid and easy to bag, or horribly exasperating, during the same day—or hour.

According to most book accounts, sage grouse cocks may reach maximum weight of seven pounds. I've never seen one that large and I'm skeptical, but I did kill one near Gillette, Wyoming, years ago that was almost six. Most adult males probably weigh around four pounds, with hens slightly smaller. The very largest males, however, may measure close to 30 inches from end of beak to tip of tail, stretched out, and have a wingspread approaching a yard.

Oddly, though sage grouse, like many others of the grouse family, would rather walk or run than fly, these big birds commonly do fly to water. This habit may be most noticeable where waterholes are scarce. In certain situations where low sage, in which the birds like to roost at night on a slope, is near water, they don't need to fly. They walk.

Regardless of how local flocks travel to water, any experienced sage grouse hunter in country strange to him looks first for windmills, cattle tanks, and natural seeps, and then studies the vicinity of each for signs. Watering places are the one distinctive feature of the vast all-look-alike expanses of sage. They are magnets to which local flocks are drawn.

In moist earth the heavy grouse leave

plainly printed tracks, easily identified by the thick, segmented toes. Droppings are also an important sign. These are usually curved, one inch or less in length, and about three-eighths of an inch in diameter. Wherever a grouse has squatted to rest or roost, there will be a pile of droppings. Making a swing out around a waterhole—the birds usually water morning and evening—and checking thoroughly will soon indicate whether a group of birds is using the area. Dropped feathers with their black, brown, gray, and white mottlings also are a clue. Hills within a half mile of any water source with sign, or on either side of a creek, should be thoroughly combed.

The most delightful, and easiest, shooting occurs occasionally at a waterhole habitually used early in the morning. One fall two of us took a stand at a windmill on U.S. Bureau of Land Management land where sign was thick. Sage grouse, as I've said, roost on the ground, up on the slopes and the ridges. We simply sat down before daylight and waited. With the sun came the birds, flying in. It was almost like shooting over decoys, or a bit like dove shooting at a waterhole, but giant-size.

Sage grouse are rightly named. They are tied to sage as with a lifeline. They are highly specialized creatures, feeding so diligently on sage that they have no need for a muscular gizzard for grinding firm food, like other grouse. The gizzard wall is thin and soft. They do eat other greens, but sage is the staple of diet. They nest in it, roost in it, live out bitter winters through violent blizzards and still get their only food and protection from sage.

I have hunted—in northwestern Colorado, for example—where sage had been sprayed over large areas to kill it so grass would grow. Where the grass had grown tall up through the dead, blackened sage

bushes, in a tract where sage grouse had always been abundant, we found not a bird. As soon as we moved into unsprayed sage, however, there they were.

In most sage areas of the West, ranches are located along stream bottoms, and vast fields of alfalfa or other hay are grown here. Alfalfa is especially attractive to sage grouse. They feed avidly on it as a succulent green change from sage. The stuff is easy for them to walk in and hide in. It produces several cuttings, so usually there is one about when the season has opened. I recall one hunt during which we went from bale to bale of alfalfa in a freshly cut field, jumping birds from the shady sides of the big rolls of hay. They soon get smart to this tactic, however, and move off the moment they see a distant hunter or vehicle.

Most references claim that cock sage grouse may reach a maximum weight of seven pounds. This one, shot in Wyoming, weighed about six. Average is closer to three or four.

One season I hunted out of Pinedale, Wyoming, with local friends, and we had permission to hunt a ranch where alfalfa had been cut. Incidentally, if you hunt Wyoming, a top state, read the laws carefully. You need permission in writing, the signature of the landowner or his agent on your license, to be legal on private property. We drove along high sage ridge trails above the fields, using binoculars to find birds.

That's a trick widely employed in sage grouse hunting. Against pale backgrounds such as the cut-over hay fields, the birds look dark, their size exaggerated by distance. Most of them don't stay in the fields during the day. This is true throughout the West wherever ranch bottomlands draw them to feed. They fill up, then retire to rest in the sagebrush hills. Late in the day, a couple or three hours before dusk, they walk down from the hills to the cut-over fields, or fly in, sometimes from a mile or

more away. This late-afternoon shooting can be some of the best, although it will try your patience as you try to get within range of birds.

A tactic that has worked well several times for me is to take a position about 4 p.m. on the outer edge of a valley feeding site such as I've described. This places the hunter next to the rising slopes of sagebrush, along the line between sage and cut-over hay field. I've had birds walk out of the sage within short range, and others fly down to alight nearby, then walk into the field. Sometimes you get pass-shooting, or you can make a sneak in the sage and flush a group or singles, or even ease up within range in the open cut-over.

Binoculars can be used to advantage elsewhere, too. We located birds one year by steadily glassing the undulating sage hills. The upthrust heads of grouse show plainly on a ridge, but their black breasts blend with black sagebrush shadows in this

Tracks, dropped feathers, and droppings found near a waterhole tell you grouse are using the vicinity. Some hunters then use binoculars to search for grouse out in the sage.

brightly lighted open country. Where sage is thin on a slope, or a patch of vegetationless alkali ground makes an opening, it is not difficult to find groups or singles if you learn to glass slowly and with patience. If the season where you hunt is long, packs of birds usually grow larger and larger in numbers as the season progresses. They also become more wary. The problem now is to locate the one big group that perhaps is ganged up in a large sweep of country. Once it is located, you need to plan an approach carefully. When one bird gets nervous and goes, probably they all will, flushing wild and out of range.

Certainly sage grouse can be dropped with any shotgun. However, I stick with a 12 gauge, full choke for long shots, modified for closer ones. A choke device or a double-barrel solves the problem best. No. 6 shot is fine. Smaller will do, but when birds are wild and shots long, which commonly occurs, I go to No. 4 high-base shells. A sage grouse is not a difficult bird to put down. Occasionally a wounded bird may run, but most of them don't, or even try to hide, as a pheasant or quail will. They make little effort to get away when wounded. Nevertheless, it pays to mark down carefully each fallen bird. A sweep of short sage all looks alike, and a dead or wounded sage grouse blends perfectly.

A few sage grouse hunters use dogs. In Colorado a couple of years ago we ran into two parties the same day who had dogs along. Most dogs aren't very staunch where large flocks are involved. The flushing birds make too much racket. When single birds from a flock are scattered, they'll often lie snug and a dog can help, or be used to locate downed birds. However, consensus among sage grouse hunters is that a dog isn't necessary, and that an unsteady one can be a nuisance.

Years ago sage grouse were awesomely abundant throughout most of the sage country of the West. Populations have drastically declined, due chiefly to ever diminishing habitat. Destruction of sage to improve ranges for livestock has depleted them over vast areas. In most states that still offer an open season, a sage grouse hunt dovetails nicely with antelope hunting, the grouse season usually opening in early fall. In my view, a special trip just for sage grouse is worthwhile. The vast, near-treeless surroundings and the unique personality of this bird join to give a rare flavor to the experience.

However, in planning a hunt it is wise to make certain well ahead that there will be a season where you intend to go. Some states have had to temporarily close seasons; others with only token sage grouse populations may suddenly close hunting permanently or for a period of years. The preponderance of the birds are in three states: Montana, with heaviest populations in the north-central and east-slope sagebrush foothills; Wyoming, where most birds are in the southern-central and central counties; and Idaho, the best counties scattered across the southern part of the state.

Colorado has good shooting, especially in the northwest and west, as does Nevada in the northern counties. Both of the Dakotas and Alberta have a few sage grouse. So do eastern Oregon and Washington and northeastern California. Whether or not any of the low-population states will have an open season in a given year is not predictable.

Almost as interesting as the bird itself and the experience of hunting it are the diverse attitudes of gunners toward its table qualities. I know a Wyoming rancher who calls them "sage buzzards" and claims he'd as soon eat a real buzzard. I know other

Sage grouse perched on a distant rock looks as big as a young turkey. Indeed, it is. Birds keep heads up when disturbed, or get where they can see and then run or flush wild. This grouse was photographed in eastern Montana.

westerners who have hunted them for years and eagerly await opening day as much for the table experience as afield. I've hunted them off and on for some 30 years, and I've never had a bird I didn't eat with praise and delight. It's undoubtedly true that an ancient cock killed in midwinter when sage was 100% of its diet might be both tough and strong. In fall, however, with food a bit more diverse and some succulents present, even old bulls are delicious if you handle them properly. I suspect it's the heavy-handed cooks, not the grouse, that have created the often-alleged poor table qualities.

Sage grouse are dark-meated, and admittedly distinctive in taste. Because of their soft food and the generally warm weather during hunting season, they should be drawn as quickly as possible. Old bulls and hens should be separated from birds-of-the-

year. Dennis Almquist, a Wyoming game-warden friend, showed me how to do this easily. Feel the lower end of the breast bone. If it's pliable, that's a bird-of-the-year. If it's stiff, the bird is older.

The "fry cook" who cuts 'em up and throws 'em in a smoking skillet is certain to add to the bird's reputation for poor edibility and tough meat. Young grouse are excellent when left whole, floured and seared in a Dutch oven. Then, with a small amount of water and perhaps dry red wine added, the pot is covered and the heat turned very low, allowing the birds to simmer gently until extra-tender. Other seasonings, of course, can be used. The gravy, thickened, is superb.

Bob Carpender, a Wyoming friend, showed us how he treats old birds. He bones the meat. The big breast is cut into fillets about a quarter inch thick. Legs and wings are boned, and the meat is cut into whatever shaped pieces one can manage. Flour the meat, place the pieces in melted butter or margarine in a skillet, and sauté them—gently. My wife sprinkles rosemary over the fillets. Cover the skillet, and turn the pieces occasionally, cooking until tender, possibly as long as 1½ hours. The oldest bull grouse, so prepared, is guaranteed gourmet fare.

The sage grouse will never again be abundant enough to be more than a specialty experience. Nor will it ever gain the sporty reputation accorded certain other uplanders such as bobwhites, ruffed grouse, and pheasants. The fallacy, however, is in trying to compare it to others. It is a most distinctive game-bird personality, fitted to a most distinctive feature of the continental terrain where the others couldn't survive a week. Naive and lumbering it may be, but it offers a variety of hunting drama unique in the world of upland gunning.

18

Tame Grouse of the Timber

In all the years I've been reading about hunting, I can never recall seeing any magazine story or book chapter concerning the spruce grouse. Book references brush off the poor bird as quickly as they can. For magazines there presumably isn't enough that's exciting to say about this bird to make any editor's adrenaline move. I can understand this, but for some quirky reason I have a soft spot for this unbelievably naive bird.

The spruce grouse is roughly comparable in size to the ruffed grouse. It has an enormous range encompassing practically all of Canada and Alaska, and spreading to the south over upper New England, the upper Great Lakes region, and into portions of the Rockies in Washington, Idaho, and Montana. Within the U.S portion of the range, the birds are not abundant, and in

portions of the eastern areas they may indeed be entirely gone.

Most bird hunters have never seen one. The areas of optimum habitat—the deep conifer forests, especially of spruce—are simply too far removed from the majority of the bird-hunting population. Further, though a number of birds have long been called "fool hen," this one probably deserves the name. The ruffed grouse, tame as domestic chickens when early settlers first knew them, learned swiftly to adapt to man's incursions and to take crafty care of themselves. The spruce grouse never did.

I remember several decades ago when I was hunting in Michigan's Upper Peninsula and saw several spruce grouse. Long before that, in the 1800s, they had been reasonably abundant there. With removal of much of the dense conifer forests, their habitat was destroyed. When their hushed, remote wilderness pockets of habitation had been removed, the naive birds could not adapt.

The pair of birds I saw in Michigan perched on a low jackpine limb and looked at me. Tame or not, game or not, they're handsome grouse. The male has a small reddish comb above each eye, a dark crown without a crest. Its face is black, outlined narrowly with white. The upper breast is black, graduating lower down to black feathers edged with white. The back and wings are mottled gray and brown. The main feathers of the tail, which fans out like that of the ruffed grouse, are black with an orange-brown band at the tips. The more subdued female is brown with the underparts flecked with white, and with bars and streaks of brown and black over most of the body.

The Michigan birds I saw were not legal game. I presume all are gone from that state today. I also saw a bird, a female, in Montana one fall while I was fishing. This one, too, just stood and looked at me and then went on about her business, walking a little way along the stream where I fished, unconcerned and disinterested.

Wherever found, spruce grouse are seldom abundant, always scattered. They don't gather in large flocks. Pairs apparently stick together. However, trying to hunt them, especially in their western mountain range, is seldom very productive. You may come upon a couple of birds, and then never see another. The western grouse were at one time classified as a different species and called Franklin's grouse. Now they are considered only a slightly different race or subspecies, of which four are recognized over the vast range.

There are many tales about the naivete of these grouse. Some claim to have picked one up, then released it and watched it just fly up to a nearby limb and perch there

Seldom is the dapper spruce grouse ever credited as being a game bird. Most of the time, it isn't much of one. *Ontario Ministry of Natural Resources photo.*

The tail of the spruce grouse fans out much like that of the ruffed grouse. These birds never have learned "wildness," but at times they furnish interesting shooting. *Ontario Ministry of Natural Resources photo.*

unconcerned. Natives in the Canadian bush and elsewhere over the Far North kill them with sticks. One account relates how a subsistence hunter regularly sought out family coveys in early fall, when the young were about grown. He would drive them enough so they'd flush up into a spruce, lining up on low branches; then he'd whack them off one at a time.

Nevertheless, the spruce grouse is far from useless, and it occasionally offers some basic sport hunting. I was on a moose hunt in the English River region of Ontario one fall when we ate spruce grouse in camp regularly. The guide's helper, a rough log-camp type who slept the whole time in a virtually rainproof spruce-bough hogan he threw together in a few minutes, had a .22 rifle along.

I'd go with him each day during the camp's after-lunch rest period, and we'd collect spruce grouse for the pot. The interiors of the spruce stands where he always looked for the birds were eerie, silent places, dark as evening. Spruce trees grew so tightly packed that there was no under-story whatever. The sun filtered in only during midday. The places the fellow picked, knowing his grouse, were always boggy and wet, with moss carpeting the ground so thickly we made not a sound as we prowled.

He moved like an Indian. He'd spot a grouse on limb or ground, and walk slowly toward it. Some would make a subdued *putt, putt* sound. Most were silent. His .22 was a single-shot with open sights. Every bird, even in the dim light, was neatly head shot. Later in fall and winter, he told me, the birds weren't as tasty as now. Then they'd feed entirely on spruce needles. Now they were getting some berries and other forage. Unlike the ruffed grouse, spruce grouse have dark meat. I like dark-meated game birds and found these very good. I've never eaten one later in winter, but natives in the northern bush country eat them all year long.

Although this kind of pot shooting might be scorned by discriminating bird hunters, I found it intriguing, and had a go at it myself on a couple of occasions. I also confess to popping a few perching birds at close range, head shots using a full-choke 20 gauge. However, every now and then the spruce grouse switches its personality and acts like a fine little wilderness game bird.

As an example, one fall I was making a fishing trip into Ontario, and the owner of the lodge where I was going told me to bring along a shotgun. We'd get in some ruffed grouse hunting. We did, and found abundant birds.

A railroad ran into the northern bush a few miles from the lodge. "I believe," he told me one afternoon, "we ought to check out the railroad right-of-way. There are loads of berries of several kinds growing along it, and only one train goes through a day. It should be a perfect place for grouse."

We drove to a crossing, left the vehicle, and began walking along the outside edges of the tracks, one on either side. The right-of-way made perfect edge cover. We flushed a couple of ruffed grouse in the first few minutes. Then we came to a mossy bog where the tracks cut through a stand of thick spruce. The opening had allowed the growth of varied brushy cover, and here bunchberries, short blueberry bushes, and several other kinds of fruit had taken hold.

To our surprise and delight, the first bird to flush here was a spruce grouse. It rattled up out of the cover, headed straight along the track, then veered toward the dense timber. I caught it right at the edge and dropped it. As I trotted ahead to pick it up, another flushed and my companion collected it. Before we had gone across the

heavy spruce stand, possibly half a mile, and broken out into an area of white birch and ferns, we had flushed a half dozen spruce grouse. Every bird had buzzed away as sporty in flight as any ruffed grouse. Given wide open shots, we downed every one.

That didn't quite end it. At the far edge of the spruce stand, we found both ruffed and spruce grouse in the birches. Spruce grouse eat birch buds just as ruffed grouse do. The experience was as enjoyable a wingshooting session as anyone could wish. And to think the so-called fool hens had furnished most of it!

Another grouse of the timber that exhibits all too trusting ways is the blue grouse, a westerner. Nevertheless, it furnishes dramatic wingshooting far more often than the spruce grouse. Blue grouse are big fellows. They weigh from an average of two pounds to as much as 3½ or four. This bird ranges over much of far western Canada, south in the United States in the forested mountains throughout the Pacific states, and in similar terrain in western Montana, much of Idaho, and portions of Wyoming, Colorado, Nevada, Utah, and New Mexico.

A casual glance at a blue grouse reminds one of a king-sized replica of the ruffed grouse. It is blue-gray and grayish brown, with subdued markings of paler hues. The tail fans out like that of the ruffed grouse, but is dark, slate to black, with a gray band across the end when the tail is fanned. There is a small comb above each eye, differing in color among subspecies from yellow to orange to red.

The different populations in various parts of the range have long produced arguments among ornithologists and hunters. Years ago several were considered distinctly different species. There was the sooty grouse, the dusky grouse, the Sierra grouse, the Richardson's grouse. It is generally conceded nowadays that these and several others are simply races or subspecies of the same bird. Including the type species, there are eight of these. A few references still insist on whacking them up, claiming that the dusky and the sooty, or Oregon, races are separate species, and allotting the several other races between those two. To hunters, a blue grouse is a blue grouse, wherever found.

The first one I ever saw acted as stupid as any bird possibly could. As teenagers my brother and I were spending part of a summer with an aunt in Oregon. She lived in the Willamette Valley, out in the country. At that time the area was a patchwork of forest and farm fields. Blue grouse, I

learned later, often came out of the conifer fringes and fed in grain stubble. My brother and I were wandering in a stubble field along the edge of a swath of forest when we saw this big bird perched on a low limb. It looked as large as a chicken.

When we walked under it, the bird simply looked down and cocked its head. Curious, we found a stick, reached up and poked it gently. It wasn't five feet above us. The bird reacted by simply moving over. We poked it a bit more. Again it moved over. It made no sound, no move to fly. As we walked away, puzzled by its actions or lack of them, it was still calmly perched.

Years later, when I next met up with blue grouse, the routine was quite different. I was in western Wyoming, enjoying fine fall trout fishing, having a sage grouse shoot,

The blue grouse of the western mountains is a big bird, weighing an average of two pounds but at maximum as much as four. *Judd Cooney photo.*

and waiting for antelope season to open. A rancher on whose property I had fished asked if I'd like to make a blue grouse hunt. The season was about to open.

"I've got a few coveys located," he told me. "These birds, like all other game birds, have highs and lows here. This is a high year. I've been keeping tabs on them all summer."

As it turned out, the terrain layout was classic for a virtually surefire blue grouse hunt anywhere. Anyone who uses it as a basic pattern for finding birds is almost certain to get sporty shooting. It was based on a small, rollicking creek that came tumbling down from the mountains. Way up, probably at 10,000 feet and above, there was dense pine, fir, and aspen forest. At possibly 8,000 feet the rolling hills were solid sagebrush, with scattered small pockets of aspen. Still lower, perhaps at 6,000 or 7,000 feet, there was more pine forest, but not so dense except along and out from the creek.

Blue grouse have odd habits. Many spend the summer nesting season at modest altitude, then when full winter arrives move up into the thick conifers where snow may be heavy. There they perch for days on end in conifers, eating the needles. Come spring, they drift down, usually flying, to lower country again. Another curious habit is that coveys based at modest altitude on slopes begin their foraging in the morning by moving from roosting sites *uphill*, walking, feeding as they go. If you come down on them from above, they may flush wild and sail back downslope. If you move upslope just as they have done, they'll hold sometimes as beautifully to a dog as any ruffed grouse. We didn't have a dog. We were going to walk up our birds. Regardless, if they have good cover they usually hold tight until you're right on them.

When they do flush, they invariably plunge back downhill. This puts them over the guns—at least some of them, if the brush and trees aren't too thick.

The rancher's scheme, which he assured me had worked successfully year after year, was to work up the creek. "The birds feed up it until they're full, then rest during midday and feed again, then most of them fly back down at dusk to where they've been roosting."

He pointed out to me that the pines quickly thinned as we climbed. Soon there were only scattered large trees, pines and aspens, along the creek, with open sagebrush covering the hills. It didn't look much like blue grouse habitat. Along the creek, however, were masses of chokecherry bushes that stretched way on up, even where the pine and aspen entirely petered out.

I now saw the beauty of this layout, and I describe it in detail because there are many similar places in western mountains where blue grouse dwell. Find one, and if birds are present you are in high shooting clover. The cherries were the key. Wild fruit is always a magnet for blue grouse. In the vast mountains where they live, you might search for days to find only scattered birds. However, if you first find wild fruit in abundance and then look for birds in it, you are way out ahead in this game.

It was late in the morning when we got into the first cherry thickets. Immediately a bird was in the air. Like ruffed grouse, the big blues can get up and glide off in utter silence. This one did. We missed it. At the shots, two more flushed. These weren't silent. They burst up out of the cherry shrubs with a high-decibel roar and rattle.

There were scattered aspens here, out from the cherries. Beyond those was only open sage. The birds, forest oriented, wouldn't fly out over the sage. They wheeled above the cherries, cut through the aspens, and plunged downhill. But there were patches of open sky they couldn't avoid. We swung on them as they crossed the first one and brought both down.

From there on the shooting was unbelievable. The several coveys the rancher had been watching apparently had all walked up the creek. They were bunched up one after another. I purposely didn't count how many birds we missed. After perhaps a half mile of fighting the cherry thickets, we paused to blow and counted up. We had only one bird to go to fill limits for each of us.

After we'd rested, the rancher grinned at me and said, "You look happy. Want to go on up and get happier, try the sage chickens?"

I was thinking of the weight already in my game vest, and of how weary I was from the climb. Add several four-pound sage grouse, and it would be like packing out part of a mule deer. I said, "I don't believe I could stand being any happier." We started back down the creek, flushed a sit-tight blue that had let us pass on our way up, and levelled off our limit.

Wild cherries, it should be noted, are only one of numerous fruits that draw blue grouse. Depending on when the shooting season falls in relation to ripening of fruit, elderberries, blueberries—especially blueberries—snowberries, blackberries, and salal berries all are eagerly sought by the birds. In Washington and on Vancouver Island, where wild blackberries in some seasons are unbelievably abundant, blue grouse eagerly gorge on them.

If you know where there are thickets of thornapple in a vicinity where birds are present, during a good bearing year they,

too, will have grouse in them every day. Any abundant fruit will draw them. One early fall we were in southwestern Alberta and found an area where bushes loaded with what natives call "saskatoons" were abundant. We picked several quarts to stew and eat. This is a local name given to serviceberries or, as they're called in the East, juneberries. Blue grouse occasionally flushed from among the shrubs.

Wild fruit isn't available everywhere that blue grouse live, but it is the hottest clue to finding them if you have choices. At high altitudes, often a covey will live all summer and fall in a bailiwick based on a mountain meadow. When New Mexico game biologists were trying to trap birds for transplant, they'd locate a covey in summer in a high meadow and build a net-covered trap in the tall grass, with long wings out from it. Then, when they found the covey feeding, they'd circle wide and very slowly move the birds ahead of them. Reverting to their "fool hen" personalities, the birds occasionally could be slowly driven, without flushing, right into the trap.

In the country up near timberline, blues are drawn to boggy meadow areas and creek courses with willows and other brush. Logged areas, clearcuts, and burns that have resprouted also are likely places to find them. The best shooting will always be where thickets are dense enough to hold birds. Blues sometimes get up wild in open country and fly for a mile or so down and across a mountain valley. There's no follow-up when they act thus. These mountain birds have endless room and are often inclined to use it.

Also, they commonly flush from a feeding area, sail downhill at sizzling speed, then brake and alight in pine or spruce trees. They're difficult to see then at close range, even if you have an eye on the proper tree. When you do flush one from a conifer, it usually leaves with a tremendous racket of wings and dives downslope again. This is one of the most difficult aspects of blue grouse shooting. Most shots are downhill. You've got to hold *under*, but few gunners learn this. Further, the big birds may barely skim the cover, leaving no "under" that you can drive pellets through.

Wild fruit, and a creek which it borders, are the main ingredients of the most successful hunts for blues. The creek isn't so important for its water but rather for supplying congenial conditions where the food will grow in a narrow swath and guide the birds. In the authentic high country, up to 10,000 feet, seeps, springs, and boggy places are spots where coveys base their activities. In fact, in dry years a spring anywhere blues live will draw every bird from a large expanse.

You will read here and there that you won't find blue grouse until you are at or above 9,000 feet in altitude. It's true that these birds are addicted to high forests, and indeed many do live out their lives at high altitudes. It's not true that they aren't ever present below 9,000 feet. Some of the best hunting at times is in foothill terrain, par-

ticularly where the season opens in early or mid September.

During big-game seasons, when the blues are back up in the high pine and spruce country, hunters often pot them with pistols for camp meat, and even collect a few with bow and arrow. Some of this pot hunting is done, unfortunately, when the bird season isn't open. Hunters who observe blues under late fall and winter situations are convinced they couldn't possibly be sporty game birds. Happily, this is only one side of the blue grouse personality.

For those who own well-trained dogs and seek places such as I have described, hunting these big-timber grouse comes close to matching ruffed grouse hunting. Be assured, however, that it is exhausting labor. The thin high-country air, the steep slopes, and often the long search required to locate birds adds up to a combo for which any flatlander needs a long fitness tuneup. That rancher with whom I hunted the cherry thickets told me, "Learning to hunt blue grouse successfully takes time, and will wear any hunter down. When you finally get the hang of it, you're old enough so you should have the good sense to quit!"

19

The Immigrant Partridges –
Birds of Paradox

Dan Clements called it "the chukar hole." It wasn't a hole at all, but a treeless plateau high atop a small Nevada mountain. Rocks from basketball size to boulders were scattered over it, and it was cut by ridges and jagged rock outcrops. Among this rough expanse there was ground cover of cheat grass in tufts and in larger patches. There was also scattered sage. Along the plateau edge in the direction we were headed, a cliff of reddish rock dropped 15 feet or so to talus and shady clefts, and from there the steep slope plunged to the valley below. It was a place that any chukar hunter would recognize as a choice spot for these birds.

The time was near noon. A quail hunter would have pointed out that this was no time for coveys to be feeding. Chukars are also covey birds, and on average days they are not likely to be feeding during midday,

either. We knew that. We had bet, however, that they'd be ganged up here, resting.

From the edge of the red cliff we could look far down across the rocky, rolling, steep-slanted, sage-covered spines and draws, down to the bottom where a dammed-up wash had formed a runoff stock pond that winked blue and clear. Dan's 4WD was parked a hundred yards beyond the pond. It was here, when we'd come into this backcountry several hours earlier, shortly after full light, that we had heard chukars galore taunting us from the slope base, daring us to chase them, calling *ka-ka-ka-ka-ka*.

Dan, an old hand at chukar hunting, kept his pointer leashed and restrained me from rushing into things.

"If we move toward them, they'll either flush wild or run," he said.

The chukar is a handsome bird, well established in numerous states. It likes the rough country of western slopes and mesas. *National Rifle Association photo.*

I knew that, but their clamor had me roiling inside with excitement, and my better judgment was crumbling. I fought it. I knew very well that there isn't a hunter on earth who can beat a bunch of chukars up a slope. When chukars are come upon in valleys and foothills, they invariably run uphill. They have a habit of running over a minor side ridge just enough to get them out of sight and *then* flushing. An average flight for flushed chukars is anywhere up to a quarter mile or more. When a bunch runs and then flushes out of sight, you don't know where they'll be.

There were obviously many birds here. Dan's scheme was to move away from them, circle around the base of the mountain, and keep moving on a slant, always upward, to deal with them later. We'd leave this big bunch without further disturbance. Maybe we'd pick up a few birds as we trav-

eled. Circling the mountain, we would come out on the far side of the plateau and work its perimeter and a hundred yards or so into it, coming back around to where we could look down on our starting point. Dan knew that chukars not only try to escape uphill but also *feed* uphill almost without fail. If the plan worked, we'd get into the whole bunch ganged up on top during midday.

We flushed several other small coveys as we traveled. Dan let the dog free as soon as we were over the first ridge. When chukars flush wild in groups, singles or two or three at a time are inclined to drop off here and there as the rest fly on. The curious paradox of the chukar is that it is an utterly exasperating runner, yet drop-out birds or birds from a scattered flock will sit so tight you seldom can find or get them up without a dog. We nailed three sit-tight birds en route, thanks to Dan's pointer, but it was the big concentration we were looking forward to—if Dan's plot worked.

Now, up on top near the red rock cliff, the pointer straightened out, nose aimed toward a small rock surrounded by grass. We moved widely left and right of the dog. A bird flurried up under the pointer's nose. We both missed. The air was suddenly a blizzard of wings as chukars exploded all around us. Maybe 50 birds. The shooting was all we had hoped for, far enough in from the edge of the plateau so we had

The chukar is an extremely sporty bird, but also a determined runner. Open ridges where cheat grass grows are a favorite habitat for it. *Oregon Department of Fish & Wildlife photo.*

shots at level-flying birds. On the slopes they invariably plunge downhill or fly the undulating contours, and are much harder to hit. Guns were booming, and the pointer was running toward two falling birds before they hit the ground.

Suddenly the long, hard hike seemed worth it. The scheme had worked. Before the late flushers were all in the air, we had put five chukars on the ground. Dan trotted ahead to meet the dog, which was fetching a bird, and behind him a single exploded. His gun was empty. He paused and reloaded, muttering, and at that instant the pointer, holding a bird in its mouth, froze, facing Dan. Beautiful! He took one step, and a chukar swirled out of a cheat grass tuft that seemed far too skimpy to have hidden it. Dan brought it down.

That exhilarating sequence of action was not a normal routine. The chukar, which has become an extremely important game bird over much of the West, causes great anguish and breast beating among the many hunters it exasperates. Nevertheless, those who know how to hunt it agree that it is a wonderful and immensely challenging addition to our upland game birds.

The unique aspect of this foreigner is that it has been established and is most at home in scattered locations in the West where native game birds are either entirely lacking or far from abundant. It fills a habitat niche little used by native game, in arid, high-desert situations.

Although its diet is varied, depending on what is available, the chukar is especially fond of cheat grass, which grows among the rocks, along the talus slopes, and over rocky foothills and canyon sides where sagebrush paints the rough highlands gray. It eats both green shoots and the seeds of this grass. Many hunters don't even look for other possible forage, although stream-course alfalfa and clover fields often draw birds off the ridges, and so occasionally do fields of wheat.

The chukar has been present in America almost long enough to be called a "native." The first birds imported were released late in the last century, in Illinois. Since that time they've been tried in all but a very few of the contiguous states and most Canadian provinces. It took a long time for game managers to realize that chukars can't sustain themselves in humid or even moderately moist areas. They require a dry, up-country climate.

Numerous subspecies of the bird have been tried in the U.S. In some areas where they've been successful, the races no doubt are mixed. The most successful strain came from the foothills of the Himalaya Mountains in Nepal. Today the chukar is well established in suitable habitats in the Pacific Coast states, in British Columbia, in Idaho, Montana, Wyoming, Utah, Colorado, and Nevada, with small populations scattered elsewhere.

Nevada tallied the first success with chukars over 50 years ago. Today the chukar is that state's most important game bird. Although chukars, like all uplanders, are somewhat cyclic, having excellent and poor reproduction years, by the late 1960s Nevada hunters were taking as many as 175,000 a season. Several other states now show kills as large or nearly so. In Oregon, for example, the chukar most years is second only to the pheasant among upland bird species in numbers bagged.

The chukar — whose name derives from its varied crowing calls, *chuck, chukar, chukara* — is a beautiful partridge. Adult cocks average 1½ to 1¾ pounds. Females are slightly smaller. Male and female are almost identical in plumage and colors. The beak, skin around the eye, and the legs

are red. Upper parts and breast are soft gray-brown. The crown is paler, gray-white. A black swath runs across the forehead and through the eye area, then curves down and around to encircle the throat and cheeks, which are white. The flanks are strikingly barred in black and white. The overall appearance of the chukar is of a very plump, short-tailed bird.

Dan Clements told me with a grin, "You can't look at a chukar without smacking your lips. It just simply looks like wonderful eating." It is.

Sometimes the chukar has been called the "red-legged partridge." Actually the authentic red-legged partridge, which has been tried here and there in North America, is a chukar relative, a native of Spain and France, where shooting for it has long been renowned. It has been successfully introduced to both Scotland and England. It looks rather similar to the chukar but requires a far different habitat, as is evident from its successful transplants to England and Scotland. Presently Oregon is experimenting seriously with the red-legged partridge. It's believed the bird will do well in the humid, moist region west of the Cascades. If this bird does establish itself there, it's possible that this chukar near-replica may eventually be successful east of the Mississippi, too.

Even though the chukar is popular, it still is underutilized, mostly because of the tough terrain it inhabits and the physical difficulties of hunting it. The birds are found at elevations anywhere from 4,000 to 9,000 feet, invariably in steep canyonland and talus slope terrain. They're rugged creatures, able to tough out below-zero winters on windswept ridges. Snow, if deep, does force them to move down to lower elevations. They can't scratch through much of it to get food. Some hunters like to hunt them late in the season, when there is snow. This concentrates birds at lower elevations where snow is light, and late in the season they often gather in packs of 100 or more.

Also, some hunters, those without dogs especially, like snowtime hunting because then they can easily find tracks of chukar flocks. A great many hunters are successful without dogs, by always getting above the birds and hunting downslope. However, they miss many birds that lie close and refuse to flush. They also lose quite a few. Even a hard-hit chukar, hurtling downslope, may fall into sage far down and be impossible to find without a dog.

When I first hunted with Dan Clements, he told me there was a shortcut to locating chukars. "In this country," he said, "you could wander over hundreds of square miles of sage and grass and rocky stand-on-end slopes and perhaps never flush a bird. So I don't begin by hunting birds. I first hunt water."

The system works admirably. All chukar country is arid. Summers are usually dry, and that condition continues into fall hunting season. The birds must have water. Therefore they invariably converge on watering places in their domains. If a fall happens to be an unusually wet one, birds may find water at numerous locations and be somewhat scattered. However, chukar country isn't noted for abundant rainfall. Besides, any permanent water source out in the sage and cheat-grass foothills will have numerous coveys raised within a half mile or so of it. If a fall is a drought period, hundreds of birds may converge on the vicinity of permanent water, even a very small waterhole.

Dan took me one day to a small creek that wound along the base of rocky, grass and sage-covered foothills with higher country above. The creek was bone-dry. He started along it anyway. Soon I understood. I heard chukars calling. These birds talk to each other a lot, and always talk when disturbed. Listening for chukars is an important part of the hunt. Presently we came upon a tiny waterhole in the otherwise dry creek.

The dog was working nicely, and in some high sage it suddenly stiffened. Acting like the paradoxes they are, a small group of chukars burst out of the sage. We both shot, and down came two birds. The rest glided down to hit the ground running 100 or more yards out. We could see them afterward, running up the slope.

We worked along the creek clear around the turn of the foothills, finding birds near every small puddle. This was about the middle of the morning, a time when chukars commonly go to drink after feeding. Finally Dan motioned for a rest, and then we started climbing. The big ridge we'd paralleled was cut by numerous offshoot spines slanting toward the valley. When we were well above the creek, we began working back across the spines.

This is another trick of successful chukar hunters. Birds often fly over a crest and alight, then run a bit. By hunting high up a slope along the general contour, you come over spine after spine and with luck are on birds at close range before they know it. We got into a covey first thing. Talk about tricky shooting! Some hurtled straight downslope. I tried to force myself to hold under. It never seems right, but it is. Some of the birds flew the contour course, which took them over the next low, close-in spine before we had shooting time. We did chalk up limits before we reached the vehicle. I was never happier. If we'd been short and Clements had suggested one more round, I'd never have made it.

Remembering that hunt recently, I recalled with amusement another experienced hunting friend with whom I was discussing the chukar and that other immigrant partridge, the Hungarian or European gray partridge, usually called simply "Hun." He insisted that the chukar was the most frustrating and exhausting game bird ever created. I insisted just as emphatically that the Hun had an edge in both categories.

"Not a chance," he said. "At least you hunt those darned things on almost level ground!" I had to agree he had a point.

The Hungarian partridge is so named in America because early transplants to this country came from Hungary. It earns the title of "paradox partridge" on at least three counts. It has been in this country on a self-sustaining basis for about 75 years, and hunted for at least 45, yet only a scattering of North American bird hunters have ever

seen or hunted it. At least five Canadian provinces and a dozen states have Huns in huntable abundance, yet in every location they are far underutilized. Perhaps the third leg of the paradox is responsible for the second: when you hunt Huns, you can be sure that whatever the birds do won't be what you expected!

The Hun has a most intriguing history. It is the most wide-ranging of the world's game birds, found in numerous locations in Asia, throughout Europe, the Scandinavian countries, and the British Isles, and has been successfully transplanted around the world. Undoubtedly more Huns were brought into the U.S. and Canada—several hundred thousand of them—than any other species thus far tried. The first record of U.S. introduction was in the late 1700s, when a relative of Ben Franklin released some in New Jersey. It is believed that every contiguous state and most Canadian

The Hungarian partridge, usually called "Hun" by hunters, has been in this country for at least 75 years and hunted for 45, but still is underutilized. *North Dakota Game & Fish Department photo.*

provinces have tried Huns at one time or another, either officially or by private leases. Most were unsuccessful.

In 1908 a release of 180 pairs of birds—Huns are monogamous—was made near Calgary, Alberta. This transplant tripped the jackpot. There was an eruption of partridge, which swiftly spread in all directions over hundreds of miles. Alberta has for years been a kind of hub of Hun population. However, southeastern Manitoba and southwestern Saskatchewan both have excellent shooting. Presently the top states and general high-population areas in them are as follows: eastern Washington, eastern Oregon, southern Idaho, northeastern Nevada, eastern Montana, much of both Dakotas, western Minnesota, and northwestern Iowa. Modest widely scattered

populations are found in a few other states and provinces.

The Hun is a handsome little partridge, about twice as large as the average quail—from 12 to 15 ounces. The neck and breast are soft gray, the back and wings brown and gray. The head and face have cinnamon hues, but with the crown gray. There are russet bars on the flanks, and the outside tail feathers are the same color. There is often, but not always, a large, rich, brown patch, sometimes horseshoe shaped, on the lower breast, surrounded by white and gray. The sexes look quite similar. Many hunters claim the breast patch marks a male. This is incorrect. Either sex may exhibit the patch. Most males have it, but in some it is lacking.

My first experience with Huns was in

Huns were first established on a large scale in Alberta near Calgary. They're tough birds, able to withstand the severe winters of the plains. These Huns are shown in open, windswept country in North Dakota. *North Dakota Game & Fish Department photo.*

northwestern Iowa. The region is farm country, and I was reminded at first of pheasant hunting. I hunted with a land-owner who was reluctant. Why not, he proposed, just hunt pheasants? Probably one reason Huns are underhunted in many places is that local hunters are used to pheasants. Huns are emphatically not birds of the wild places; they do best where agri-cultural operations are pursued in prairie or rolling grassland terrain.

"One cock pheasant," the landowner re-minded me, "sure would feel better in the game pocket than several Huns!"

Indeed, in that region as in many others, Huns are taken mostly as incidentals while pheasant hunting. However, I soon began to understand additional reasons for my host's reluctance. We had no dog. We started off along the edge of a wheat-stub-ble field. It seemed to me there wasn't enough cover to hide a sparrow, let alone a partridge covey. Besides, why would they be out in the open?

To answer my thoughts, a covey whirred up at least 100 yards in front of us. It flew several hundred yards and came down, not in the cover of a nearby creek course but in the short stubble. We hunted two hours and jumped six coveys. The closest we got was to one that held until we were about 30 yards from it. When birds as fast and explosive as these little partridge flush unex-pectedly that far out, you have to shoot fast to catch one still in range. We weren't fast enough.

Finally the farmer said, "I'm going to do you a favor, knowing how badly you want to collect at least one or two of these birds. There's a home covey that stays in the shel-ter belt near the farm buildings. We never bother them, but I'm going to make an exception."

I protested—rather weakly. We headed back toward the narrow shelter belt of trees near the buildings and put the covey up almost immediately, at short range. There must have been at least 15 birds. They streaked through the trees. I shot three times. Not a feather came down! I suspect the farmer felt relieved.

Huns aren't always so difficult. Neverthe-less, their habits perplex many hunters. I learned later on that flushed birds time after time will alight on open ground rather than heading for brushy cover. If you find them in picked cornfields, or where stubble is dense, or in grass, for example, you can often get within range. A dog for Huns must be a close-in worker.

I hunted once with a pussyfooting little Brittany that knew all about Huns. She'd never try to get in close on a covey. Her nose was exceptional. She'd stay only a few yards out front of us, working very slowly, and the moment she got scent, she'd stop. Her owner worked her into the wind, of course, and on the prairie farm fields, wind is never hard to find. You had to get used to judging about where the birds would be. Some points she made were from as much as 50 yards away. She could do this only on feeding birds. We never followed up flushed coveys that came down compactly. They didn't put out enough scent, the owner claimed, when first aground.

Scattered birds from a covey will hold snug as can be at times, especially if they are down in tall grass or a hay field. On one hunt this same Brittany flushed the same covey twice, and instead of flying together the last time, they scattered into a hay field. We moved in. It was dramatic to watch the little dog change tactics. She knew precisely what those singles were going to do.

On her first point, as we moved in a single buzzed up, barely missing the dog's nose. It cut to my side, and I dropped it. At

A covey of Huns hurtles into the air. They often flush wild and are difficult birds with or without a dog. *North Dakota Game & Fish Department photo.*

the shot another arose 20 yards out. The dog's owner instantly put it down. We worked the hay for other singles and took three birds each. A great hunt.

Picking up his third partridge, my companion said with a grin, "You know, in Alberta in the early 1940s they had a limit of 20 Huns per day and 250 for the season." He paused, looked at the Hun in his hand, and added, "Don't say it—I know what you're thinking."

"Sure you do," I said. "How the heck could anybody kill 20 of these darned things in a day regardless of how plentiful they were?"

In some of the rolling country of the West where Huns are abundant, hunters take advantage of the fact that a flushed covey often heads toward a low ridge and flies over it. Experience has taught them that the birds probably will alight just past the crest, and may not run after coming down. A quiet sneak over the ridge occasionally puts one in easy range. Other successful hunters claim they locate water first, and always find several coveys within a half mile.

One of the most successful Hun hunters

I know dotes on creek courses in farm country. "There's one I know about," he told me, "that meanders across a wheat farm. Wheat fields border it on both sides. Along its course there are willows and varied tall grass and bushes. The birds use it for resting and dusting, and for protection against the cold."

He explained that he doesn't hunt early and late here. The Huns then are feeding in the wheat field edges and are inclined to flush wild. He hunts it during the middle of the day, paying special attention when he gets near the buildings of a long-abandoned farm. "There's always a covey near the buildings," he says. "If I hunt quietly, they'll stay put in the creek cover until I'm within range." Then he grinned and added, "Well, sometimes."

True. As I said earlier, whatever Huns do, it won't often be what you hoped they'd do. There is one facet of Hungarian partridge hunting, however, that is infallibly predictable. That's when a few have cooperated and are brought to the table. Huns are darker-meated than pheasants, but they are superb fare.

Part IV

THE PHEASANTS

The only original American representatives of the large family to which the pheasants belong were the several species of native quail. No true pheasants were native to this continent. Pheasants have been here so long, however, that many a modern hunter thinks of them as natives. Worldwide, the family *Phasianidae*, which includes the quail, partridges, and pheasants, is extremely varied. There are representatives in almost all countries. The pheasants are the larger members of the vast tribe, and are the most colorful and highly varied, with dozens of species.

Pheasants of practically every gaudy color and color combination are found in various habitat types around the globe. Most, but not all, of the male birds are long-tailed. An outstanding specimen of one variety with an astonishing tail was measured at almost eight feet long from beak to end of tail. For centuries numerous colorful pheasants have been reared in captivity as display birds. Ancient Greeks raised pheasants as chickens are raised today, for food. Pheasants have also been sporting birds dating back in history to when the Romans introduced them into western Europe.

The first known release of pheasants in America occurred almost 200 years ago. During George Washington's first term as President, English black-necked pheasants were released on the grounds at Mount Vernon. A few years later the governor of New Hampshire set free some English pheasants on his estate. It was hoped they might colonize along the Atlantic Coast. Neither release was successful.

From that time forward, hundreds of releases of pheasants have occurred. Mongolian pheasants, Japanese pheasants, Chinese pheasants, and countless others from throughout the world were brought to this country. Up to the present, virtually every state has either privately or officially experimented with pheasants. All of the early transplants, and the majority in later years, eventually disappeared. It was not until 1881 that the pheasant became a success in this country. What a success it was! In fact, this transplant made history as one of the most astonishingly successful ever accomplished of any game species anywhere.

The U.S. Consul General in Shanghai, Judge Owen Denny, collected several dozen Chinese pheasants and had them shipped to Oregon, where they were released in the Willamette Valley. Apparently they found this new home perfect for their needs. The birds nested so successfully that there was a veritable population explosion. During the ensuing decade, pheasants simply overran the Valley. The first hunting season, 2½ months long, was held in 1892. Whether or not the harvest count was correct, it was claimed that during the first day of the season hunters downed 50,000 pheasants!

Game departments were not then the smoothly run and knowledgeable organizations they are today. The Oregon success obviously excited people in budding game departments all over the country. Scores of pheasant strains were transplanted and widely tried, most of them close replicas of this ring-necked bird that came out of northern China. Today no one can say precisely what race the so-called American ringneck is. It has evolved undoubtedly from many strains, and has become in general a truly American pheasant.

At the present time, experiments with new pheasant species, hybrids, and races have slowed down, largely because all game departments are running on short budgets nowadays. However, our American bird

habitats are constantly and swiftly changing as our population grows. Pheasants are birds that for centuries have adapted well to man's civilization throughout the world. Most varieties are distinctly tied to agricultural lands. Undoubtedly, in time other pheasant varieties will be established on this continent, filling niches the American ringneck cannot tolerate.

Meanwhile, hunters can derive immense satisfaction from the fact that they have witnessed, in the astonishing ringneck colonizations of the past, one of the world's phenomenal wild-game transplant successes. It's doubtful whether many of today's hunters realize just how immense the ringneck success was at its peak.

In South Dakota, center of the pheasant eruption range, hunters were harvesting an average of two million birds each season by the late 1920s. I remember hunts there two decades later during which we were allowed 16 birds daily, either sex. Natives then told us that things had slowed down, that even higher limits had been allowed previously. I was also told tales of commercial trappers, operating illegally during depression years, who boxed up 300 to 500 birds, drove them to Chicago, and sold them for as little as 50 cents each.

The peak years were in the mid–1940s. It was claimed that during the 1946 season 7½ million birds were shot in South Dakota alone. After that, kill figures and numbers of birds began to decline. Land use began slowly changing after World War Two. Nevertheless, in the middle 1960s total annual pheasant harvest throughout the United States was tallied at an average of around 18 million birds. Today it may not be that high, but it still is in the two-figure millions, and the pheasant population coast to coast remains relatively stable.

Although hunters have always been enthusiastic about abundant pheasants, not everyone was when the birds were first developing high populations. I remember my father, who was not a hunter, being disgusted because of the depredations pheasants caused in our Michigan farm-country garden. A "garden" in those days was no minuscule backyard plot. We lived in the country and lived on what we raised. My mother canned dozens of jars of a wide variety of vegetables. Those that kept well, like potatoes and carrots, were put in crates in our dirt cellar.

We always had possibly a half acre of sweet corn, for fresh summer corn-on-the-cob and to be canned for winter. All garden work then had to be done by hand. My father and my brother and I laboriously put in the rows of corn hills, hoeing out the small holes, dropping in a few kernels, covering them up. Several years, the minute the sprouts appeared above ground, pheasants walked the rows and jerked each one up to snip the still-attached kernel from the base. They completely cleaned us out.

They worked on our grapevines, too, arrogantly perching in them and gorging on the ripe grapes. As my brother and I grew older, we put a stop to some of it. We had a single-shot 12-gauge shotgun and a single-shot .22. We punished the pheasants as much as we could, but it was a losing game. They swarmed. I recall one time asking a neighbor down the road if we could hunt some on his place. He said we could, if we'd promise to kill every pheasant we got a chance at, hens and cocks. He had tried to raise tomatoes near his house. Unless he stayed out there watching constantly, which of course he couldn't do,

they incessantly combed the patch. He finally poisoned the lot of them.

Those were minor depredations compared to what some of the plains-states farmers had to put up with during those explosion years. Hunters might have been pleased, but landowners weren't. I was browsing recently through Morris D. Johnson's excellent "Feathers from the Prairie," a book published some years ago by the North Dakota Game and Fish Department. A letter written by a landowner to the Department in 1945 caught my eye. It complained of serious damage to haystacks, cornstalks, and corn still on the cob by pheasants during the winter, and crop damage during summer. One sentence states, "There are between 600 and 800 birds at our buildings continually and between 6,000 and 8,000 on our land." And later, "The only means of scaring them is by shooting, although we are unable to get shells at the present time. We also have thought of poisoning them."

Today the pheasant phenomenon has struck a better balance so far as the landowner is concerned, and hunters everywhere still have good shooting. Over the years, I have been privileged to shoot our American ringneck in numerous places. In addition to its beauty and sporty qualities before the gun, two attributes have always immensely pleased me—the bulk and weight a couple of cocks make in my game vest, and the delectable presentation they make on the table. "If someone could invent a chicken that tasted like pheasant," a hunting companion once told me as we worked on a brace of baked birds, "he'd be a millionaire overnight."

20

The Gaudy Cock That Changed American Shotgunning

The big Lab was crisscrossing out front, within shotgun range, through dead weeds and wild sunflowers so dense and tall the dog was hidden. Motion and crackling of the stalks told us where he moved. This dog had been brought up on pheasants. He was doing just right, going very slowly, careful not to overlook the scent of close-lying birds. They couldn't run in this cover, and the dog knew it.

There were cut-over crop fields bordering both sides of the strip of weeds. Undoubtedly the birds had fed in those earlier. It was midday now, and Paul Young and I, following the dog, knew as well as it did that this time of day the birds would be in the cover, and that any we got up would hang tight until the dog or one of us all but stepped on them.

The place was northwestern Kansas, near the town of Norton. I liked this kind of pheasant hunting far more than the big drives I'd made on many occasions in the plains states. This was the way I'd hunted pheasants when I was a teenager, except that most of the time then I didn't have a bird dog. Much of the time my brother and I had hunted without a dog. Other times we used whatever dog we happened to have. I remember a bobtailed mongrel that was part Collie, a beagle that was a whiz on pheasants, and a cocker that was small and couldn't run or work fast and thus was extremely thorough.

Presently the weeds quit moving. The burly Lab was standing still. Guns up and alert, we moved in. The cock ripped up through the weeds, letting off a startled and annoyed *croo-kuk, croo-kuk*—the last syllable accented, the tone grating and raucous, a sound that, even remembered, triggers excitement. The bird swerved left, and Paul

The gaudy cock that changed American shotgunning. As a teenager I hunted pheasants without a dog, and they were always running or skulking in cover.

swung to get a lead on the "part that counts," that forward portion of head, neck, and shoulders. Too often hunters see the overall length and shoot at it, but almost two-thirds of a pheasant is tail. At his shot another rooster swirled noisily out of the cover a few yards ahead. I let it level off and then laced a successful shot at it.

Even after you've shot hundreds of pheasants, it's difficult to take one in hand without pausing to turn it this way and that, still hardly believing the rainbow colors and how they change and are patterned as light strikes them from different angles. Looking at the cock I'd just shot, it struck me that the Chinese ringnecked pheasant has been for many years now the greatest single influence toward change in American upland gunning pursuits. Many of us, of course, still hunt ruffed grouse, bobwhites, and numerous other natives. The immense success of the pheasant, however, for years now has drawn more hunter attention than any other facet of shotgunning sport.

There are logical but not always recognized reasons this occurred. At the time of successful pheasant introduction, a lot of upland shooting had waned. The once awesomely abundant prairie chicken was swiftly declining. So was the sharptail. The upland plover, about which modern gunners have almost no knowledge, also had been a sensation on the plains, but had now been protected and scarce for years. Even bobwhite quail were in trouble in many places as land-use changes decimated their habitats.

Suddenly, there were ringnecks exploding in many places, and at least huntable as modest-population game birds in many others. There is no question that the male's gaudy garb contributed to the bird's appeal. This alone made it a desirable target, to this day a kind of trophy bird. In hunters' minds pheasant cocks also had a kind of arrogant, aggressive, regal aura—perhaps imagined, but nonetheless provocative.

Added to these qualities was first of all the attribute of size. Here was a bird that put weight in the game bag. That weight has often been exaggerated by enthusiastic scribes. I read recently that adult cock pheasants weigh five pounds. Numerous game-department surveys, during which hundreds of birds were weighed, agree that an adult cock weighs on the average about three pounds. A range of 2½ to 3½ pounds will cover cocks of all ages.

Consider, now, that of all native and introduced upland game birds excepting the wild turkey, only two match the cock pheasant for size. One is the sage grouse, which is in relatively short supply and has always been a specialist's bird, with restricted range. The other is the blue grouse, adults of which more often weigh in the two-pound class. This bird also is range-restricted and lives in a habitat few hunters get into.

Indeed, when you put a couple or three pheasants into your game vest, you know you are taking home a substantial amount of meat. This, too, lent the pheasant immense appeal. We all like to claim we aren't meat hunters. The fact is, the eating is and should be one of the hunter's most important considerations. It is a culmination, a rite of sorts. And here the pheasant comes up with another attribute that has added to its impact. Lots of gunners wouldn't eat a sage grouse, because the meat is dark and has, they'd claim, a too-distinctive flavor.

The ringneck, when first savored by Oregon and then plains hunters, was eagerly sought for food. Not only was it large enough for a family meal but also its yellow-skinned, delicate meat was far tastier than chicken. Here was an upland game bird in the gourmet class.

Even beauty, size, and eating quality, however, wouldn't have brought such fame to the pheasant except for the fact that here was an *every-hunter's* game bird. If you didn't have a bird dog, you could walk up a limit. You didn't need to go on trips to remote areas, or even to places moderately difficult to reach. Pheasants were birds tied to farms and even city fringes, thus easily accessible. I can recall scores of times driving a mile or two out from some city and making quickie hunts late in the afternoon after a day's work and fetching in a rooster or two. Wherever pheasants have established themselves, or even have been released put-and-take, they are everybody's bird.

There is one more quality that helped make the tremendous impact. Pheasants are easily pen reared, but once released, they almost instantly revert to the wild. There is something so inherently wild about them that they seldom succumb to taming influences. I remember vividly how as a kid I used to watch pheasants during hard winters come into our farmyard to eat with the chickens. Eat "with" is hardly a proper description. The aggressive roosters would drive the chickens away from the feed we put out for them, and then eat!

Is the pheasant thus the perfect game bird? For a majority of upland shooters who live near it or travel to enjoy pheasant hunting—average hunters, not specialists—it may just be perfection.

On that Kansas hunt with the late Paul Young Sr., a Texas friend, I remember thinking, as we rousted out the abundant cocks, that I really had not had to learn much about pheasants since my teens and early years. I don't mean that I knew it all back then, but I grew up with pheasants, swarms of them that amounted to nuisance proportions as far as small-farm people were concerned.

As teenagers, my brother and I hunted them winter and summer—admittedly not paying much attention to regulations, and I suppose there were some, although we didn't know of a warden anywhere near. We ran them out of our garden and into Mother's cooking pots. We tracked them in snow during midwinter in a red willow swale behind our house, and popped many with a .22 single-shot. We learned year by year more and more about the birds: what

travel routes they followed, where and on what they fed, which places they'd hide or laze in, which ditch banks they'd sit tight on and which they'd run down. We knew what kinds of places they liked for roosting—for example, in heavy marsh grass along swale edges where the ground was dry. We knew what time they'd leave the roost site and how the temperature and weather dictated that. This is the lore any accomplished pheasant hunter must have.

What we learned through enormous experience before we were out of our teens was the basic fact that, depending on the time of day and the cover, pheasants have two deeply ingrained habits. Disturbed in thin or so-so cover, they run like the devil and as far as a half mile if chased. In heavier ground cover they sit so tight you can be

Beginning a pheasant hunt on a small farm. The pheasant is every hunter's game bird, always easily accessible.

standing astraddle of one and never know until it rattles up behind you, scaring the wits out of you.

I have watched a dog, wildly excited, hunt frantically all over a six-foot circle in dense, uncut alfalfa with three hunters standing nearby watching—and all the time a cock was laid flat out in the cover, not moving until the dog actually poked it with its nose. I remember hunting dogless with my brother when I was a kid, pausing to rest a minute, looking down and seeing a cock lying flat right in front of my feet. I reached down slowly and in naive kid style grabbed it by the tail. It had flown 200 yards before I realized I was standing there clutching its tail in my hand.

The point to be made about what I learned of pheasants as a young man, and saying I've never needed to know much more, is that almost every year for the past 20 or more some magazine runs a highly ballyhooed piece about how the pheasants are changing. The writer tells about some scientific study, and how pheasants now exhibit totally different habits from those they brought to America with them—and then tells how to thwart the wiles of these "new" pheasants. These instructions may grab readers and sell magazines, but they are utter nonsense. Pheasant *habitats* certainly have changed since the '30s and '40s. The birds have had to vary basic routines here and there because of habitat influences. Nonetheless, the ringneck's personality hasn't changed one whit. They still run, they still cling tighter than bark—whatever best fits the situation as regards their safety. No game bird is more sly, more crafty.

During the high-kill years at the peak of the ringneck's success, hunters never would have bagged as many birds as they did except for the finesse that was brought to

pheasant drives by large groups. Most were plotted for the huge corn fields in South Dakota and elsewhere. Many fields were a half mile or more long and half that wide. In standing corn the rows are open underneath. Pheasants wouldn't flush out of such cover—or only a few did. The rest ran down the rows.

Driving a field that large required at least a dozen hunters for highest success. It's still done the same today as it was years ago, in corn, in cut-over maize, in sorghum fields, in any row-crop feeding field that has cover enough to allow birds to run. I've taken part in many a drive, in the big-limit days and even within recent seasons in places like the Texas Panhandle. No question: the big drives are thrilling when birds are abundant.

One fall near Faulkton, South Dakota, an area famed for ringnecks, I booked a hunt during which we stayed at a large old farmhouse. There were a dozen hunters in various parties. The operator brought us all together and explained the drive plans to us.

Four of the older hunters were assigned as blockers. They were let off at one end of the field and spaced as evenly as possible. They were to remain quiet until the drive began to near them. Then they were to talk and walk back and forth so birds ahead of the drivers would know they were cut off. The drivers were transported to the far end of the field. One hunter was placed on either side along the edge, in wheat stubble, and sent on ahead 75 or so yards. These men were instructed to walk at the same pace as the drivers and try to stop birds from running out to the sides. The remaining six of us were spread out evenly and began walking down the rows toward the blockers half a mile away.

Shortly after we started, I could occasionally glimpse pheasants running ahead. Now and then several flushed out to the sides. The side men were to hold fire on those, for fear of flushing all the birds in the field. We drivers were allowed to walk noisily, and to call quietly to each other, but not to be too noisy, so birds would continue to run, not flush.

The last 100 yards was the crucial part. We were to slow down, hoping to bunch the birds for a big shoot for all hands during the last 50 yards or so. I'm sure some modern-day drives gather a lot of pheasants. Nonetheless, nothing could compare to some of those drives of the peak years. On the occasion I'm relating, we drivers came to a quiet stop at last about 40 yards from the end of the field. When all hands suddenly stand quietly, the tension on whatever birds are gathered is severe.

Suddenly, from practically under my feet, two cocks burst up. I shot twice, and dropped both. That triggered an unbelievable response. The corn rows exploded with dozens of birds. Hunters who've not witnessed the end of such a drive would hardly believe the scene. I suppose there were 100, perhaps twice that many, pheasants in the air at once. Hens were not legal that year, so you had to watch closely to make sure of your targets. By the time the dispersal was complete and the guns

A pheasant drive in progress in a South Dakota harvested corn field. In the high-kill years, limits of a dozen or more birds were set in the top states, and it was no trouble to fill one.

silent—a matter of only a few seconds—
30 birds had been collected.

Small groups can't successfully make
drives of that sort. There are situations,
however, where three or four hunters can
make successful drives. I remember a small
creek course in Nebraska where birds were
tremendously abundant. You could step
across the creek anywhere. Also, it was
barely moist. Along the banks grew willows and weeds. Wild hay had been cut
right up to the creek on either side. At one
point farther up, grain fields bordered the
narrow skein of creekside brush.

There were three of us. We all walked
down through the grain fields, converging
on the place where the creek moved out to
meander across the hay stubble. I then circled and came in on the creek about 300
yards down, where it petered out and a
swath no wider than a mower sliced across
the end. Immediately past that was a small,
egg-shaped stand of tall trees with brushy
understory. I was to watch to make sure the
birds went into the brush beneath the trees.

I hunkered in the stubble a shotgun
range away from the end of the creek.
Pheasants came running from out of the
willows and weeds, having coursed down
the more open bottom of the creek. When
they hit the open swath of stubble, each
took wing, flying a foot or so above ground
and disappearing into the stand of trees.
What a thrilling sight it was! I'm sure at
least 100 birds made that flying hop across
as I watched, and as my two companions
moved slowly toward me along the creek
bottom.

When the two reached me, we moved in
around the egg-shaped stand of trees and
cover. Several birds flushed. Someone shot.
The air was instantly a mass of noisy wings
and cackling pheasants. The daily limit
there that season was three birds. We collected it in that single exciting operation.

Brief drama of that sort cannot, in my
opinion, match the drawn-out enjoyment
of the way I hunted as a young gunner. A
couple of hunters, with or without a dog,
working pheasant country where birds are
adequately abundant come to know what a
real pheasant *hunt* is like. They have to
know their birds and the terrain, as we did
as kids, not simply herd their targets
blindly.

If the weather is mild and there is an
alfalfa field to comb, pheasants may have
roosted in it, even if it was recently cut.
They're certain to be feeding in it when the
sun is fully up. Before hard frosts, they find
grasshoppers and other insects and also eat
the green clover leaves. Alfalfa or any close,
short grass requires slow, methodical crisscrossing. We used to chuckle as we
watched town hunters hurry across an alfalfa field our family owned. Even their
dogs seldom found a bird. We followed
close behind, kicking out every square
yard, and often bagged several roosters in
the field.

Some of the finest shooting in small-farm
country occurs on mornings following a
severe frost. The birds won't get out at
dawn. They'll stay roosted until the sun is
well up. They will have selected edges of
swales where heavy marsh grass grows but
the earth is no more than moist. Or they'll
penetrate dense stands of wild sunflower or
weeds. Every small patch is a bet for a bird.
We used to discover them occasionally even
in cattail stands. I recall a fence corner with
a few sumac bushes, another where sassa-
fras grew. Pheasants habitually roosted in
each, and they also used each as resting
cover, so if you made a round in the morning and another in midafternoon, you
might flush a bird or two each time.

Dredge-ditch banks and small brushy
creeks serve as travel lanes and roost sites.
You have to know, however, what the bot-

tom of the ditch or creek looks like. If it is full of water, pheasants will skulk in the heavy cover and every bird must be kicked out. If the ditch bottom is dry or only muddy, birds will move down into it as you hunt along it and run like blazes.

Hunting the small patches of cover and the possible roost sites doesn't last long, even on a frosty morning. Soon the birds move out into the edges of grain fields to feed. Small corn or maize fields can be hunted successfully by a couple of hunters, but it's best to leave the big ones alone. The birds in those will frustrate you. Midday takes you back again to fence rows, if you can find any not cropped to the wire, and to the swales and the weed patches. Then, from midafternoon on, the birds will be out feeding again, and toward dusk will slip into dense grass or weeds for roosting again.

If you're a good shot or have a retriever, you can get some great hunting—where legal quitting time doesn't dictate otherwise—very late, in the roost patches. Birds are reluctant to flush. They get up practically under your boots. Limned against a clear or glowing sky, they loom black and bulky, easy targets as your shots send flares from the end of your barrel in the dying light.

Two important facts about pheasants that every beginning hunter should know are that they are faster awing and running than you would believe, and that they are undoubtedly the toughest of American upland birds. Pheasants aloft appear bulky because they're big. They look like easy targets. Hens get up and under way quicker than the long-tailed roosters, but both laze along at 40 miles an hour, and under pressure can rev up to 60 or more. When you swing on a crossing bird, keep in mind that at full speed it is moving at 40 to 60 feet per second.

In my early pheasant days, and later when I returned to boyhood haunts, small-farm corn fields were prime places to collect a couple of cocks in a hurry.

I have no idea how fast a pheasant can run in the open. The legs are extremely strong, equipped with numerous "spring bones" that help it catapult into the air and also assist ground speed and stamina. I've often watched a dog trying to keep up with a rooster running unseen down an open ditch bottom. The dog has to go all out and even then sometimes doesn't succeed in flushing the bird.

For many years I used No. 6 shot on pheasants. As a young fellow I killed many with No. 7½ shot. I also lost too many. One error hunters make is shooting at

During midday, hunting brushy fence rows is a fine tactic in small-farm country. Birds may run or lie snug.

going-away birds with a gun choked too tight. If you're off just a bit, you break a wing. The bird cartwheels and seems to come down dead. What it actually does is come down running. If you are dogless, you'll seldom get it, even if it has a shot or two in the body. It will run until it drops.

Crossing or quartering shots give better chances for sure kills. These are presented most often when two or more hunters are working together. However, always force yourself to use ample lead, and to discount that long tail. Years ago I measured a good many cocks from tip of beak to tip of tail. There were even contests here and there for the longest rooster tail. My brother and I

measured a venerable rooster one time that had spurs grown inward, toward the opposite leg, and almost two inches long. We'd seen the bird in our garden several times and thought it limped. The limp was caused by the spurs tripping it. This tough old rooster was 33½ inches long overall. In the air, broadside, you'd think you couldn't miss one like that. The fact is, in order to be sure to drop that bird, you'd have to put the shot into the first 10 inches. Up-front shooting is what puts pheasants in the game vest.

Today's hunters are not likely to get a chance to shoot so many pheasants that it becomes easy for them. Maybe that is just as well. The period when the birds were at peak, when limits might be 20 per day, was certainly a unique shotgunning era and experience. I believe, however, that we didn't appreciate each bird bagged as we do today, when limits are two or three and not always easily collected.

Several years ago I was able to take my older son, Mike, on his first pheasant hunt. He had been hunting a dozen years, had taken numerous deer, wild turkeys, and other game, but had never had an opportunity to try pheasants. We hunted most of one day without flushing a bird. At last Mike and a friend decided, late in the day, to walk out a long cut-over maize field that had heavy stubble rows. I claimed the old gent's privilege of playing end blocker.

As I walked back and forth at the end of the field, knowing birds could easily get around me, I watched the two come slowly down the field. Presently I saw a cock rise before Mike. He was so far away that I saw the rooster keel over and fall before I heard the shot. At that sound another cock arose, and the same routine ensued. I was delighted. Two cocks filled his limit.

Now I watched closely, knowing full well what he would do. He collected the roosters and held them up before him for a long moment, turning them. He tucked his gun under his arm, held the birds laid out across his hands, and studied them, shaking his head in wonderment. He didn't put them into his coat. He came on, carrying both by the legs in one hand, every few seconds pausing to look at them again. It took me back a long, long span of years. Trophy birds. No matter how many he shot in years to come, I knew that he'd have the urge to pause and look each time at the remarkable, beautiful prize and, like all other pheasant hunters, shake his head in wonder and disbelief.

21

New Pheasants for the Future?

Deaf Smith County surrounds the town of Hereford in the Texas Panhandle. It is one of the state's leading counties in livestock production. Thousands of acres of corn, sorghum, wheat, and cattle feed lots spread across its high plains. As we drove out to our hunting location shortly after daylight, a gaudy cock pheasant raced across the road and disappeared into stubble. Two hens swirled out of the grass, flushing close to the car, and followed the rooster.

"That's just unbelievable," Bob Benton said. "In fact, I'm not even sure I do believe it."

Many years ago Bob and I, as young fellows of high-school age, had been hunting buddies. The first birds either of us ever shot on the wing were pheasants. We shot so many of them every fall that my mother used to resort to canning some. There were no freezers in those days, and though

pheasant was a standard meal all during hunting time, it was hard for two families to eat their way ahead of us eager bird shooters—what with the swarms of birds on our own place and on the farms of neighbors where Bob and my brother and I hunted.

A half hour after we'd seen those first pheasants along the road, we were walking a cut-over maize field, the landowner's mongrel dog casting about in front of us. We were primed for a shot. Bob had written earlier that he'd be in Texas in mid-December and maybe we could get together. I thought it a great idea to renew acquaintance after all these years, over a flushing pheasant or two. But he had thought at first I was pulling his leg. Pheasants in Texas? It hardly seemed possible.

Suddenly, however, there was a raucous cackle and a cock exploded from the stubble. I remembered how we'd learned way-back-when to let 'em go straight up, using the several spring bones in their sturdy legs to push them into the air, rising with wings beating furiously with a downward push to get the heavy body airborne. Then, at the height of the rise, the bird would heel over into a flat and proper flying position. At that instant, the peak of the rise, it was almost literally standing still, and vulnerable. All you had to do was hold fire until that instant, and the bird was easy pickin's.

Bob hadn't forgotten. He waited it out and shot, and down the bird came. Grinning broadly, he said, "I just don't believe it—pheasants in Texas."

He gathered in the bird, and, of course, we had to turn it and stroke it. We yammered about the way we used to shoot too quick and shoot under, and then how we tried to cure that and shot over, before we learned the top-of-the-flush trick to bust one every time. I was thinking about how many pheasants my guns had pointed at over the years, and in what a widely scattered variety of places.

Today many hunters who knew pheasant shooting in its heyday are saying the bird is as good as done for. There is no question that today the ringneck, at one time the world's greatest upland-bird success story as a transplant, has run its high course over most of its once-optimum range. It probably will never again tower to the phenomenal populations it once reached. But game-management people are far from ready to give up on these grand game birds. The search for varieties other than the ringneck, other strains and hybrids that may be able to make it in varied habitats not suitable for the ringneck, still goes on. Here and there it has brought some startling and little-publicized results—not in swarms of birds, but in the beginnings of establishment of pheasants in specific areas once believed to be totally unsuitable. It is pos-

In numerous states the search for suitable pheasant varieties goes on. This is the pure-strain Afghan white-winged pheasant.

sible that, as land uses change, many a modern hunter will see the day when he'll be shooting pheasants of unusual varieties and in places he'd not have believed they'd ever be found.

When I was growing up in Michigan, pheasants transplanted from Oregon during the 1920s had caught on until they actually were nuisances to farmers. I've seen 40 or 50 birds in a group in winter literally tearing a corn shock to pieces. Even up until the early 1960s Michigan hunters were bagging over a million birds each season. That, of course, was nothing to what was happening westward, particularly in the Dakotas.

I was one of those who saw what the South Dakota pheasant shooting was like at its peak. I thought I'd seen pheasants in Michigan—but I hadn't seen anything. I vividly recall drives a group of us made in the country west of Redfield, South Dakota, when we listened, awestruck, to a breathtaking rush of wings and cackling at the end of the drive and saw an estimated 250 birds rise into the air at one time. Imagine a 16-bird-a-day limit, easily filled if you could hit 'em! No one knows how many birds, total, that state had during its best seasons. The official estimate of the peak year was 50 million.

I shot in South Dakota later on, in the late 1950s, when three birds a day was the limit. There were still an unbelievable number of pheasants. But by 1966 it was evident that a debacle had occurred. The estimate: a flock of possibly two million. The lower-Michigan country I'd lived in and hunted as a young fellow was as good as finished, too. Nowadays some public hunting areas there are stocked in the morning and most of the birds have been shot by late afternoon.

There is no great mystery about what

happened to the pheasants either there or in the Dakotas, although many people have tried to make it one. Changing land use, intensive farming, the end of the Soil Bank, and other degradations of optimum habitat left the ringneck little nesting and hiding room.

I watched it happen where I grew up. We had lush fence rows and red willow swales, shocked corn in small fields, timothy hay and alfalfa and buckwheat. Then slowly the fence rows disappeared, the swales were drained and plowed, crops were switched, and land refitted as soon as harvested. A pheasant had hardly a bush to hunker under.

Today in the once-prime plains states the ringneck is reduced to making-do largely with roadside ditches and rights-of-way for nesting and hiding. Of course, the bird always did use these. But in both South Dakota and Nebraska today biologists estimate that over 25% of the total pheasants produced come from the unmowed portions of roadsides. Both states have worked with programs to mow narrower swaths and in some places none at all. This succinctly illustrates the degradation of the once-vast living and producing room of the ringneck on millions of acres of range which was originally optimum.

The very success of the ringneck for a time held back experimentation with other pheasants. The ringneck was tried in practically every state, with numerous failures. Some years ago transplants to Mississippi lived to furnish some hunting, but were unable to propagate. It was believed then that no pheasant could breed successfully below the 40th parallel. That idea was obviously erroneous. Kansas, for example, which has the 40th as its northern border, became one of the top pheasant states and continues to offer excellent shooting. Texas

New Mexico made pheasant history when the Afghan white-winged variety was tried in the southwestern part of the state. Note that it has no white ring around the neck.

Panhandle birds immigrated from Oklahoma over 30 years ago, and in the Pecos Valley and portions of the Rio Grande Valley in New Mexico the ringneck pheasant, a transplant there, has been present in breeding numbers for close to a half century. So much for the 40th-parallel theory. What is true is that the original ringneck strain, at least, never has been able to sustain itself in the humid Deep South states.

However, it is in the so-called non-pheasant states of the South and Southwest that some of the most interesting and determined experimentation has been done with new varieties, new strains, and hybrids. Game managers of the region finally became convinced that the ringneck was a precarious gamble, capable of establishing itself in only a few places. Thus it was obvious that other varieties of pheasants—the world has over 100 species, subspecies, and crosses—would have to fill the gaps.

New Mexico made hunting and pheasant-management history some years ago when it established a wild breeding population of pure-strain Afghan white-winged pheasants down in its southwestern corner. I made a trip there to get in on the first hunt that was held. It was a dramatic experience. The Afghan whitewing is slightly smaller and more streamlined than the

ringneck. It is also an illimitably wilder bird, seemingly untamable even in hatcheries, nervous and jumpy. You can sit quietly beside a penned cock and it will run back and forth and sometimes die from the stress of your nearness. The whitewing is a sensational flyer, fast and handsome. It is easy to distinguish the cock birds from ringnecks even at a distance. They do not have the white ring on the neck, but they do have a large whitish area on the shoulder.

Several game-department personnel and I launched that first hunt on a frosty dawn near Red Rock, in tall weeds, grass, and catclaw brush along the Gila River. The surroundings seemed incongruous to me. All of my pheasant hunting had been done in farm fields and woodlot edges of the Great Lakes region, in rather similar surroundings in Oregon where the first U.S. ringnecks were established, and on the vast grain-growing plains of the Dakotas, Nebraska, and Kansas. Before full light I was catching my hunting pants on thornbrush and dodging cactus clumps. Across a narrow flat of grass and weeds beyond a small stock tank, a red rock cliff towered, and beyond that was a rock pile of mountain, barren except for brush and cactus.

It certainly didn't seem like pheasant country to me. The pheasant we were after is native to the Oxus Valley in northern Afghanistan. That region of southwest Asia is quite different in climate from the original home of the ringneck. It is rather arid, and warm. I had been told that the native range was remarkably similar in terrain and climate to this portion of southwestern New Mexico.

In some respects all pheasants, I knew, are alike in habits. On a cold night they roost in the heaviest cover they can find. As light came up and one of the party released his dog, I swept a glance across the immediate terrain. The dog was casting about in dead grass about six inches to a foot high. It was likely cover, but off to the left there was a stand of tall weeds and brush with heavier ground cover of interwoven dead grass. I was remembering my early days of ferreting out ringneck cocks on cold mornings, and that seemed just the stuff.

I angled off into the head-high cover, not sure what to expect. Would these super-wild birds flush at a distance? Or would they on this cold dawn let me all but step on them? My question was quickly answered. The dog was still working the short grass. I crashed ahead, pushing aside dead weeds with my left arm, holding my gun high. Then I paused to look around—and a beautiful cock catapulted out of the weeds right at my feet.

I remember the thought racing through my mind that this was an astonishingly swift flush. I tried to get my gun around into position, but got tangled in tall weeds. Desperately I ripped free and tried to get on the bird. By then, of course, it was too late. I had never witnessed such wild, fast flight by a pheasant. But I'd had so far only half of the surprise. That rooster headed for the red cliff, veered aside, and towered up, up, up, not lowering and sailing on set wings as I'd seen thousands of ringnecks do. It headed right for the mountain, and it went

up and over. When they'd told me this bird was wild, they'd certainly told it correctly.

As thrilling as that flight had been to observe, I was utterly frustrated to miss this opportunity. I knew we'd not find the birds abundant. I was allowed two, and frankly I wanted them desperately. Muttering, I took three steps, and another rooster exploded practically in my face. That time I wasn't tangled. The bird didn't waste time rising perpendicularly, in ringneck style, but swirled up and leveled and was away. I blotted it out as it rose at a shallow angle, and as the shotgun noise bounced off the far rock wall, the bird cartwheeled into the brush.

Texas began to work with the Afghan whitewing at about the same time as New Mexico. The imports were released a number of times in the western counties in the general area of Lubbock, Plainview, and Brownfield. Encouragingly, they have in some instances established themselves temporarily. Farther to the southwest in Texas, in the arid Trans-Pecos region, the whitewing also temporarily caught on in very limited numbers. Apparently the small amount of suitable habitat available is what restricts sustaining populations.

Texas also tried the Korean pheasant, a bird much handled by several other states but one which seemed promising. These were stocked along the Red River, which forms part of the northern border. They were unsuccessful. Missouri also has tried this bird, and Michigan got the idea of testing it from its moderate Missouri success. Missouri, along with several other states, also worked with the Reeves pheasant and the Iranian blackneck. It was in Texas, in a most interesting and exciting program, that the Iranian black-necked pheasant finally got a foothold.

For some years Texas had been trying to establish ringnecks in the rice country of the humid Gulf Coast. It didn't work. Finally a hybrid bird was produced, a cross between pheasants wild-trapped in the Sacramento Valley in California and the western Iranian blackneck. The idea behind this careful breeding was to "build" a bird with a tolerance for a humid climate and a substantial amount of rainfall. Over several years the birds did so well that it was possible to have a brief season in portions of two counties. These have continued.

These hunts have not been highly publicized, but are unquestionably a tremendous breakthrough in the new pheasant culture. Both the Iranian blackneck hybrid and the California pheasants, also released along the Gulf, appear to be taking care of themselves, nesting and feeding in the rice and the after-harvest stubble. Fallow rice fields, studies have shown, are extremely important to the pheasant cycles. If agricultural practices along the Gulf do not drastically change, limited hunting should continue there.

In other states much has been done in attempts to find pheasant varieties that do not depend so heavily upon cultivated lands and agriculture. In Idaho's Panhandle, for example, the Japanese green pheasant flushed spottily before hunters' guns for a few years. In this state the ringneck, long the most important uplander, has seen just as serious difficulties as it has elsewhere, all due to changing land use and switches in agricultural practices. The Japanese green is a tough, fast bird, difficult to flush. It is not basically a farm bird, but a creature of forest edges and brushy cover. It is a bit smaller than the ringneck, with no white neck band, and a dazzlingly green head, neck, and breast. A few years ago it had gotten to a point where over 70% of ringneck pheasants killed in northern Idaho were pen-reared releases. The green was tried as a ringneck replacement.

In the rough Gila River country of southwestern New Mexico, a white-winged pheasant heads for the rocky ridges as a hunter swings his gun. This is an arid-country species. Other exotic pheasants may still find a niche in U.S. habitat.

This same pheasant is established in Hawaii and has been used in Virginia. There it established itself meagerly some few years back in Eastern Shore counties, and even learned to roost in pine trees! Another interesting pheasant tried in Virginia and elsewhere in that region of the U.S. is the white-crested Kalij. This is a grouse-like pheasant, a woodland bird. Years back, it was stocked in Virginia's Jefferson National Forest. There was at least one open season on it, in the mid-1970s. Far to the west, Arizona has had several pheasant seasons in past years, the Afghan whitewing the target.

Several years ago I was on one of the most delightful mixed-bag bird hunts I've ever experienced. It took place in New Mexico. I had plotted with friends in the Game and Fish Department there to set up my trip so I could jockey beginnings and tail-ends of seasons on several birds to put them all into a single hunt. We bagged two varieties of quail, plus doves, ducks, lesser prairie chickens, and pheasants. Well, I guess I should say pheasants were taken during my trip—but not by me. It was one

Crosses of ringnecks and Afghan white-winged pheasants have proved hardy in some places. Some of today's birds in New Mexico may be these hybrids. Here one hides in tall grass.

of those last-hour-of-the-day situations that I like best to remember. Two of us were working a hunk of brushy cover along the Pecos River near Roswell.

My partner, a native, said, "We'll do a little sneak and maybe jump-shoot a duck or two en route. But the big reason for this welty is that I know there are some pheasants along this stretch, hybrids of ringnecks and Afghan whitewings."

Near the river the cover was dense. Beyond it, cultivated fields flowed away. I worked my hunk of cover until my boots weighed 50 pounds. The sun was getting ready to give up for the day, and I knew with that low feeling any hunter gets when he fails to connect in the stretch that I was not going to round out the hunt with a long-tailed bird.

Suddenly a duck arose from a bend, quacking loudly in surprise and fright. I'm not even sure to this day what kind of duck it was. I beat at the riverside brush, clawing for an opening to shoot through. I jumped to one side onto a hummock to get a clear view and started to pull on the bird. Instantly I was transported far back to my young-hunter days in Michigan. *Croo-kuk, croo-kuk, croo-kuk* — the raucous cackle of a rooster crashed upon me, from spang underfoot. The beat of wings against the cover accompanied the sound, and adrenaline exploded into my bloodstream as a gaudy bird swirled aloft.

I tried desperately to turn in the proper direction. I fell off the hummock, crashing and stumbling to regain balance. My last glimpse of the rooster was of a far-off bird, wings set and gliding, drawing a swift line of color across an opening, the low sun burnishing its feathers with red-gold.

That scene has been etched in memory in intricate detail ever since. I see it nowadays as a kind of symbol that pheasant hunting in the U.S. may be changing. Never again will there be the millions of ring-necked birds there once were. There'll be just "some." But additional tastes of exotic gourmet fare served up in exotic settings are certainly as exciting as gorging on heaping portions of home cooking. That just may be what the modern pheasant hunter has in his future.

Part V

THE WILD TURKEYS

You can take your pick of the several tales about how the turkey got its name. The most likely one begins in what is now Mexico, 466 years ago as this is written. This was the beginning of Cortez's ramblings around that region. The wild turkey, largest of the world's gallinaceous, or chicken-like, birds, dated back millions of years previous to that, to the Pleistocene era. It was present nowhere in the world except North America.

Cortez presumably discovered that the Aztecs had thousands of these big birds domesticated—undoubtedly the variety now known as the Mexican turkey. Some accounts have it that Columbus had already discovered similar birds during one of his trips on coastal islands near what is now Honduras. Some say turkeys had been taken back to Spain previous to the Cortez period.

As the big bird spread elsewhere in Europe, there was confusion as to its origin. Communications then were, of course, most primitive. The peacock had been brought into Europe from India and the guinea fowl, it is said, from Turkey. The birds from the New World apparently were confused with one or the other of those. Their name may have arisen from the country where they were mistakenly assumed to have originated or from words used in parts of Asia that sounded somewhat similar to the word "turkey."

It's interesting to note that when the naturalist and taxonomist Linnaeus gave the turkey its scientific name, *Meleagris gallopavo*, which it still carries today, he was calling it quite a mixture. The first name means "guinea fowl." The last name's first portion means "chicken," the second portion "peafowl." Apparently Linnaeus was trying to satisfy everybody, or else he simply didn't know what kind of bird the turkey was. One of the wry slants on the turkey's history is that it was domesticated over most of Europe and on into England only briefly after it had been brought to Spain. Later on, the colonists brought domestic turkeys to America, and lo and behold, they found thousands of wild replicas already here!

The original wild turkey range in America covered most of the eastern portion of the present contiguous states, except for the northernmost Great Lakes region and upper New England. The upper plains in general lacked turkeys, but there were scattered populations in wooded areas and along stream courses. The Rockies region in Colorado, parts of New Mexico, and eastern Arizona had turkeys, and so did eastern, southern, and far western Texas.

Because of their size, abundance, and excellent table qualities, wild turkeys were a staple in the diet of early settlers. As civilization pushed westward, market hunting for them accounted for tens of thousands. They weren't difficult to collect. Flocks of several thousand were not rare. There are records of hundreds being brought out of the woods in numerous places and sold for as little as 10 cents a bird. By the late 1800s and into the early part of this century the wild turkey was cut down to remnants.

I had the good fortune, years ago, to visit with an old man in Saginaw, Michigan, W.B. Mershon, who killed the last wild turkey ever recorded in Michigan. It was shot in the vicinity of the village of Reese, in the "Thumb" area not far from Saginaw, in 1886. Mr. Mershon told me numerous dramatic stories of the abundance of wild turkeys in Michigan during his years as a young hunter. At the time he was relating these stories, it was hard for me to realize

that few Michigan hunters then alive had ever seen a wild turkey. However, the situation was similar over most wild turkey range. I remember the years when everyone in the game-management business—it was not very advanced then—was saying the American wild turkey was doomed.

What actually happened, of course, was that game managers learned how to not only reestablish wild turkeys on their original ranges but also transplant them and nurture them to establishment in states and habitats far removed from their ancestral ranges. The comeback of the wild turkey is one of the great conservation success stories of the century. Presently every one of the lower 48 states has resident, self-sustaining wild turkeys. Turkey hunting has been for some years now one of the fastest growing gunning sports. No one knows exactly how many wild turkeys on average are bagged each season, but it runs into the hundreds of thousands. Further, many states have seasons in both spring and fall, with bag limits of several birds.

Wild turkeys differ substantially from region to region. Five subspecies are, or originally were, found within U.S. borders. The turkey that had the most extensive original range was the Eastern subspecies, scientific subspecies name *silvestris*. This bird is large. Old gobblers occasionally weigh 25 pounds, although the average is probably about 17 or 18. This turkey has much rich brown in its color pattern, and the tail when spread shows a band of chestnut to dark chocolate around the end. Originally the range of the Eastern turkey blanketed most of the eastern two-thirds of the U.S., reaching even into eastern Texas.

For some curious reason a quite different turkey developed on the Florida peninsula. The Florida turkey—subspecies *osceola*, sometimes called the Osceola turkey—is a darker, less colorful bird than the Eastern, and distinctly smaller. Its main range is restricted to Florida, but it overlaps northward into southern and eastern Georgia, into the domain of the Eastern subspecies. Where this occurs, the two birds intergrade.

The Rio Grande turkey originally was native to most of Texas, except far-west Texas, spilled northward into southwestern Oklahoma, and reached far down into eastern Mexico. Nowadays it has been widely stocked northward clear to North Dakota, and west into parts of the Pacific Coast states. In Oklahoma it has been so successful that it has spread by transplant and natural colonization over much of the state. The Eastern turkey, extirpated from its original range in eastern Oklahoma and Texas years ago, has been reestablished. Undoubtedly intergrades between the Rio Grande and the Eastern birds occur where they come into contact.

The Rio Grande turkey averages slightly smaller than the Eastern bird. We have this turkey in Texas where I live, and have them on our own ranch. The largest Rio Grande I've killed over almost 30 years of hunting them weighed 18 pounds. This turkey, subspecies name *intermedia*, is a bird of more arid ranges than the Eastern. It is somewhat paler in overall colors, and has a buff band across the end of the tail.

The native turkey of the mountain states, now widely transplanted elsewhere, is the Merriam's, named for the naturalist who first described it, and given the scientific subspecies name *merriami*. These are large, handsome, striking birds. Twenty-pound gobblers are not unusual. I killed one that size in the Pine Ridge country of northwestern Nebraska a few years ago. The gobblers appear glossy black with varied sheens of color. The distinctive markings are white feathers on the rump, a white band at the end of the tail, plus on most toms a double band of white across the middle of the tail.

One other subspecies—of little consequence and perhaps not present nowadays in pure strain—is the Sierra Madre turkey, *mexicana*. This turkey ranges throughout the Sierra Madre far down into Mexico, but originally spilled northward into small areas of southwestern New Mexico and southeastern Arizona. The turkey of the type species, *gallopavo*, is actually the Mexican turkey, which ranges in southern Mexico and doesn't reach U.S. borders.

This is the lineup of turkey varieties as they occurred on ancestral ranges. In our modern times it is often difficult for a hunter to tell which turkey he has collected. Strains have been intermingled as transplants were made, and often they were mixed up as intergrades on overlapping ranges as the wild turkey made its remarkable comeback. Nevertheless, if you hunt in Florida or in most of the rest of the eastern half of the U.S., you will probably see turkeys of the original kinds, of quite pure blood. The same is true if you hunt in Texas, for example, where the Rio Grande has not been too much intergraded, and in the Western mountains, where pure-strain Merriam's turkeys are standard fare.

One influence that has to some extent degraded wild turkeys in many places comes from domestic stock. There are probably thousands of instances where a farmer who keeps a few turkeys has contributed to infusions of domestic blood into wild pure-strain birds. Many a wild gobbler has tolled off a domestic hen during spring breeding season.

I hunted one year in Texas on a ranch where turkeys were tremendously abundant. They were, presumably, Rio

Grandes. However, I noted every now and then a bird that showed a few white feathers. Undoubtedly somewhere far back, white turkeys, commonly raised for the market in large numbers, had mingled with wild birds. When I was a youngster we raised a few birds that were called in our area "bronze" turkeys. They were big, brown birds. Some were mottled with tan and white. There were no wild turkeys for them to mingle with, but birds similar to those have been and are raised in numerous areas of the East and South.

Most domestic turkeys that appear at casual glance like wild ones wear a very distinct telltale badge, a white band across the end of the tail. It has amused me now and then to see color photos of "wild" turkeys from the East or Midwest in magazines—every gobbler with a white tail band. I suspect always that the photographer had found domestic birds easier to photograph than the wild ones. Some turkeys of this description do show up in the wild, outside Merriam's range, but they definitely carry domestic blood and usually lack the inherent wildness of authentic stock. Further, a good many turkeys infused with domestic blood that are bagged annually will on close inspection have a broad, rounded breast and a bulky overall appearance, evidence of domestic interbreeding. Full-blooded wild turkeys are tall, slender, and, as one turkey expert has said, "snakey looking." The breast is narrow and V-shaped.

To the eager and excited turkey hunter, it's likely the shape of the body or the color of the tail band won't make much difference when one of the big birds comes into gun range. Nor will he care whether it is a Florida bird or a big Merriam's. Wherever the hunt, the thrill is certain to be unmatchable. It just may be that Ben Franklin was right a couple of centuries past when he suggested that the turkey should be chosen as our national bird.

22

Fall Turkeys Without a Call

With the great popularity of turkey hunting nowadays, everybody has a call but darned few are able to tell a turkey anything it wants to hear. This is especially true in fall, when turkey calling is possibly the most inexact and uncertain art known to hunting. It's true that calling a turkey successfully is a prideful experience. It's also true that bushwhacking one fair and square is altogether as artful. No one should be so determined to use a call that he ruins his fall hunting.

The most ludicrous fall experience along that line I ever had occurred in Texas when I hunted for the first—and last—time with a gentleman determined to use his yelper. We glassed a group of gobblers half a mile away. After an anguished hunching, crawling stalk, I was elated. We'd gotten close enough to shoot. But suddenly my companion leaped up, yelling, firing his gun in the air. The flock flushed every which way.

I was dumbfounded. He was beaming. "Beautiful!" he said. "Now we hide, like the book says, and call them back together."

Indeed, that's what most books do say for fall: scatter a flock, then call it back together. To make certain birds flush into the air and scatter, you have to get shotgun-range close. Birds that run off in a group won't come to a call. What puzzles me is why, after a clever stalk close enough for a flush, you don't just shoot. Calling isn't *that* much fun.

Many modern-day turkey hunters have been brainwashed into believing wild turkeys are profoundly intelligent and can seldom be outwitted. They're wary, that's certain, but not omniscient. Any crafty hunter can beat them—some of the time. Hunting

Bushwhacking gobblers like these oldsters is as much an art as calling one in. You have to know their habits and read sign correctly.

fall turkeys much as you'd hunt deer is a real challenge, and it offers the best odds, especially for a so-so caller.

The procedure is to first comb your hunting area for sign. Tracks are most important. Search along moist or muddy creek bottoms, near shallow crossings, on sand bars, around ponds, in muddy or dusty places along old roads and game trails. Check especially for tracks going both ways, which means birds habitually use this travel route between destinations.

Tracks indicate birds are present. In an either-sex area you needn't worry whether hens or gobblers made them. If you're after an old gobbler, however, look for BIG tracks that sink in and show rough bulges along the broad toes. Concentrate on the area where these are most abundantly printed. Once established on fall range, turkeys are creatures of habit. They also follow a loose caste system: hens together, often in the largest groups; young gobblers in groups up to perhaps a dozen; old gob-

blers alone or in small groups, to possibly a half dozen.

While searching for tracks, keep other sign in mind: scratchings among fallen leaves where turkeys have been feeding; dusting patches where birds squat or lie, fluffing and dusting their feathers. These signs, if fresh, tell you turkeys have recently used that place.

Droppings and fallen feathers are among the most important signs. One fall I discovered scads of droppings—many old, some fresh—upon an open knoll by a creek. Abundance indicated heavy use. The differing ages of the scat told me the spot was long used, and in use. Across a creek at the foot of the knoll were several large sycamores. Beneath them on rocks were splatters of dung, and on the leaves were numerous well-formed droppings. Here was a current roosting site.

I checked whole droppings carefully. Many were large, round, and had a small curlicue on top. Under trees a short distance up the creek, all were long, slender, and of similar diameter throughout. The big, round ones are invariably from old toms, roosting apart from hens and young gobblers. This "reading" may not always be accurate, but it usually is.

Under these trees also were numerous feathers, both fresh and old. They indicated a roost used for some time. Large flight and tail feathers are seldom numerous except under a massive roost. Small, easily loosened breast and body feathers are the most important clues anyway. An ash-gray scallop on one indicates a hen. A shiny or iridescent black one tells of a gobbler.

Although roost sites are the most valuable find for the fall hunter, familiarity with fall turkey foods *where you hunt* may occasionally lead to a bushwhacking possibility. Waste grain is one of these. Succulent green feed such as a winter oat patch along a woods edge is another. After frosts turkeys love winter greens. Acorns are prime fall forage; trees with especially heavy crops are magnets. Hackberries also draw turkeys. I've watched them in fall flying up into hackberry trees to walk limbs and pick off the berries.

Appraise places where wild grapes, barberry, or wild cherries are abundant. Areas of tall, seeded grasses are also worth noting. I've often watched turkeys on our ranch walk along a valley or slope base, stripping off heads of grass seeds. They seize a stalk

In fall, turkeys follow a caste system. Hens run together. So do young gobblers. Old toms, like this one about to be turned into a candidate for the oven despite hunter's incomplete camouflage, may be loners or run in small groups.

just below the seed head, strip upward with the bill, and never lose a step as they go.

Roosts are undoubtedly the most important finds. But you must be certain how turkeys are using one or more roosts. On our ranch, for example, birds use a certain roost several nights, then switch to another location. This practice is common in many areas. Conversely, one time in far northwest Nebraska, we found a Merriam's turkey roost in pine-clad hills among a stand of venerable cottonwoods in a creek bottom, with dung literally a foot deep below them. It had been used endlessly, and still was. I know a roost in western Texas, in an area where large trees are scarce, that is used year round by both sexes and all ages of turkeys, maybe 100 or more birds constantly.

Roost sites are usually along creek courses, at the head of a draw or canyon, on southern slopes in wooded valleys, and in flatter country in a conspicuous stand of large trees. Good-sized trees are virtually mandatory. Sit quietly on a high point near a roost late in the afternoon, and you can hear birds fly up. Depending on weather, they go to roost anytime from before dusk to almost full dark. Their wings make much noise as they strike branches. The birds change positions noisily after they're on a roost, getting settled for the night. Once you've put some turkeys "to bed," you know right where they'll be come dawn.

Ordinarily, undisturbed turkeys are not especially talkative in fall at dusk. But they are noisy at dawn, uttering clucks, whines, and the full wild-turkey vocabulary. Don't believe the nonsense you may hear that toms don't gobble in fall. At dawn particularly, you can locate them by their occasional "gobbles," never as raucous or incessant as in spring, but distinctive nonetheless.

On our place we go out during the fall season while it's still pitch dark to listen as dawn sneaks in. We note wing sounds as birds come to ground. We listen for gobbles and varied other turkey talk. I listened one season to a flock coming off a roost in our creek bottom and identified several old gobbler voices, some hens farther upstream, and what I suspected were voices of young gobblers mixed in somewhere. You can deduce their travel direction, once they've come to ground, by following their voices. Then you try to get ahead for a stake-out.

If they don't talk, or you haven't heard any flying up at evening or down at dawn, make a sound at dawn. Slam a car door. Mimic an owl hoot. This is a great way to find out where a gobbler is, because often he'll shower down his gobble in reply.

If a roost you've located is in a fairly flat area, birds will probably come off it the same way they went to it—in reverse. So if you observed them, by binoculars or by listening to dusk talk, you can guess fairly accurately where to waylay them. If when going to roost they flew off a bluff down to big trees, at dawn they'll probably go to ground in the valley and eventually feed back up to the ridges. A roost site in a creek bottom hemmed by ridges offers birds the opportunity to move at dawn upstream or downstream. Pick your gamble, or with a partner cover both directions, getting into positions silently before dawn at least 100 yards from the roost site. Shooting turkeys *on* a roost is illegal almost everywhere, and is unsporting in any case. Stake-outs near a roost for waylaying birds going in near dusk or coming off at dawn, however, are both legal and productive.

My second stake-out choice is along an old farm, ranch, or forest road, or even along a deer trail where sign indicates use by turkeys. If there are fences, especially of woven wire, check them for open gates, duck-under low places, a hole through the wire. Turkeys prefer to walk through such crossings rather than fly over. A curve on an old woods road also makes a fine stake-out. You can hide on the inside of the curve, and birds moving in either direction can't spot you until it's too late.

Using binoculars is most helpful in hills, mountains, and semi-open forest and farm-country ranges. Turkeys move about feeding until midmorning, and again from mid-afternoon until dusk. They appear black and obvious at surprising distances. Spot a group, and it's a better-than-even bet they'll stay fairly well on course, moving as the

Once turkeys are down from the roost, you can often predict their travel route by the sound of their voices as they "talk" en route. Then you can get in position to have one like this startled tom practically in your lap.

land contours dictate. The trick is to get ahead of them and hide without disturbing them where they'll be most likely to come into range.

A rifle is advantageous for stake-out hunting. The .22 Magnum with hollow-point bullet is adequate to about 75 yards. A deer caliber or the .222 handloaded down to a muzzle velocity of 2,000–2,400 feet per second is needed for shots to possibly 125 yards. Occasionally the rifle hunter also gets a chance at one of turkey hunting's top thrills, silently tracking a gobbler to within shooting range in fresh snow.

Greatest of all thrills, however, is that rare chance to take a turkey in the air. Vividly I remember one fall sneaking along a creek course with a shotgun, trying to spot turkeys up ahead. There were numerous big, fresh tracks. On my side of the creek I came upon a narrow draw on my left, a trickle of water dribbling down it to the creek. At the draw I paused to listen, every nerve tight. I lifted my right foot to take a stealthy step ahead, gun ready and my head turned left so I'd be peering up the draw just in case.

Before I could put my foot down, a big gobbler stepped out so close we almost collided. Trying wildly to turn my head, gun,

and feet all at once, I slipped and fell with a noisy splat into the mud and water. The startled gobbler sprang into the air with a great rush of frantic wing sounds. It had to gain altitude to miss the trees hemming it in. Bluffs on either side forced it to head straight downstream.

Somehow I regained my feet, having kept my gun barrel out of the mud. My mental vision to this day is of that huge gobbler beating upward, virtually standing in the air with tail down and neck stretched skyward, trying to lift its great bulk to get enough flying air under its wings. I'd guess it was not more than 20 feet up when I, dripping slime and water, swung the gun six inches above its head and touched off. There was another great splat. The gobbler was mine.

I remember shaking a lot, but not from the wet clothes and cold water. I readily admit that calling turkeys in spring is heady stuff, but come fall I'd just as soon hunt without a call. If I experienced even more excitement than I get bushwhacking and stalking—yes, even including the times I foul it up—my doctor wouldn't allow it anyway!

23

Lady Henrietta's Lovers

It was definitely love at first sight, and there was nothing platonic about it. The intentions of the strutting gobbler were strictly dishonorable.

We had staked out Henrietta, a life-sized plastic wood, paint, and papier maché replica of a hen turkey, in an open patch of low greenery surrounded by venerable oaks and mesquites. Because Henrietta stood so darned still and stiff, we had given her this day a decoration of feathers secured to her neck by a rubber band. As the breeze dallied, the feathers fluttered enticingly.

This seemed to entrance the tom, which had just walked out from among the shadows of the trees as Murry Burnham seductively plied his call. When the gobbler's beady eyes had explored fully the svelte, curvaceous Henrietta and had noted the continued come-on of the fluttering necklace of feathers, the old lecher simply came undone.

He puffed up like a balloon, spread his great tail, dropped his wings so that the stiff flight feathers trailed on the turf, made a muffled *chuff-chuff-chuff*ing sound, and grandly pirouetted. As the tom faced Henrietta once more, Murry touched the call ever so lightly, sending out a trio of lovesick *perks*. The long-bearded, iridescent suitor rammed his blood-gorged head straight forward and showered down a *gobble* that made the woods ring.

This dramatic scene unfolded before call maker Murry Burnham and myself at 4:30 p.m. the afternoon before the opening of a certain spring turkey season in Nolan County, western Texas. We had been experimenting with Henrietta incessantly all spring. Already she had attracted a dozen-

There was nothing the least bit platonic about the intentions of the first gobbler that came to strut near the decoy.

odd utterly addled lovers. Three of them had attempted, to their total frustration, to mate with her. She had also been involved with several highly incensed, crotchety old hens that had ruffled their feathers and tried to run her off as competition. Two other more friendly hens—some of the girls—had coaxed her insistently to come along with them.

This afternoon we were past experimenting. This was the beginning of more serious matters. We had schemed to get away from other turkey hunters for opening day, on a ranch to which we'd been invited, where ordinarily no hunting was allowed. We hoped to let Henrietta work her wiles without interruption or endless astonished questions.

The eager gobbler let fly again. We had selected a place for our setup near which we were quite certain, from checking sign, there was a roosting site. Our plan was to call in whatever gobblers might respond—in order to shoot some final photos, but more importantly to watch exactly where the toms went to bed. At dawn next morning, opening day, we'd be on hand some distance from them, Henrietta placed strategically to entice the first toms off the roost. If she did right, and we did right with calls and guns, two gobblers should be hanging from the windmill tower near our spike camp by breakfast time tomorrow.

As we sat there fully concealed, having made camouflaged blobs of ourselves, even to camo headnets and gloves, the sun began to fade behind the horizon. Two more gobblers came down into the open area, gobbled at the strutting tom and Henrietta, but, skittish of the boss gobbler, kept on going. Old Eager continued his display, possibly 30 steps from Henrietta and so close to me now and then as he paced around between struts that I sat slumped and rigid, head bowed, afraid the smitten bird would sense my presence—or step into my lap!—and blow the whole plot.

Dusk crept in. I was reflecting that over a

lifetime of hunting, including at least 30 years of pursuing turkeys in both spring and fall in a half dozen or more states, this decoy business was just possibly the most intriguing experience of all. Henrietta had been conceived, built to her present perfection over years of trial and error, and marketed two years ago by a dedicated old-hand turkey hunter from North Carolina. There have been many attempts dating back more than a century to toll in wild turkeys with some sort of decoy. Early Indians and colonists used crudely stuffed turkey skins. Many years ago, before laws curtailed the practice, live turkey hens were sometimes staked and tethered to fetch in ardent toms.

The original of this decoy, put together several decades earlier, was made with a wire frame overlaid with papier maché. It was too heavy to be carried for miles through turkey woods. Weight and bulk have been, in fact, a deterrent in several decoy experiments. Some amusing incidents have occurred in attempts to lick that problem. For example, Joel Vance, with the Missouri Department of Conservation, told me of one of their wardens seeing, a few seasons ago, a hunter hauling a heavy homemade decoy into the woods in a little wagon. Claimed he got his gobbler, too.

A wryly comic approach was suggested in print by a Missouri decoy aficionado. You purchase a domestic hen turkey from some farm, remove the innards, and freeze the bird, feathers and all. Then you take it out and use it, stuck on a stick, as a decoy. One person who tried this claimed it quickly went limp and drew no gobblers but swarms of flies!

One of the most hilarious incidents concerns a Texas turkey hunter, a prominent

While shooting pre-season photos, I found that the decoy approach was my most interesting experience in 30 years of hunting turkeys. Here a gobbler struts beside Henrietta while an irate, jealous hen, head outthrust and feathers ruffled, gets between the tom and the decoy.

electronic-call manufacturer, who went to the trouble of having a wild hen turkey mounted. It is illegal everywhere to use live-turkey decoys. This strikingly realistic mount, although expensive—it cost $150— looked like the final answer to any turkey hunter's prayer. Worked fine, too. Drew a gobbler right in the first time it was used. A wild gobbler of 18 or 20 pounds, as any turkey hunter knows, is an exceedingly strong critter, and often extremely rough with his lady friends. This old tom took the mounted hen so seriously he tried to breed it, and in his mounting frustration and perplexity tore it to smithereens. Punch line: the hunter was so astonished, confused, and incensed that he sat with his mouth open and finally jumped up and ran the gobbler off, forgetting to shoot.

While I was researching the Henrietta matter, Stephen Capel, with the Kansas Fish and Game Department, related to me how, during a turkey-restoration study he was making, he hit on the scheme of decoying gobblers for close observation. Many times callers, as all of them know too well, make some error and "un-convince" a partially convinced tom. Capel got from a friend a fresh turkey head with the neck skin on down to the breast. He skinned it out and mounted it on a piece of doweling. "I thought," he related, "that I could sit behind a tree, stick this head out, bob it around, and lure a gobbler right in. It would be the convincer."

The first several sharp-eyed toms saw his arm and called it quits with a loud *putt*. Then he learned to refine his act, and sure enough it worked. Elation was short-lived, however. He attended a wild-turkey symposium in Missouri and told proudly about what he'd done, and it was quickly pointed out to him that he was just asking some overeager turkey hunter to shoot him. He dropped that head in a hurry.

Perhaps curiously and conversely, the use of a full-bodied hen decoy, which is far more realistic than the homemade silhouette cutouts and full-bodied foam mockups a few hunters have tried, is considerably safer. It is a fact that there have been more and more shooting accidents as turkey hunting has grown in popularity along with the astonishingly successful restoration of wild turkey flocks, including establishment of the bird in states where it was never native. A good caller, well hidden, convinces some other hunter he's the real thing, is stalked, and. . . . Several states, worried sick, have been reticent about publicizing such accidents.

The hen decoy is placed in an opening, where it is easily seen from a distance by both turkeys and other hunters who may be present. The focus of the gobbler on the plainly seen decoy keeps its attention from the hideout of the caller. It just as effectively focuses the attention of another hunter away from the caller. Presumably he'll recognize the decoy for what it is—but don't bet on it.

While I was experimenting with Henrietta, I found a flock of state-park turkeys that had become somewhat used to people and were not quite as wild as average hunted birds. I plotted their usual course toward their roost for several days in a row, then placed Henrietta where she'd surely be seen. I hid behind some bushes to observe what might happen. The turkeys came strolling along. A gobbler veered off and circled Henrietta several times. Hens followed. They gathered and talked to her.

Suddenly there was a clatter behind me. A man came on the run, gesturing. Apparently he'd been out walking and had seen the birds. "Hey," he yelped, "you see them turkeys?" The turkeys, of course, flushed like quail. "You see that funny damn bird among 'em? What the hell kinda bird *is* that?" He now realized that "funny bird" hadn't flown off, and he swiveled his embarrassed gaze to meet my furious one, then slunk off without another word. If he had been a hunter, I reflected, I'll bet he'd have shot the decoy and tried to cook it! Some caution should be used in carrying and placing the decoy. After that, if somebody blasts it, at least it takes the heat off you.

All the legal aspects should be checked in the state where you hunt. In some, turkey decoys are illegal. Recorded or "electronic" calls, hunters should be aware, are illegal for turkey calling almost everywhere. Using one in conjunction with a decoy would therefore be illegal. And, for crafty tinkerers, that goes for a decoy containing a recorded call.

One wild-turkey biologist told me there was no difference in hunter success between using and not using a decoy. I thought about that as Murry and I hunched in growing darkness, watching that darned gobbler that simply wouldn't give up and go to bed. By then we had spotted eight gobblers that at least ogled Henrietta in passing and going to roost, and had heard them in the still evening fly up possibly 200 yards distant. Murry had by now quit using his call, hoping Old Eager would get his passion under control and take to roost, too. Every time he gobbled, all the others gobbled, apparently including some we hadn't seen and counted. Because the Texas season is set rather late, the majority of the hens were already nesting. Thus only a few had come in to the roost.

We agreed later that the feathers we'd attached to Henrietta's neck were definitely a help. I had correspondence with an Arizona decoy user who sticks on a few tail feathers. Slight movement in any breeze adds to the authenticity of the live-hen illusion. When a gobbler comes to a call, it fully expects to see another turkey. Many chances at birds are lost because an incoming one, failing to spot what it expects, becomes suspicious and sneaks away. The decoy bridges this gap, and slight feather movement is an attention grabber, helping allay suspicion.

The old gobbler that had fallen for Henrietta was unbelievably persistent. At flat dark, when I had to squint along the ground to make out any image at all, it was still *chuff-chuff*ing and dragging its wings. Finally when we could no longer see it, we followed its progress by its gobbling as it reluctantly strolled off toward the big trees. We sat quietly for a full half hour after it finally went up to its limb. The danger was that we might somehow disturb all the roosting birds and flush them. That would nix tomorrow for sure. Finally I eased up, sneaked silently through brush, out to the field, and far around, circling away from the birds, which were still gobbling from their limbs. Murry loomed beside the vehicle half a mile away when I padded in.

We ate a cold supper in a dark camp, to avoid any possible disturbance, even though we were well away from the roosting birds. We discussed experiences so far. Was the newfangled turkey decoy an unfair advantage, a surefire gobbler mesmerizer? I had been fiddling with Henrietta for over a year, so my experience now covered two spring mating periods and one entire fall and winter. All the incidents I witnessed, plus correspondence and visits with others who've tried a decoy, convince me that using one simply gives a careful, adept hunter an edge. It is by no means a cure-all for turkey-hunting problems, but it adds a provocative new dimension to a grand and difficult old sport.

Time after time, during experiments in spring, I watched gobbler reactions to live hens, to the decoy, and to a call with no decoy in sight. Turkeys, as long-time hunters well know, are exceedingly individual birds. Personalities among them differ widely. Reactions to the decoy seemed to depend on how ardent a gobbler is on a given day, how early or late in the breeding season presentation occurs, and how professional the caller is. An inept caller seldom will convince a gobbler, decoy or none. A so-so caller may give himself an edge because the decoy adds to the illusion.

Fully camouflaged hunter working his call. A so-so caller can give himself an edge with a decoy. Experts probably can do as well either way.

Most expert callers can bring in the shyest gobbler without a decoy as well as with one.

Hesitant gobblers, which so often and exasperatingly come almost but not quite into range and then slip away, appear to be influenced—maybe 50% of the time—to come closer to check out the decoy. As mentioned earlier, I watched hens try to consort with the decoy. In a state where hens are legal at least in fall, this might indicate help from the decoy. I watched hens several times that were definitely irritated at the presence of the decoy. They ruffled up and talked to Henrietta in indignant terms.

Curiously, during the pre-opening couple of days of our west-Texas hunt, we had several hens come into range, talking incessantly. Murry talked back. They paid no attention to the decoy. Oddly, two different gobblers that came with intermittent strutting paid no attention to the live hens, preferring for some reason dear old stand-still Henrietta.

Where young gobblers and old longbeards are vying for hen attention, a young one curiously looking over the decoy occasionally brings an otherwise disinterested oldster on the run, simply to put the youngster in his place. I watched one such incident, and after the youngster had left, so did the old tom. Undoubtedly such scenes are sparked by jealousy. Breeding-age gobblers seldom rush up to a hen. They strut, and the hen comes to *them*. This is one drawback of the decoy. Over several weeks of experiments Murry and I watched several gobblers come out to strut but never move closer to the decoy than 50 yards or so.

During our actual hunt, I carried a shotgun, and we agreed I'd shoot first if there were two gobblers. Murry used a scoped

.222 rifle with a down-loaded handload. Hunters who use rifles and hunters in the more open turkey range of the mountain West, where one can see far off, have less need for a decoy. It is of greater advantage to those who use shotguns, which means the target must be within 35–40 yards at most, and to those who hunt in dense cover.

Henrietta's mentor actually began developing his decoy during the fall-winter period back when hunting with dogs was legal. Specially trained dogs would find and flush a flock, and were "broke" to stay quiet thereafter in a makeshift blind while the hunter used a call to rally the scattered birds. By late winter, Henrietta's maker told me, turkeys had been shot at by squirrel and deer hunters and anybody who came along. Calling one in after flushing a flock was difficult and sometimes impossible.

"I thought that if I just had a decoy set out there, I could take my pick. But no decoy was available. I decided to make one."

Over the years, using various experimental models—even cloth cut to look like a turkey and sewed over balloons—he killed many birds that responded. He claimed that how well the hunter hides is the most important part. He emphasized that the decoy must be placed in an opening, even though the only ones available may be small. A friend of mine who works for the Louisiana game department says that many smart old gobblers in his region, particularly on open river sand bars, simply won't come within shotgun range unless they see a hen. Thus a decoy can be the convincer.

"It's very important," the manufacturer cautioned, "to place the decoy within 20 or at most 30 steps of your hideout. At least for shotgun hunters. This helps assure get-

ting an interested turkey within range. A decoy placed 40 yards off may simply result in influencing a gobbler to stay on the far side, out of range."

Some of my own experiences with too-ardent turkeys were comic. I heard similar tales from others. Jim Bisbee, a Stuttgart, Arkansas, turkey enthusiast, told me how a friend of his had his decoy knocked over twice during the same afternoon by two different gobblers. I watched three different toms bump mine, seeming irritated because she didn't "squat." The most curious experience was when Murry Burnham and I watched a buck deer stalk Henrietta, knock her over—bending her "leg" in the process—and then try to gore her.

One interesting switch on standard turkey-calling technique that can be accomplished with the decoy is influencing gobblers to move downhill. Most old hands claim that in hilly country you should never try to call from below but instead get atop a ridge, because a gobbler will move up but not down. When the decoy was placed in plain sight, my trials—and tales related to me by others—proved that toms were just as eager to come down as go up, occasionally flying downslope to the sight and sound.

There are experienced hunters, too, who claim you should never call, at first light, to gobblers still on a roost. The birds will wait, it's claimed, for that "hen" to come to them. Neither Murry nor I believed that, and long before daylight of opening morning we were back at our stand, with Henrietta staked out in the open facing the roosting area. Gobblers were already sounding off, and our excitement was high.

We sat together this morning, hidden in scrub mesquites. Finally, as weak light slid gently along the opening from our left, we heard a turkey fly off, then saw it. Excitement ebbed. It flew the length of the motte of tall trees, far past us to our right, and alighted 100 yards or so out in the field. A hen followed. The tom began to strut and gobble. If they all did that, we were fouled up for certain. Presently a hen flew to ground within 10 paces of us. She fluffed her feathers, turned spang at us, and walked toward the bushes where we sat. I suppressed a groan. She came on, talking. In the dim dawn light she passed so close between us that either of us could have grabbed her—and went on, talking away. We let out breath slowly, elated. We must have been camouflaged indeed.

The conclusion was almost anticlimax. We heard birds come to ground possibly 100 yards to our left. A double gobble ensued. And another. Every turkey still on a limb let fly, too. The two buddies that had passed Henrietta the previous evening—I guessed—were on their way. Presently, through our headnets we could see them, both long-bearded toms. Then came a bad moment. They were veering off, toward the edge of the woods. Murry touched his call gently. Like marching soldiers responding to command, they thrust out their heads and gobbled, turning straight toward Henrietta.

I raised the full-choke shotgun in slow motion, letting them come. They paused before Henrietta and gobbled at her but did not begin a strut. They started on, separated now by mere inches. Too close. I'd kill both if I shot now. Then they were a foot—two feet—apart while I breathlessly held fire. The 12-gauge shattered the creeping dawn. The rear gobbler hit the ground. The other, startled, trotted a few steps, and as turkeys often do at a shot, did not fly but stopped, head high, perplexed. Murry touched off the .222, and at its sharp crack we knew that both of us, and Henrietta, had done right.

Should you conclude that a decoy assures success? Not necessarily. Like ladies everywhere, Henrietta snared a number of passionate lovers with her stand-still wiles. Also like ladies everywhere, she was eyeballed by scads of girl-watchers who didn't think she was much. Using a turkey decoy is fun, and offers at least some help in a sport where most hunters can use all they can get. Some biologists have worried that the decoy will mean debacle for the nation's turkeys. I doubt that. Most of us, even decoy equipped, will still be abundantly able to foul things up at the crucial moment!

Part VI

MIXED BAG – SHOREBIRDS AND OTHERS

It has long seemed to me that numerous bird hunters miss much by keeping their focus too narrow, and because of overdedication to a favorite target. The bobwhite hunter in some areas is irked when his dog points a woodcock. The duck hunter with prime jacksnipe shooting underfoot pays no attention to it.

One of the influences that led me to wander widely over the years was the incessant urge to sample as many varieties of wing-shooting as possible. It seemed to me that the chance at a bird I had not hunted deserved as long a trek and as great an expenditure as a try for a trophy elk or a big bear. Size of the quarry should not be a consideration. A successful woodcock hunt where birds are numerous, or a chance to collect a few chachalacas in southern Texas or across the border in Mexico, is equal in my view to the enjoyment and thrills

of any big-game hunt. They're simply different kinds of enjoyment. Having tried both the bear and the chachalaca, frankly I enjoyed the chachalaca more.

I've always believed the shorebirds were among the most intriguing of all game birds. Perhaps this is because modern hunters are so severely restricted as to what species of shorebirds they can hunt, and yearn for "the good old days." Early in this century, due in great part to overhunting, most of the shorebirds declined so drastically that they were placed on the protected list.

There are some 30 or more species of shorebirds. The ones still hunted today are the woodcock and the jacksnipe. The woodcock always has been one of the most beloved of American game birds, especially in the Northeast, where hunting it is a kind of elite ritual. It is odd that so much sports-

men's love has been lavished on such a pre-
posterous-looking little bird. It is plump
and dumpy. Its bill is thick and about three
inches long, the tip flexible and sensitive to
enhance accurate probing for food in soft
soil. Female woodcock are larger than
males, about half a pound as compared to
six ounces. The general appearance is of a
buff-colored bird mottled over the back and
crown with dark browns, black, and flecks
of white. Although many hunters consider
the woodcock an upland game bird because
of its habits, it belongs to the family *Scolo-
pacidae*, which includes sandpipers, the
jacksnipe, and the curlews.

The jacksnipe is smaller, a trim, dapper
little gent of about five ounces average.
Its three-inch bill is more slender than that
of the woodcock. Standing, a jacksnipe is
about six inches from ground to crown,
with the legs, bent slightly at the knee, 2½
or three inches long. The back is brown,
buff, and black with streakings of white,
the underparts off-white with dark specks
and with the flanks barred. The sexes look
the same, except that females are slightly
smaller than males.

Both of these species, though among our
smaller game birds, are large enough to be
counted among them. Numerous shorebird species were too small ever to gain
much shooting popularity. However, the
yellowlegs, at least three times the size of a
jacksnipe; the willet, twice jacksnipe size;
occasionally the game-sized godwits, do-
witchers, the closely related turnstones and
avocets; and the larger species of sandpipers
all were hunted heavily throughout early
settlement and until early in the 1900s.

All of those were in scattered abundance.
The cream of the shorebird crop and their
relatives, in the sportsman's eye, were the
plovers, especially the upland and the
golden plover. These were not seashore or

lakeshore and marsh birds like most of the
others, and in fact are not true shorebirds
but members of a closely related family.
They were inhabitants of the prairies and
the farmlands. They were also naive birds,
and never learned otherwise. Like most of
the flocking species of shorebirds, they
were easily decoyed. They and the others
mentioned above often swirled in to decoys in compact flocks. Shooters—market
hunters especially—used large-bore, open-
barrelled guns. It was common to kill a
dozen or more with one shot.

An old gentleman in Erie, Pennsylvania,
told me back in the late 1930s many tales
of shorebird shooting in his younger days.
He explained how he fashioned several decoys the size of yellowlegs, using wings
from the birds themselves. He had devised
them so that when he pulled a string from
his blind, the wings would flap. This attracted passing flocks. He told me one shot
often got him 10 or more yellowlegs. His
largest shorebird bag for one shot, he related, was 18 upland plovers. The largest
daily bag that he remembered was on
golden plover, somewhere over 100.

Upland plovers were shot on the midcontinent plains and on down into Texas in late
summer by the hundreds of thousands.
They fed there on abundant grasshoppers,
and gathered in vast concentrations for migration on down into Mexico and South
America. All of these shorebirds were superb eating, and popular on the market at a
few cents each.

The plover seasons were over when I was
old enough to begin bird hunting. I remember what a thrill it was when, in the early
1950s, I saw an upland plover and heard its
liquid call in the northern Lower Peninsula
of Michigan. It was perched on a fence post
beside a meadow, a mile or so east from the
village of Wolverine. For several summers

I saw a plover or two in the same area. Although they're not extinct, today they are nowhere very common.

The big long-billed curlew, a bird of a pound or more that sports a sickle-like bill eight or nine inches long, was another shorebird highly prized and diligently hunted. The curlew originally ranged abundantly almost across the continent. It was most sought on farms and plains. There the flesh was indeed tasty. When shot along marine beaches, however, where it fed on small mollusks and other available forage, it was not considered palatable.

Some years ago, before Mexico began cooperating with the U.S. in protection of certain migratory bird species, I was hunting there and had the opportunity to sample the curlew shooting. It was a nostalgic experience, like stepping back many years into history.

Fortunately the woodcock, a shorebird even though it doesn't act much like one, continues in ample supply. It is especially abundant in certain areas—New England, Nova Scotia, the Great Lakes states for nesting and fall shooting, the Mississippi Valley and especially Louisiana in winter. Woodcock have their ups and downs, and their problems. Severe freezes on wintering grounds occasionally decimate the population. They can't probe into the ground with their long bills. Use of pesticides, it is believed, also harms woodcock to some extent, because they feed predominantly on earthworms, which may ingest the poisons.

Nevertheless, anyone who wishes to hunt woodcock today can fill limits in most seasons by doing intelligent where-to planning. The woodcock is a bird tailor-made for hunting with a pointing dog. It is indeed a delight to hunt, and again on the table. The meat is dark but with a most delicate and distinctive flavor. Curiously, on most game birds the breast is lighter than the legs. Woodcock are just the opposite. The meat of the plump little legs is quite light when cooked.

The jacksnipe, or Wilson's snipe, also is in good supply, with legal shooting each fall almost coast to coast, and with generous bag limits and a long season. The jacksnipe problem is not lack of birds but rather underutilization. Few hunters purposely go out for this sporty little bird. Oddly, very few are shot incidentally by waterfowlers and others. The general attitude seems to be that jacksnipe are too small to bother with (or else hunters are unaware of them), and that the dark morsel of meat isn't very tasty anyway. The truth is, jacksnipe are among the sportiest of game birds, and if you like dark meat they are an authentic delicacy.

One of the puzzles of the modern wing-shooting world is the lack of popularity of the sandhill crane. For over 40 years there was no open season on these birds. They eventually became so numerous and concentrated on certain northern nesting grounds, and especially on wintering grounds, that they severely damaged crops. A season was allowed, and has continued now for over 20 years, in a few states down the migration route from Canada to Mexico. The most massive wintering flocks are located in eastern New Mexico and western Texas.

I took in the first modern season on sandhills back in the early 1960s, and have hunted them many times since. These big gray-blue and brownish birds average seven to 11 pounds, have a six-foot wingspan, and measure as long as four feet from tip of toes to tip of bill. They are in my opinion warier than geese. Their flight speed is deceptive. Hunting them is a grand experience. Because they are grain feeders, their table quality is excellent. Misconceptions and myths about these birds—i.e., they're fish eaters; they're half tame—probably have encouraged hunter reluctance. After all these years the annual kill is minuscule, but the opportunity is wide open. The sandhill crane is a bird everyone should experience at least once—which will almost certainly lead to further temptation.

As I have said, any unusual bird hunting has always intrigued me. I've made many a long, arduous trip to collect a few birds of species scorned or neglected by most hunters. I never have made comparisons. That's just a good way to ruin a current experience. Bobwhite hunting is neither more nor less exciting than ruffed grouse, or woodcock, or bandtail pigeon hunting. Each has its individual atmosphere and flavor.

I will say, though, that the most distinctive atmosphere and flavor of any bird hunting I have encountered surrounds the drab-colored, long-tailed, noisy chachalaca. I'm not even certain the lovable chachalaca, a bird of about 1½ pounds, deserves to be called a game bird. If it qualifies, it is certainly the wackiest game bird on the continent. It lives in the cactus and thorn jungles along both coasts of Mexico, and spills northward on the east side across the border into a few counties of extreme southern Texas in the lower Rio Grande River Valley. It might be called the rarest U.S. game bird because of its miniature Texas range. Hunting it is not necessarily a dramatic wingshooting experience. Fundamentally, chachalaca hunting is a battle with the habitat, a challenge to see how gracefully one can suffer. You can read about that as the windup for this book.

24

How to Find and Hit Woodcock

The woodcock, or timberdoodle, classed as a shorebird, seems more like some curious cross between an upland and a lowland game bird. It's a delight to hunters—when they can find it and are able to hit it, which in the case of many is frustratingly seldom and uncertain. It is an odd woodland character, described by one authority as having been put together from parts left over when all the other birds were created. It seems to use these mismatched parts with uncanny adroitness to purposely perplex and exasperate hunters.

Indeed, since the first one twittered unsteadily up before the gun centuries ago in what appeared to be tremulous, uncertain flight, hunters have been wondering how on earth they so regularly manage to miss it. In addition, a hunter who stumbles into a bonanza of birds today, then goes back tomorrow to find yesterday's teeming cov-ert empty, is often too puzzled to continue. The woodcock is a mystery bird, a riddle. Yet it's not really that tough either to find or to hit, if you thoroughly learn its habits and eccentricities and analyze its really quite simple but deceptive flight patterns.

When I was learning about woodcock a good many years ago, I couldn't have chosen a better place for my lessons. We lived then in the northern part of Michigan's Lower Peninsula, in a small village on the edge of a large state forest. It was laced by trout streams and their tributary creeks. Woodcock nested abundantly in the region. I fished trout incessantly all summer, and at dusk each evening on some stream stretches dozens of woodcock would begin what has been called "trading," arising from a thicket, making a short, dawdling flight on twittering wings over to the other side or to a nearby thicket, and plummeting

Though classed as a shorebird, the plump, rather ridiculous-looking woodcock appears to be a cross between upland and lowland birds.

down again as if struck dead in the air. Often I've had one bump into my fly line or brush my hat as it passed.

Driving home in the dark, I'd see them standing in their comically dumpy stance on the forest roads. Occasionally, too, we'd spot a whole family, the young even more ridiculous in appearance than their parents. Through the long summer and into early fall I came to know intimate details about what kinds of coverts they invariably favored, and their precise airborne routines and antics. Then as fall advanced and storms swirled over the Upper Peninsula and southern Ontario, where thousands more woodcock nested, flight birds would pour across the Strait of Mackinac some nights, dropping into specific locations that suited their whimsies.

Year after year, the birds used many of the same spots—*exact* spots, to the square

yard. Occasionally, when weather formed up just right, the migrating birds and our locals would all be on hand at once. I vividly recall one triangle of cover at the confluence of two streams, an area of probably no more than 50 acres, where one fall two companions and I and a small black cocker spaniel—the breed named originally for its use as a woodcock dog—put up over 100 birds in the course of a single hour.

No American game bird is so uniquely selective about feeding and resting places. Nor is any quite as specialized as the woodcock. The specialization, in fact, is what dictates so narrowly where it will be, and when. The bird's diet is almost entirely earthworms. Woodcock do eat some ants and varied insect larvae. The long—2½ to three-inch—thick bill with sensitive, flexible tip is, however, designed for probing in soft ground for earthworms. Although much research has been done on the subject, no one is certain how the bird locates the worms. Perhaps it's by acute hearing. Obviously, because the bird depends on earthworms for its living, in order to locate his quarry the hunter must think in terms of where earthworms will be abundant, reachable, and in ground soft enough for the bird's bill to probe.

Even then it's tricky until you understand more about woodcock. They are basically night creatures. Almost all their feeding is done beginning at dusk and on through the night. Thus woodcock may not be on their feeding grounds during the day—although they may be, if suitable resting cover and ample food are both available in the same location. However, because they do not usually fly more than a brief distance at dusk if they must move to feeding grounds, resting cover will at least be close to low-light feeding areas.

Because of their specialized feeding,

woodcock are fine-tuned to the effects of weather. They're always jittery about what's happening, or about to. Frost is their nemesis. Even a light crust on the ground may effectively shut off their probing and make them uneasy enough to leave an area.

I recall a classic situation that illustrates how concerned they are about weather. One fall immediately prior to the season opening, I scouted a spot in northern Michigan where invariably there were birds. I walked through it and kicked up 16, all of which circled behind and plopped down again. I had a friend coming the next day to hunt. Everything was fine. He arrived and was excited about my find. That night the temperature began to drop. Next morning white frost was everywhere, and skim ice on puddles. I knew before looking that my hotspot would be empty. It was. Those nervous birds had gone on.

However, I knew another place where flight birds always dropped in when they came south across the Strait of Mackinac. That over-water night flight is rather long, often with buffeting winds. I reasoned that perhaps flight birds chased out by more severe weather farther north might have been forced to come in to rest in that quite protected covert I knew of. We went there and had a great shoot—but the next morning all birds were gone from there, too.

A weather eye therefore is of prime importance in the timing of hunts. Also, never plan on finding birds just because they were there yesterday. Migrations begin in the North in September or, during a balmy fall, no later than October. Temperature will control how long good hunting will last on both local and flight birds. It lasts longest, of course, on the southernmost wintering grounds.

Cocker spaniel with a woodcock beginning to flush. The cocker was named for its use in woodcock hunting. Years ago in northern Michigan, I used one on many hunts.

When severe weather farther north arrived, woodcock sometimes tumbled in amazing concentrations into coverts I knew. Here I'm in the process of making a double on woodcock, a rare occurrence. Two birds are in the air above me—one folded, the other about to be.

By far the greatest concentration of wintering woodcock is in Louisiana. The fact that as much as 80% of the continental population winds up there gives hunters a hot clue to how to find these oddball birds almost anywhere. One strong key is water. Biologists feel certain woodcock migrate chiefly by following stream courses and their bordering valleys. As they funnel down from nesting grounds, they drift southeastward or southwestward along tributaries of every big river.

In the North they nest by the hundreds along streams, even to the smallest creeks—not necessarily right along the bank, but within a few to several hundred yards of it. When they are moving southward in mountainous or hilly country, they may rest on ridgesides, invariably tumbling in

after a night flight onto southern slopes. Nevertheless, their lives are tied to stream courses everywhere because these and the valleys spreading out from them are where soft earth—suitable for earthworms—has been collecting for centuries. You may occasionally find woodcock far from a stream, but you seldom find *abundant* birds away from valleys where streams flow, and often they'll concentrate near the stream banks. The living there is easiest.

I've hunted woodcock in Maine, New York State, Michigan, Wisconsin, Mississippi, Louisiana, and eastern Texas. I made it a point years ago never to scout aimlessly. I followed a creek or a river, hunting a wide or narrow swath depending on the size of the stream. I remember bagging three or four birds every day one season when we lived in northern Michigan, by selecting and following each time a step-across creek with proper cover along it. Sure, you may find woodcock elsewhere, but if you make a rule to focus on stream valleys, you'll spend less time looking and more time shooting.

Precisely what to look for gets us to the tricky part. Some hunters think of woodcock as marsh birds. They're not. They shun marshes. In some ways they are similar in habitat preferences to ruffed grouse—they like the edges, timbered edges. But their needs and preferences are precise and specific. A heavy, tangled matt of grass never appeals to woodcock. Soft earth—commonly black loam where worms thrive—is a magnet. Usually it's moist, but not soggy. I've hunted successfully where low places held puddled water, but the birds aren't waders, and dislike resting in sopping areas.

In the North, mixed woodlands of poplar, white birch, and maple intermingled with conifers such as scattered balsams form typical *general* cover. In such forests, stream borders will have alder thickets, stands of blackhaw, willows. Here and there along lower hillsides thickets of wild plum, chokecherry, or Juneberry may be present. In the South, vegetation differs and the birds select what suits them best. Hardwood bottoms of mixed, mature timber will often have an understory of catbriars and varied shrubs, often dense. Much willow is often present. In addition, I've hunted places well down toward the Gulf where palmettos on the forest floor were thick and nearly head high. It seemed to one with experience only in the North like a ridiculous place for woodcock.

Once you fix in mind the valleys and stream courses, and the kinds of vegetation I've noted, then you get down to pinpoint preferences. Moderately dense grass such as is usually found below tall, shady timber is acceptable. Fallen leaves are invariably present during hunting season. In general, cover at ground level and immediately above should be open. But the woodland understory is invariably distinct, from scattered shrubs to thickets. Woodcock prefer neither bright sun nor heavy shade. Dappled sunlight and shadow filtering through tall trees or through the middle-height cover is perfect for them.

As my woodcock experience grew during my first years of hunting them, I came to realize that you could describe each detail of what they like—as I've tried to do here—but still you need a kind of sixth sense. This is developed simply by noting well the exact places where you find birds, or don't. A weed patch that might have open ground at the stalk bases, but with dense tops thick above, you mark off as not worth checking. It's too difficult for birds to fall into and flush from such cover. A clump of blackhaw at the edge of a woodlot where a creek meanders hits you as precisely the kind of place a woodcock will be resting. You walk up to it, or your dog—wise to woodcock ways—approaches it, and there's your bird.

After you've got the broad-scope picture and have narrowed it down and accomplished a few flushes, you find yourself always keeping an eye peeled for comparable places. Soon you've developed what purist woodcockers sometimes call "timberdoodle telepathy." Always file in memory every place where you've located woodcock, whether a tiny spot where a single flushed, or a 100-acre expanse that held many. Year after year, as long as the cover does not drastically change, birds will almost unfailingly utilize those same coverts. They've got that sixth sense, too.

Writing that, I'm reminded of a location

in northern Michigan that friends and I a long time ago called the "Sawdust Pile." Years previously there'd been a sawmill in the forest there, and the enormous pile of sawdust had rotted down. Second-growth timber had grown—poplar, maple, scattered young balsam and hemlock. A tiny creek wandered near. Scattered alders, highbush cranberry, and serviceberry were present.

To any woodcock hunter of experience, this was a birdy oasis. I didn't get to use a dog often in those days. Though dogs, especially slow ones that stay close, work well on woodcock, which lie extremely snug as a rule, the dogless hunter can do very well walking them up. That's what I was doing when I first discovered the sawdust pile. I flushed my first bird right at its edge. Along perhaps 100 yards of creek and the surrounding area, I flushed four more. I hunted that spot every year for five seasons. Always it produced a few. I was back there for a visit after a 20-year absence and, making the identical short tour, I killed two and missed two.

Lots of beginning woodcockers know about that—the missing. Curiously, woodcock have long been touted as difficult birds to hit. Actually, even though I miss my share still, they are not difficult. Shots are almost always short. The cover is not conducive to long-range tries. You need a fairly open-barreled gun of any gauge you wish, and small shot. No. 8 is a good choice, in field loads.

The problems of hitting woodcock are tied to their curious manner of flushing, the gunner's confusion over the crisscross of cover, and the illusion of tremulous, weak, zigzag flight. The entire flight pattern, from flush to alighting again, is so different from that of the standard uplanders—quail, ruffed grouse, pheasants—that it puts the hunter off. Once analyzed, however, the pattern is so simple that shooting also becomes simple.

Woodcock invariably flush straight up. How high they tower before leveling off depends mostly on how tall and dense the general cover is. In big timber with shrubby understory, the birds burst up, often liter-

These springer spaniels, wise to woodcock ways after hunting them each fall of their lives, knew where to look. Here one fetches a bird while its companion honors the occasion.

ally right by your boots or before the nose of a dog you've been able to walk up to because the birds lie so tight. They climb vertically or nearly so until they clear the lower cover. It's no trick for them to fly among large, tall trees. However, if you're in second-growth that's perhaps spindly but thick and 20 or 30 feet high, birds may tower that high before leveling off.

Try to think of a woodcock as being out in the open. It must lift its weight almost vertically. Thus the upward flush is relatively slow. A quail zooms off at a narrow angle, nearly in horizontal flight from its flush, and is going 35 to 50 in short order. Ruffed-grouse flight is much the same. But if you had the woodcock out in the open, hitting it would be ridiculously easy. At short range, just swing above until you blot it, shoot, and it's yours. The vertical lines of the cover, plus having the bird move upward into it, is what fools hunters. They shoot too fast or shoot below, hurrying before the cover cuts them off. Deliberate shooting is the first rule of putting woodcock down.

If you miss as a woodcock towers, wait for it to tip over into level flight. At that point it is extremely vulnerable. Just put the confusion of cover out of mind. Fire through it as if it wasn't there. Also, put out of mind the idea that woodcock are zigzag, uncertain fliers. It's an illusion. If you miss as the bird flies on, watch it closely. Woodcock seldom fly far. You may be able to put it up again.

Woodcock may seem swift, but they fly slower than any of the quail, grouse, or pheasants. Steady flight has been clocked at around 35 m.p.h. or so, short flights between flushes as slow as 23 m.p.h. However, woodcock have a greater wingspan-to-weight ratio than the other game birds. A ruffed grouse with two feet of wingspread weighs an average of 24 ounces. The wood-

The woodcock is one of the grandest of game birds. It may seem confusing because of its habitat and curious flight, but once you learn, many a still-life like this will be yours.

cock, spreading 18–19 inches, weighs only six or eight ounces. It cups those long wings distinctly, however. The wing motion in that stance, plus tilts to avoid trees and saplings, give the appearance of teetering zigzags, when the flightline actually is about as beeline as that of quail or grouse.

So pay no attention to the grid of lines the cover seems to draw, shoot with deliberation, use an open or improved-cylinder barrel, take 'em at the top of the tower, and you'll be an expert woodcock shot by the time you've put one limit in your game pocket. The woodcock is too grand a game bird to be passed up because it's presumed to be hard to find and hit. In numerous places it's underutilized for those very reasons. They're not valid, and with a pinch of woodcock wisdom, you can prove it.

25

The Other World of the Woodcock

Since the beginnings of American wing-shooting, the woodcock and woodcock hunters have enjoyed a decidedly elite status. This in-between game bird, seemingly part uplander and part lowlander, borders on the ridiculous in appearance, what with its pop eyes, long bill, and tremulous flight patterns. Yet it has always been associated with the tweed shooting-jacket set, with fine double shotguns highly engraved, with after-hunt gentility and gourmets who know the proper wines and to whom a serving of broiled woodcock bound in bacon would serve as a valid excuse for shooting the chef.

The clean, handsome woodlands of Nova Scotia, New Brunswick, New England, the Great Lakes region—these are the prime coverts wherein the woodcock has always been gunned on crisp, golden fall days. They are without doubt contribu-

tory to the aura of elitism—shining white birches with yellow fall leaves; neat balsams, poplars, and gaudy maples; tag alders, thornapple, and haw thickets fringing rollicking crystal trout streams. Classic woodcocking grounds.

Long before we settled in Texas, I had shot those places countless times. Where else does one shoot woodcock? Those are the places where the woodcock *are*. Anybody knows that. Yet I wasn't there. I was hundreds of miles south. It was January, and I was on a woodcock hunt deep in the infinitely tangled swamps of the Atchafalaya River Basin in southern Louisiana, only a short run northwest of New Orleans and the Gulf of Mexico.

Tommy Prickett called, "Listen!" He stopped. So did Bruce Hammatt and I. "I don't hear Tammy's bell. We've got a point."

We went wallowing through the bottom-

Near the Atchafalaya River in southern Louisiana, Tommy Prickett stands ready for flush of woodcock as both setters are on point.

land timber toward where the bell had been tinkling. Great leafless hardwoods towered above us. On our level, king-sized cat-briar vines and giant berry canes clawed at us, some of their thickets so dense and thorny even the dogs shied from them. A galaxy of understory species of shrubs and scrub crisscrossed our vision and blocked every step. And in this particular sweep of cover, at knee to head height below the brush and vines were interlocked palmettos, an endless maze of great green fronds rustling and crackling.

Woodcock? It was preposterous, I reflected, crashing and ramming noisily through the palmettos, trying to keep up.

My partners, both natives here, were much younger than I. Their idea of a slow, short hunt, I had already gathered, was a 10-mile swamp jog. Rubber boots were mandatory. We incessantly moved from patches of only damp ground through spreads of water anywhere from an inch to mid-calf depth.

"Hold up," Tommy called to me. "The dog's right in front of you. Not four feet."

A white setter, and I couldn't see it four feet away in the palmettos!

Bruce said, "Go ahead. Flush the bird. We'll back you up."

I elbowed gingerly into the rattling palmettos. Ah! There was Tammy—beautifully rigid, one hind leg trembling in excitement and restraint. Suddenly the bird went up. It *looked* like a woodcock. It *flew* like a woodcock. The unusual surroundings faded, like a dissolve in a movie. I was swinging up my gun, trying to separate the wing-dancing bird from the grid of branches, then squeezing the trigger, and in the abrupt clatter of gun sound the bird was tumbling.

So this was the "other" world of the woodcock. For many years I had yearned to shoot on the bird's wintering grounds. I was remembering, as the dog brought in the bird, the countless articles I'd read—and quite a few I'd written—about the kind of cover woodcock demand, and recalling the detailed studies done on this grand game bird, all telling only how it is in the spring, summer, and fall worlds of the woodcock. In my own rather extensive library of outdoor books, there are only a few meager words about the wintering grounds.

Tommy said, "I kind of hope it won't be like last week. That was *too* fast."

Tommy Prickett was at that time a biologist, Upland Game Study Leader for the Louisiana Department of Wildlife and Fisheries. He related how, the previous week, he'd lifted one dog over a wire fence—a fence we'd just climbed at the edge of this timber, separating it from open crop fields. Before he could get over the fence himself, the dog was pointing. He flushed the bird and shot it; the dog ran to retrieve and accidentally flushed a second, which he also shot. During the retrieve of those two, the dog pointed again.

"By the time those three were in my coat, I bumbled into a fourth, and the setter was pointing again. The whole hunt—five birds bagged, a daily limit—lasted 20 minutes and covered maybe 100 yards. I was half annoyed at myself for shooting—but it sure was fast and exciting."

Bruce Hammatt, a native of the area, had told me earlier that some days, if you hit the right places, it's possible to flush 200 woodcock in half a day. The reason is simply that Louisiana is wintertime woodcock mecca. The birds nest over a vast east-west spread of the northern U.S. and southern Canada, from the Maritimes and New England to southern Ontario, Manitoba, and the Great Lakes states, with a few stragglers southward in middle latitudes. But when migrations begin in fall, the birds follow stream courses and north-south valleys. Tangent flights set a course down the Atlantic states and along the western edge of the Appalachians, but the majority of the birds begin to converge along the Mississippi River system.

By mid-December an estimated 95% of the entire continental flock has located in only six states, from Florida across the Deep South to Arkansas and eastern Texas. In a several-year Fish and Wildlife Service study done over 30 years ago, it was estimated that because of the fix the birds have on the Mississippi, at least 50% of the entire population winters in Louisiana. Later studies by Louisiana researchers indicate that the percentage may be much higher, up to possibly 75%. Whichever is correct, Louisiana packs in somewhere from four to 7.5 million woodcock every winter out of a total continental flock estimated in normal years at eight to 10 million birds.

Even that doesn't tell the whole story of the astonishing concentration. The bulk of those millions winters in a relatively small part of the state, but it happens to be the largest swamp region within the contiguous U.S. This is an area measuring roughly 100 miles north-south and 60 or more east-west. It encompasses the entire length of the Atchafalaya River Basin, from Lafayette and the Bayou Teche area on the west to

Baton Rouge and the banks of the Mississippi. Three parishes (counties) gather the majority of the birds: St. Landry, Pointe Coupee, Iberville.

There's good woodcocking elsewhere in Louisiana. The area north of Lake Charles is one spot. The Florida parishes—the region north of Lake Pontchartrain, south of the east-west Mississippi border with Louisiana, and east of the Mississippi River—winter excellent populations. There is fair to good shooting at times in the northeast, too, from Union, Ouachita, Caldwell, and Lasalle parishes east to the Mississippi River.

Why has the woodcock never become renowned in Louisiana? Simple enough. When you go "bird hunting" anywhere in the South, any southerner knows you're talking about bobwhite quail. It is the South's dearly beloved. Yankees should easily understand that. Most of them think likewise about ruffed grouse—and perhaps never would have become avid woodcockers except that in the North both birds are commonly found in the same coverts. Woodcock in the South have always been shot just as incidentals come upon while quail hunting. To be sure, in modern times there are a few dedicated timberdoodle hunters, but the average bird hunter thinks of the woodcock—and will tell you so—as "not much compared to a quail." Tradition dies hard.

In addition, for years in the South woodcock were poached and market-hunted by devious and far from sporting means. Late in the last century and early in this, a brace brought about $1.50 in eastern markets. The birds do almost all of their feeding from evening through the night and dawn, most of it in open areas, flying out from cover to favored worming grounds. A pine torch to shine the big eyes of feeding birds

and a stick to whack 'em with sacked up woodcock by scores. Some Cajuns still call woodcock "bec de nuit," which translates as "snipe of the night," or "bec de bois," meaning "snipe of the woods." "Becasse" or "becada," the first French and the second Spanish, used rather interchangeably for snipe or woodcock, are heard occasionally.

In addition to the stigma attached to a bird that could be killed with a stick, many southerners wouldn't have been caught drunk working good quail dogs on such quarry. Further, woodcock hunting in the South, compared to Yankee woodcocking, is darned hard work. A friend in Mississippi once told me how his granddad would gather a group of black boys and have them make a drive through swatches of cane brake while he and friends covered the open fringes. Scads of woodcock would come jittering out to a racket of guns. This, mind you, was a diversion, not serious bird hunting.

That first morning we didn't put up any 200 birds, but I'd guess in three hours we found at least 50 and had no difficulty bagging limits. Like woodcock anywhere, some sat unbelievably snug, some ran, some flushed wild. Many less-than-experienced woodcock hunters don't believe these birds will run. The fact is, every now and then one will skedaddle long before the dog gets close, and either flush wild or never be located. Conversely, I've never seen woodcock sit as tight as some of these wintering birds did.

Tommy told me, "We've actually caught a bird by hand once in a while, just to see if it could be done."

One day of my hunt I carried only cameras. Both dogs were exceptionally steady, and on one point Tommy located a woodcock flat on the leaves not a yard from the dog's nose. I moved in, not quietly—there

I retrieve a bird from beside a trickle of water. The first morning of my Louisiana hunt, we put up at least 50.

isn't any such thing in that cover! — pointed a camera from a range of four feet, and took three photos before the bird finally burst up and away.

The following day Tommy and I hunted alone, with his two setters. There were no palmettos that day, but the vines and canes were just as tangled. Birds were everywhere. I used to believe, when I lived in northern Michigan, that I had seen the best woodcock shooting in the nation when the fall flight came tumbling into the northern

Lower Peninsula from the Upper and added to our locally raised birds. I thought the same one time in Maine. I now have to agree, however, with what one Louisiana native told me: "Shoot, you Yankees don't know what lots of woodcock look like!"

For those who try the Louisiana hunting, there is another kind of cover that holds birds. This is waxmyrtle, or bayberry, a shrub that grows in heavy stands in meadows and swamp hammocks and near shores. It has grayish berries along its twigs all winter, and the leaves are evergreen.

"This is surefire woodcock cover," Tommy told me, "and when you get the birds up, you get them in more open shooting situations because there usually isn't the tall overhead hardwood growth."

The best Louisiana shooting is during January and early February. This is because late in the season more and more cold to the north keeps pushing birds into the prime parishes. Normal season length is from early December to the first week or more of February. Tommy explained why we didn't find birds by the hundreds, as he had on several occasions a bit earlier. On their winter grounds they are exceedingly touchy about weather.

"We usually continue to have good hunting right to the end of the season," Tommy said. "But meanwhile, weather causes minor migrations back north a hundred miles or so, and then the birds return. Whenever we get a warm spell, the birds dislike it almost as much as they do the cold. They'll move to a cooler area, and then come pouring back in to the southern extremes as soon as a cold front pushes through."

The late-running season is an advantage for a visitor. After practically all the major hunting seasons have closed down over most of the country, Louisiana woodcock are at their peak concentration in the vast lowlands of the Atchafalaya Basin. A trip there interferes with little home-state shooting and is a grand opportunity for nonresidents to extend their season.

The region is not only another world for woodcock, but distinctly so for visitors. This is Evangeline country. It is also the country—near St. Francisville, north of Baton Rouge—where Oakley Plantation is located, dating back to 1799. This was where Audubon resided for some years, where he painted 84 of his Birds of America series and undoubtedly learned much during the winters about woodcock. The general region is the "English Louisiana" of history, with numerous restored antebellum mansions and plantations.

I'll issue one warning: Cajun woodcock country is no place for weight watchers. It is the crawfish capital of the world, the only area on this continent, in fact, where freshwater crawfish are big business and gourmet fare. Tommy and I hunted one day within a short distance of the bayou-front village of Henderson, a few miles east of Lafayette off Interstate 10, and lunched there. My wife and I had spent a couple of days previous to the hunt trying the several restaurants for which the town is famous.

Pat's, a delightful, big, sprawling place on the bayou, famous in the area, was our favorite. It claims to be the location where the business of pond-raising crawfish originated, because the owner couldn't get enough to supply the popular restaurant year round from the Cajun fishermen who trap them in the swamps. We gorged on crawfish pie, stew, gumbo, bisque, etouffée. I bought a platter of boiled whole crawfish—four or five dozen to the order—and went through them the traditional way, getting almost as much smeared on me as in me. The entire region is a welter of ex-

cellent seafood restaurants, with Louisiana oysters on the half shell or any way you can dream up, fresh shrimp, and numerous varieties of Gulf fish, all cooked in Creole and Cajun fashion.

To illustrate how plentiful and easily accessible the woodcock are—if you can still waddle after sampling the regional food—one day we hunted barely outside the city limits of Baton Rouge, a city of about 200,000. A couple of warm days, my companions said, had evidently pushed most of the birds farther north. They kept apologizing for poor hunting. We flushed "only" 40-odd birds from that tract in two hours!

Admittedly, it isn't like hunting the neat New England coverts. Three times I swung on an easy shot and had the gun all but jerked out of my hands by a cat-briar vine. Once I made the error of wearing regular hunting boots and was soaked all day. Rubber boots made little difference the next day. A woodcock sat on a tussock and allowed the dog, almost belly deep in water, to point it. I got in over my boots—but I bagged the bird. To wind up that hunt I fell down in the slick gumbo of a creek we crossed and was soaked to the waist.

"Everybody bleeds some," Bruce Hammatt told me with a grin when I complained about the countless cuts I had on hands and face from greenbrier vines and cane brakes.

Although it's best by far to have dogs, when the woodcock are fully concentrated a hunter without a dog can't help walking up an ample number of birds. He'll usually do best by hunting the edges of a timber stand or other cover, rather than wandering deep into large tracts. The reason is that birds which feed in open fields or along woods edges at night don't necessarily fly far back into cover. Many of them spend the daytime within sight of the edge.

There are some problems for nonresident visitors looking for places to hunt, because of clubs leasing hunting lands. However, there are numerous state-owned Wildlife Management Areas in Louisiana, each containing from a few hundred to upwards of 60,000 acres, a few of them in the first-choice woodcock areas. Further, it is no insoluble problem for an ingenious visitor to find someone to take him out, or to get permission to hunt on private unleased lands, especially for woodcock, which are locally second-rated and receive little serious hunter attention.

Driving back toward Texas and home after that hunt, I paused to put fresh ice on my possession limit of birds. Packing the fat little timberdoodles securely, I reflected that this "other world of the woodcock" may be discordant with northern tradition, but it unquestionably produces the fastest action the species offers anywhere on the continent.

26

The Jacksnipe —
Feathered Frustration

"How can I keep my mind on a dog and a rabbit," John Peterson said, "when *that* keeps happening?"

What he meant by "that" was the flush of a small bird intricately mottled in brown, black, and white, from almost beneath his boot. It burst out of the frost-bent marsh grass and swirled away low in a swift but tottering flight as if it were using first one wing and then the other. Over the first few yards it called in annoyance, the sound like a small, rusty door hinge—"*screak, screak, screak.*"

John had lurched around at the flush, swinging up his gun reflexively, startled, then lowering it. The bird was most difficult to see as it skimmed the grass. Out of gun range, it towered high, circling the pond nearby. Now the jittering flight was gone. With astonishing speed the little bird

came around, scimitar wings biting deep and three-inch bill outthrust.

"Why didn't you shoot it?"

"Shoot it!" John exploded. "How the heck could anybody *hit* one of the darned things?"

We had started out across the fields that crisp midmorning in November with a single beagle casting about. This was to be our first cottontail hunt of the season. There'd been a couple of chases, and we'd bagged one rabbit. Then the dog had started working the marsh grass around this small pond, perhaps hoping to find a cottontail in a cozy form there, but immediately a jacksnipe had flushed. Then another, and another. The grass was full of them.

No doubt they had fallen in here during a migration flight a day or so ago and had stayed, finding good feeding in the soft

The jacksnipe, a sporty little bird that gets little attention from hunters.

mud of the pond border where they could probe with their long bills. To stumble upon such a gathering of snipe was a rare find indeed. Both John and I had stood it for several minutes now, but we both knew we weren't going to put up with it much longer.

I chuckled at John's exasperation. "We really didn't need this many," I kidded. "Give each of us one snipe and two boxes of shells and I suspect we could make an exciting day of it." Then I said impulsively, "Let's tie up the dog and have at 'em."

With the beagle moaning sadly at his plight, John and I put 40 yards between us and began slowly walking around the pond. Up from underfoot went the first bird. In characteristic fashion it skimmed away close to the grass in what has often been termed a "corkscrew" flight pattern. John's 20 let fly to no avail, and mine followed with like result. The bird now reacted in typical jacksnipe fashion. It towered high and flew away over the fields, but presently turned and came back, circling the pond, not in corkscrew motion now but in level, all-out flight.

"Blot it out and keep swinging," I said to John as the bird coursed straight in high above him.

His gun gave its command; the bird folded neatly and fell on a long slant into the marsh grass.

The poor beagle felt sorry for himself for several hours that day. This hunt occurred many more years ago than I like to admit, and was the first real all-out jacksnipe hunt I ever experienced. Previously I had taken a pot shot at one here and there, but until that fall day, I'd never known what truly wonderful sport these little birds, which weigh only four or five ounces, offer. Oddly, few gunners do. And that is unfortunate, because nowadays, with so many hunters afield and civilization crowding everywhere, we need to utilize all of our species. A tremendous recreation potential for gunners goes begging every season because of lack of interest in or knowledge about this diminutive though superbly dramatic lowland game bird.

In pioneer days, when unrestricted sport shooting and market hunting were at peak, jacksnipe were present in untold thousands. They ranged—and still do—over the entire continent, nesting and summering above the middle-latitude states and northward throughout most of Canada and Alaska, and wintering in the southern states and on down clear into South America. They swarmed in coastal areas, and inland over wet meadows, around the fringes of bogs and ponds, and along stream courses.

One of my favorite pastimes years ago was walking the courses of small creeks in the Thumb region of southern Michigan where I was brought up, kicking occasional snipe out of cover. If I missed a bird, it would fly on up or down the creek, and I knew I'd flush it again as I hunted on. Many an enjoyable shoot had only a half dozen birds as its basis. It was sporty and provocative shooting.

In early settlement and market hunting days, it was common to see bundles of snipe hung by the necks outside marketplaces. Some market shooters, using decoys, brought in whisp after whisp of birds—that was a term used to describe groups of snipe that flew together—then unloosed fine shot from enormous guns, killing dozens at one blast.

There are old and all-but-unbelievable kill records from the last quarter of the 1800s and the first decade of this century. One tells of over 350 snipe shot by one hunter during one day. Another notes that one enthusiast shot almost 7,000 birds during a single winter.

Probably some of these massive kills were for the market. All the shorebirds hunted for market were delicious, but the small jacksnipe was considered by many the ultimate delicacy of the lot. There is the tale, often told using different settings, about the waiter in a plush hotel who served to a gourmet a half-dozen broiled snipe. The customer stared in horror, noting that each had been wrapped in bacon. Then he flew into a towering rage, arose, and shot the waiter dead. Whether true or not, it illustrates the esteem held for the pure and delicate flavor of this dark-meated morsel.

The jacksnipe, as well as most other shorebirds, lays no more than four eggs to a clutch. None of the species could tolerate market hunting or uncontrolled hunting long. In addition, in early days the birds were rather naive, and would even decoy again and again to wounded or dead birds. They also were shot in spring and fall, and were even during nesting season victims of nest robbers, because the eggs were palatable.

Protection early in this century undoubtedly saved all shorebirds from extinction. Hunting continued, however, for the jacksnipe. Its range spread over much vaster territory than that of other shorebird species. And the population was distributed thinly by comparison. Even though enormous concentrations of snipe were present during market days and previously, this bird was not fundamentally the flocking kind.

Everyone has observed flocks of various shorebirds along marine beaches or inland lakes arising as one, circling as one, dipping and swerving as one. The jacksnipe at its peak moved in large concentrations simply because there were so many of them. Seldom, however, did—or do—jacksnipe flush or fly as a group. Indeed, today's moderate numbers never consort in large groups, but more commonly trade here and there as singles or small, loose groups of four or five to a dozen. However, when several are flushed at once, they usually fly in all directions and don't stick together. Further, the snipe is warier than most other shorebirds, and though it can occasionally be decoyed, it is not naive or eager. To the average wing-shooter, it is an exasperating, easily missed target.

I had the good fortune to hunt these birds in the Great Lakes region when they and the marshes that drew them were quite abundant. Small swales of a few acres were scattered everywhere over farms and pastures during those fine days when draining had not become an obsession. A farmer following his plow usually skirted the wet spots and left them, though probably not with any really dedicated thought in mind for wildlife. But as time and land use marched along, the wetlands and the snipe population dwindled. Finally, in 1940, U.S. seasons were entirely closed. Some Canadian provinces continued to allow shooting.

Because wintering snipe are scattered over a very wide area, it has always been difficult to tell precisely what their population is. Without question the Louisiana marshes nowadays get the vast share of wintering birds, and undoubtedly always have. During the 1950s biologists began to develop much better methods of determining bird populations, and with protection the jacksnipe made a substantial comeback. At last hunting seasons were opened again over almost all states and provinces where snipe nest, migrate, and winter. To date the bag and possession limits have been eight and 16 most of the time and in most states.

Snipe hunting has always been something of a specialist's game, with a very small number of addicts. During the era of full protection, young shooters coming up never made acquaintance with the jack-snipe over a gun barrel. When the species appeared again on the game list, few of the new crop of hunters even knew what it was when they flushed one. Meanwhile many a duck and goose hunter had hung up his decoys because of low bag limits. But besides that, few waterfowlers had ever been dedicated snipe hunters. For them the jack-snipe was just too small a target to be interesting.

And so, oddly and unfortunately, during the late '50s and through the '60s snipe hunting actually became for all practical purposes a lost art in all but a very few localized spots throughout the wide range of the bird. In my contacts with game departments through the U.S. recently while I was doing research for a large hunting book, the invariable answer to my snipe query was: "Little or no interest among hunters; a few bagged as incidentals by hunters after other game."

Only a few states are primarily waterfowling and lowland-bird hunting locations. Louisiana is the classic for jacksnipe because of its abundant wetlands and the migration patterns of the birds. Nevertheless, even in states where wetlands are limited, enough jacksnipe are present each season to furnish many memorable days afield for a number of purist-type gunners. Their skill may not be large, but a shoot that gathers four or five snipe is, I can assure all readers, a dynamic experience. It will keep you going back and wondering where these little demons have been all your shooting life. And if you do go back time and again, and save your birds well-wrapped in the freezer until you have garnered enough for a meal, I can make another prediction: you will really be hooked.

I cannot at this point resist an anecdote. Some years ago I happened to hunt pheasants in Pennsylvania with two friends in a piece of habitat that was quite marshy and exactly right for migrating snipe. Apparently a flight from up across the lake had tumbled in recently on its way toward the Gulf Coast. There were a lot of them. The pheasants weren't much, and the three of us got to shooting snipe. The two others had never previously done this. They had a ball, but when we finished, they confessed they didn't know what to do with their birds.

"Are they any good to eat?" one asked.

"Them little things!" the other scoffed.

Now we, like other hunting companions, often played little pranks on each other. I said, not actually lying but just messing around a bit with the truth, "Some say they taste terrible." I paused. "Funny, though, I know somebody who loves 'em."

So far as we knew, there was nothing to prevent them from giving me their birds to pass along to "that person," especially if we made it official with a written statement to that effect so I would not be outside the possession limit in the eyes of the law. The upshot was that the whole bag wound up on the table of that person who "loves 'em"—me! And one of my sons, who had previously said he thought they tasted terrible, didn't get a bite! If you can work this on some unsuspecting friend, feel free.

It was interesting for me to reflect, after the reopening of seasons on snipe and my return to seeking them, that they certainly had not changed one bit. The spots they selected were the same, their flight was precisely as I remembered it, and my misses had not changed much, either! I suspect that woodcock hunters might make the best snipe seekers. They know how to ferret out special coverts. No dog is used, of

Colored cardboard cutouts inserted in split twigs serve as jacksnipe decoys. Occasionally the birds come in to decoy sets.

course, but a woodcocker gets used to looking for exact conditions of cover where he knows woodcock are almost certain to consort. He also looks for the "whitewash" or droppings which indicate that birds are, or at least have been, there. The same applies to snipe.

Snipe locations—or at least locations usable by snipe—are not as difficult to find as those for woodcock, simply because they are always based on water or other wet areas. But in many instances a search resembles one for a special woodcock covert, because a very small marsh may have exactly what the jacksnipe desire and may attract them in substantial numbers, whereas the large and more obvious marsh may for unknown reasons be less attractive.

In one instance I discovered a small dredged ditch whose banks were sparsely overgrown with small willows, and with marsh grass near the trickle of water. It was no snipe bonanza, but season after season about a mile of it, cutting across several farms where I had permission to hunt, held a few birds. The shooting was lovely indeed, for the snipe acted as they always do. That is, when I jumped one, either it flew on a short distance to be jumped again, or it circled and came down some distance behind me, where I could flush it again on the way back.

This habit is just as strong in a marsh or around a pond. Birds using the place do not like to leave, particularly if a pond with surrounding marsh, or a low place with marsh grass and openings where snipe can easily probe, is a fair distance from any other suitable cover. The birds just about defy being driven away. They rise and corkscrew away, and if they are missed they circle high.

The flush is a difficult shot for many gunners because they think the bird is flying far

more erratically than it is. Use No. 9 low-brass loads if you can get them, No. 8 if you can't. Use a fairly open barrel, and don't worry about the crazy flight pattern. Just pull tail-on and let fly, and the bird is yours. If you miss, hunker down and wait. In numerous instances the bird that towers and circles will come right back over you. Now its flight will be straight as an arrow, and though it'll be swift, the shot will not be difficult.

After you've missed the same bird a couple of times, of course, it won't play this way so easily. If there is a gully or small creek with cover along the sides that comes into or leaves the marsh, almost every bird that you scare away will fly off over the fields but will circle and come back into the creek bed, perhaps unnoticed and a goodly distance from the pond or marsh. Leave such places alone until you are through with the marsh. Then work them. Missed birds will head for the marsh again.

Especially on the southern wintering grounds, wet meadows or crop fields furnish more prime snipe hunting than marshes do. The going is often tough, slogging through mud. The birds may flush wild, or they may lie snug in virtually no cover at all, getting up with that *screak, screak* call of protest well within gun range. On these moist meadows, most missed birds and those that flush out of range will circle and come down behind the hunters. These can be flushed on the way back, although they may not hold if they've been shot at. I recall one hunt where two of us walked across a meadow, separated by 40 or 50 yards, and a companion trailed well behind. He picked off more birds that circled back than we shot flushing them.

For beginners, the basics to be learned start with the general habits of the bird. It is not a swimmer, although it is capable of doing that, and though classed as a shorebird, it is not much of a wader. Occasionally one is seen wading the shallow edge of a pond. But fundamentally this species is an open-country wetlands bird. Wet meadows, as stated, may suddenly blossom with them. Harvested rice fields in the South offer excellent hunting. Yet they like best the sedge and other low vegetation common around ponds and marshes. Scattered willows or other trees and bushes are acceptable. But snipe are never the "thicket" birds woodcock are. They feed to some extent on worms, just as woodcock do, but the diet is made up largely of such items as small crustaceans, snails, larvae of aquatic insects, and the worms other than angleworms that are found in muddy and boggy earth. What to me is most remarkable about the jacksnipe is that it seeks its favorite surroundings even in mountain valleys and rocky terrain.

I have always remembered a fall in New York State when I was climbing forested ridges after ruffed grouse, and also discovering occasional woodcock in the scattered copses on more open slopes and beneath alders along a valley stream. The general terrain was rocky, and the casual observer would call it forest cover. I came off a ridge and into an opening where scattered clumps of poplar and evergreens grew. In a tiny basin surrounded by poplar there was a seepage rimmed by soft soil and fallen leaves. The water area was no more than 10 feet across and the depth possibly three inches. A few clumps of tall grass such as grows commonly beside a permanent spring were here.

This was no place for a grouse or a woodcock, and I let down my guard and laid my gun over my shoulder as I skirted the spot. Instantly a brace of snipe rocketed up. I finally got into action, but astonish-

Hull flies as hunter drops a snipe that flushed from pond edge. Flush shots seem more difficult than they really are. When a bird drops into a pond, as here, you have to wait for a breeze to move it to shore, or carry a casting rod and surface plug with which to retrieve it.

ment and lack of alertness were worse enemies than the flight paths of the birds. They passed over the ridge unscathed. The lesson is that all such spots, particularly in hilly country, can be secret hides where this fine little game bird consorts during migration. It pays to overlook none.

Beaver ponds are also excellent bets. The edges, cleared by the beavers, attract snipe. Creeks that have any soft soil at all along their courses, slow, vegetated bends on large streams, the old-time typical "swale" of which we see all too little nowadays—all of these, plus the duck marsh, may hold snipe. The so-called duck marsh, however, is not usable except along its fringes. You'll never find jacksnipe where water is more than about two inches deep. Lake edges that are marshy are good bets, but shy from the sandy shores. Sand holds little forage for the bill of a probing snipe. Mud flats are the ticket.

Though snipe do not seem to be quite as jittery as woodcock about leaving when a hard frost hits, they certainly won't hang around to face frozen ground. The fact that they feed along pond edges and on mud flats, which do not freeze as quickly as the somewhat higher ground of woodcock habitat, makes them a bit more adaptable. But my advice would be, if you live in the North, to start trying to locate birds a bit before the season and then get right after them when it opens. Keep watch also for a fresh flight of birds coming in when a severe piece of weather strikes farther north.

When you have your birds in hand, make the most of them. Though they're not easy to pluck, because of the fine undercoating of feathers that stick rather tight, by all means have the patience to work at it and leave the skin on. And if you must save birds in order to have enough for a meal and you freeze them, don't leave them too long. Snipe, like woodcock and doves, do not retain their proper flavor if left frozen for long. They're best when fresh.

The English snipe enthusiast of old much preferred to hang his snipe to "ripen." When the feathers began to drop and the head began to separate from the body, the birds were considered just right. Few of us have such culinary tastes today. But far more of us can do ourselves a large favor by forming a taste for hunting this small bird.

27

Game Bird of History

Cold rain had been falling for days, and the coastal flats of eastern Mexico were an endless sea of mud, with sparse vegetation thrusting out of it. Shivering, I lay on my belly in the stuff. I had on a rain parka and pants, but water seeped in at the wrists and ran to my elbows, and my feet squished in my flooded boots. A blob in the mud to my right was one of my partners, lying in the soggy weeds 100 yards away. Another was out in front a long way, on his feet and moving, and I now saw him turning very slowly back toward us.

Then I caught a glimpse of the birds, and my heart gave a thump. They had turned without flushing, as we'd hoped, the moment they spotted the far-distant circling hunter. Feeding on the ground, they had switched course to move toward us—10 or 12 of them. They paused occasionally to thrust their foot-long, sicklelike bills into the mud.

Now just why should a reasonably normal human being lie in this chill ooze for an hour, heart thumping each time he spied birds? It can't be explained; you'd have to have been there to understand. We were hoping desperately to get a shot that would momentarily recreate some of this continent's most romantic bird-hunting history. The long-legged reddish-brown birds stalking toward us were curlew.

Admittedly our method was quite different from that of the old-timers. But we'd been trying for several days to get shots and had failed. The curlew were everywhere on the flats and wet-grass meadows, but they wouldn't let us get within gunshot range. They seemed to have an uncanny ability to sense danger and flare away from it just

233

The long-billed curlew. Once this grand game bird was extremely abundant. It is no longer hunted, but is not endangered.

beyond reach. Frustrated, we had finally set up this drive.

I can imagine how the curlew hunters of a century ago would have laughed at us, especially when the first two drives failed. Maybe this third one would pay off. Through the dripping mesquite branch I had stuck in the mud I saw three birds, far out ahead of the others. They were going to spot me and flush, and that would flush the others. I'd ruin my partner's chances, I knew, if I got up and shot, but I had no choice.

As I scrambled up, one boot slipped in the mess and I fell on my face with a splat. The three curlew were instantly airborne, pouring out the loud, liquid cries of alarm that have rung above hunters down the centuries. In the distance the others got up, straggling, wheeling into the wind, then

cutting back. I had scrambled to my feet and now shot deliberately, grim about it, trying to push the charge with my shoulder to urge it a little farther. And to my great surprise and joy, one bird's cry ceased abruptly. The curlew faltered, then tumbled into the Mexican maize field along whose borders we had been lying. I raced toward it, throwing mud and water like a charging brush-country steer.

You'll understand my elation in taking this first curlew, I'm sure, because no modern gunner on U.S. soil has ever been able to hunt curlew legally. Indeed, few of their fathers ever shot one. But many a grandfather did. Seventy-five to 150 years ago, great flocks of curlew creased the fall skies along the Atlantic and Pacific coasts. In wedge-shaped groups they circled the marshes, filling the air with their cries, which sound much like a whistling repetition of their name—*curlew, curlew, curlew*.

This bird, largest of the shorebirds and king of all the long-legged, long-billed waders, was highly esteemed by hunters. It made a substantial contribution to the gamebag, and its flesh was of fine quality. The birds, flying swiftly in small groups perhaps 30 yards above the marsh, offered sporty pass-shooting. They had also come readily to decoys.

I remember vividly my excitement as I sat one evening many years ago in a home in Erie, Pennsylvania, and listened to tales of lowland hunting related by a man who was then in his 90s. He fondled a beautifully weathered twist-barrelled 10 gauge and told me it had been his favorite curlew gun.

Ten was a popular gauge in those days of the meat hunters. The idea generally was not to shoot at a single bird but to bring down as many as possible with a single blast—even shoot them on the ground.

There was no notion of meat shooting on our hunt; I thought for a while that my single curlew would be all I'd get. But as the rain eased and the sun dried things up a bit, we tried other hunting methods. We camped wherever night found us, and as we progressed a little farther south, we found the birds even more abundant. Having no decoys, we simply hunkered down in low vegetation wherever birds appeared to be trading back and forth, and gambled on some coming near.

Quite a number of singles came to us when we worked out a strategy. We got between a mud flat, where a large gathering of birds was busily probing for fiddler crabs, and an area where scattered birds were feeding. Then the large group decoyed the singles toward us. We practiced curlew whistling, and when we got good at

it we could coax the birds to reply and come in fairly well.

During a whistling session I was caught crossing a mud flat by several singles converging from different directions. I squatted as low as I could, my boots slowly sinking into the gray gumbo. When I thought several birds were in range I got up—and then came the most dramatic incident of my curlew shoot. I tagged one at the far right, passed up a close shot in front of me, then swung around and pelted the close bird—which by now was getting pretty far out—with high-base 6's. Down it came. A third curlew roundly cursed me as it flared high overhead. I held well out in front and brought it down with the third shell in my plugged gun.

We did not kill many—only what we could eat, because we could not take them with us back into the U.S., where they've been totally protected for many years. They are abundant in winter in Mexico. Undoubtedly a substantial portion of the entire continental flock winters there. Nowadays Mexico also gives the birds protection. However, on the northern nesting grounds the curlew is not at all rare. I've seen them often in summer in Montana and other western states and on into Can-

Nonetheless, the long-billed curlew has never been able, under protection, to make the comeback that the jacksnipe managed. No one is quite sure why. Of course, none of the shorebirds is prolific. Like the jacksnipe, to whose family the curlew belongs, the longbills lay but three or four eggs.

One species, the Eskimo curlew—smallest of the lot—has long been considered extinct or nearly so; over many decades only an odd one has been sighted. In the old days, though, fantastic flocks of these little curlew (about 12 to 14 inches long) clouded the skies each fall along the Atlantic coast. Because they always arrived butter fat, hunters dubbed them "dough birds," and they were much sought after.

The 18-inch Hudsonian curlew, next largest, was the famed "jack curlew" of the coastal gunner. An arctic breeder, this curlew, which looks like an immature specimen of the larger long-billed curlew we shot in Mexico, once came down both coasts in late summer and early fall. Oddly, the birds apparently learned the danger they were in and changed migration routes, the main flights staying offshore from New

England and coming to rest about at the Carolinas. The western birds seldom touch down in appreciable numbers until they have crossed into Mexico or gone on down to South America.

Of them all, the longbill is the most dramatic in appearance. It may be two or more feet long, with the bill extending a full foot in some specimens. Longbills have been more adaptable in their nesting habits; some never leave eastern Mexico. I have seen them in summer on meadows of the King Ranch in southeast Texas. And I recall

Of the several species of curlews, the long-billed one—sometimes called a "sicklebill" in early days—is the most dramatic in appearance. These three birds from Mexico were my taste of shotgunning history.

A curlew flies over a prairie region of central Montana. Many nest in scattered locations across the plains.

that one summer, when I was fishing the pothole lakes of the Nebraska sandhills south of Valentine, curlew often dive-bombed me in an effort to drive me away from their nest areas. They'd spiral high into the air and plummet alarmingly. Often one would sweep almost to the ground, then shoot up so close to my face that it would barely miss my cap. As it catapulted upward it would roll out its alarmed cry.

A great many of these curlew nest unobtrusively here and there on the western prairies and across our Northwest, especially in alkaline regions. The focal breeding point is probably in western Canada. In all the summering area, grasshoppers and other insects make up a large share of the curlew's diet, except along lake and marsh shores, where it uses its bill to seize crawfish and to probe for other aquatic life.

On our last evening in Mexico we sat by our little tent and watched a brace of curlew for each hunter broiling over our mesquite fire. Waiting hungrily, I tried to picture a market in New York or Boston back

in the 1870s where bunches of curlew hung by their bills and sold for a few cents each. I recalled, too, that Newfoundland coastal residents salted down barrels of curlew for winter meat. Audubon, well over a century ago, reported that he had witnessed curlew migration flights that would rival the awesome flights of the passenger pigeon.

Now we were content to have a brace apiece, even at the expense of a trip to Mexico and some mighty uncomfortable hours in the wet mud. Animal eyes glowed suddenly at the edge of the circle of light cast by our fire. We snapped on a flashlight. Their owner, a coyote, wheeled and ran. One of its brothers far off in the brush sang to the night, and a flock of geese passing over called to each other.

It could have been long, long ago, another age, when the plump, sickle-billed shorebirds drew countless Vs across the sky. We'd had an experience to treasure—a taste of gunning for a game bird of history.

28

The Twenty-Four-Square-Foot
Game Bird

Stars were still bright in the sky, but the eastern horizon held a suggestion of dawn. Camouflage jackets, heavy with high-base No. 4 and No. 2 shotgun shells, tugged uncomfortably at our necks as we felt our way across the dark pasture, trying to dodge the clumps of thorny scrub mesquite.

A steep ridge loomed ahead. Beyond it, we knew, lay small, shallow, and alkaline Coyote Lake, a prairie slough of the west-Texas Panhandle southwest of the town of Muleshoe and almost on the New Mexico border. From the lake came a weird and exciting chant of bird voices, a seemingly endless chatter.

"Once you've heard that sound," I told John Casey as we paused to blow, "you never forget it. No other gamebird has a voice even remotely like it."

"So that's what sandhill cranes sound like," he said. "There must be thousands of 'em."

We headed up the hill toward a broad saddle that we figured should be a perfect flyway for cranes leaving the lake to feed in surrounding grainfields as daylight and legal shooting time arrived. We were hoping to get some hot pass-shooting. We'd scouted the spot the previous afternoon and now were relieved to find no other car here.

"Hope nobody gets into them before they start to leave," I said. "The birds will move, a flock at a time, right into the breeze, and we'll have 'em in our laps. But if they're spooked by a hunter on the shore, they might all go at once, and every which way."

The early-November breeze was bitter, and snow was falling lightly, but the raucous and intensifying chatter from the lake made us forget the weather.

Presently we reached the ridgetop, selected bushes to hide behind, and peered over the lip of the hill. Sandhill cranes roost standing in shallow lakes. These, etched in the weak light, formed seemingly endless masses of picketlike silhouettes scattered in close groups over the shallows.

This was John Casey's first crane hunt. I had been on two previous ones.

"They chatter as they fly," I explained, "so we can hear a flock approaching. Those that gain altitude to top this ridge should be in easy range if they're undisturbed. But keep down until they're right over us. These birds are really skittish and wary—and deceptively fast."

Soon the light was up a bit and we spotted a crane swinging around us far to the left. Casey nervously checked his watch. Another single appeared, out of range to the right.

"Some hunters consider those first ones scouts," I whispered. "Maybe they are."

Legal shooting time arrived. We knelt behind our cover, fidgeting. The noise from the lake was a fantastic cacophony, but suddenly a fragment of the guttural calls stood out from the rest.

"Flock coming!" I hissed, planting one foot firmly.

The big birds, black against the sky, appeared almost magically above the edge of the ridge 40 yards in front of us. They were a stunning sight. Adult sandhills have a wingspan as wide as six feet. They fly with long necks straight out and legs trailing straight behind, and they stretch four feet from beak to toes. Their wings seemed to be barely in motion. They seemed to laze along.

"Now!" I barked, and John and I leaped up and swung our guns.

The birds flared wildly to our left. I trailed one, trying desperately to catch up and get ahead of it. I fired twice and heard John fire three times. The flock, its formation broken but its numbers intact, was now far off over the flat behind us.

Feeling foolish, I looked at Casey. His expression was one of total disbelief.

"It isn't possible," he murmured. "We can't be that bad! They looked like they were

Cranes flying from the roost lake out to feed in the morning. They roost standing in shallow "playas," sometimes thousands together.

just hanging up there."

That's how John and I launched that season on one of the finest and most exciting and yet least known and least hunted of North American gamebirds.

In pioneer days sandhill cranes were tremendously abundant, nesting on the northern prairies and in the muskeg and tundra of the Far North, and migrating south in vast hordes for the winter. There are two main subspecies: the lesser sandhill (or little brown crane) and the greater sandhill. A third subspecies, less numerous and nonmigratory, is the Florida crane.

The lesser sandhill, most numerous of the three, nests farther north than the slightly larger greater sandhill, chiefly in northern Canada. Virtually the entire continental flock of several hundred thousand lessers winters in eastern New Mexico, parts of Texas, and south across the border in eastern Mexico.

All of the greater sandhill cranes nest in the Northwest, from southwestern Alberta and southeastern British Columbia to western Montana, eastern Oregon, northwest Wyoming, and north-central Utah. But these greater sandhills winter some distance west of the wintering ground of the lessers. Some greaters are found along the Sacramento Valley in California; others pass through the San Luis Valley in Colorado and form wintering concentrations along and west of the Rio Grande River from about Albuquerque and the Elephant Butte Lake region to the New Mexico town of Columbus on the Mexican border. Limited hunting has been allowed recently for greater sandhills.

Some lessers do winter with their larger relatives, and vice versa. There are also a few "intergrades," offspring of birds that intermingle on the nesting grounds.

Hunting-area boundaries have been set up with great care, to make certain that no whooping crane is shot. That's why eastern and coastal Texas, where some lesser sandhills winter, is closed to hunting, although portions of central and southern Texas are now open. It is at Aransas National Wildlife Refuge on the Texas Gulf Coast that the carefully nurtured remnant flock of whoopers also winters.

Many people, even experienced hunters, confuse cranes with various wading, fish-eating birds such as herons and egrets. In fact, herons are commonly called blue cranes and egrets are often called white cranes. But the cranes feed almost entirely on green shoots and grains. They are easily identified because they fly with neck and legs outstretched; herons and their relatives fly with the neck crooked and the legs trailing awkwardly.

The flesh of cranes is delicious. Early settlers quickly discovered that fact. The huge and renowned whooping crane, and the sandhill cranes, were all close to extinction at the turn of the century. Many people know the well-publicized history of the whoopers. Not so much is known by average hunters about the sandhills, chiefly because hunting them was outlawed for many years.

Sandhills, considered to be severely endangered by indiscriminate hunting, were given full protection in 1918. Both greater and lesser sandhills made slow comebacks over the years, but then the lesser really zoomed in population, especially during the 1950s and 1960s. By the 1950s the little brown crane—which at six to 10 pounds is not so little—was doing serious damage on the grainfields of southern Saskatchewan. And soon on its wintering grounds in the Southwest many a farmer was claiming that cranes were literally carrying off his grain crops.

In the fall of 1960 surveys showed that at least 200,000 cranes were wintering in a relatively small grain-growing area in west Texas and eastern New Mexico. Federal authorities allowed a brief season, and on New Year's Day of 1961, I was in eastern New Mexico participating in the first legal crane hunt in the U.S. in over 40 years. There have been annual seasons ever since.

Now as Casey and I hunched behind bushes and waited for the next flock, I was recalling the respect for sandhills that I'd gained that first season. I had gone to New Mexico expecting easy pickings, but after hunting awhile I thought I'd never succeed in outwitting a crane.

"They're worse than geese," I said to Casey. "Let one flock shy off, and every following bunch is likely to take the same flight line."

Happily, I was about to be proved wrong. Since we'd stayed below the top of the ridge, our shots had been muffled and so had not unduly disturbed other cranes. Two groups loomed before us. One flock began to drift wide, but the other bunch headed toward Casey at a steady pace.

"How fast?" Casey asked anxiously.

"They cruise at 30 to 35," I whispered, "and they can make over 50 with only about two wingbeats a second."

Then Casey was up and swinging. The range was long. But he was shooting a full-choked 12 gauge chambered for three-inch Magnums, and when I heard its roar I saw a crane falter, try for altitude, then fold and fall.

"Great shot!" I yelled.

But Casey was already racing to collect his bird. He came back admiring it and grinning.

"I shouldn't admit it," he said, "but I was holding and swinging about on the head of the bird ahead of this one!"

Cranes were soon in the air everywhere, moving in long, wavy lines out over the fields. But still the sound from the lake was loud—several thousand birds were slow to get off the roost.

We were amazed to hear only a scattering of distant shots. Oddly, this scarcity of hunters has characterized crane hunting ever since the first season.

"Hunters," I was told by Billy Huey, then chief of game management in New Mexico, "either think cranes aren't worth both-

Many hunters confuse cranes with fish-eating herons and egrets. Cranes are grain feeders. Here a flock comes into a maize field in eastern New Mexico. Flocks can be extremely destructive to crops.

ering with or give it up as too tough after getting a taste of the exasperation of crane hunting."

Actually, it is an exceptional challenge.

Although the first season, in January 1961, was in New Mexico only, later there were seasons in portions of Saskatchewan, in Alaska, in certain counties of North and South Dakota, in eastern Colorado and western Oklahoma, as well as in New Mexico and Texas. Those seasons continue. The great bulk of the crane population winters in counties surrounding Portales and Roswell in New Mexico, and in the Texas Panhandle.

The total annual bag throughout all of the open area in both Canada and the U.S. is probably less than 10,000 birds. In Texas, for example, the estimated crane population one winter was 280,000 birds, with hunters collecting only 1,339.

Casey and I watched several large groups skirt our position. Then a big bunch, flying low, loomed up suddenly from below the lake side of our ridge. The cranes were striving for altitude, but were easily within range and would present perfect targets if only they did not flare. We lay utterly still.

When the lead bird was directly above us, I leaped up. I picked a bird to the left, and as it flared, showing its entire underside and wings, I had a target that seemed to be painted upon the sky. At my shot it crumpled and plummeted.

I swiftly swung on another bird, now approaching the limit of my shotgun's range. The close-choked barrel gave its abrupt command, and the crane slanted down, coming to ground far down at the base of the hill.

I was elated. The daily limit, which has remained the same for some years, was three, the possession limit six. I was well started on a crane feast.

I looked around for Casey and saw him legging it down the hill. I dropped my gun and grabbed a camera. He had a wounded bird down there, and I knew what might happen.

Sometimes a winged sandhill will run and be almost impossible to catch. It's best for the hunter to shoot again instantly, before the bird gets out of range. But sometimes that's not possible and you have to chase a wounded bird. They can be amazingly aggressive and may stab viciously with the beak at the face of a hunter. Caution pays. Youngsters, incidentally should never be sent after a cripple.

Casey's bird was down in a clump of mesquite. Its wings were beating, and it had its head up. As we closed in, I yelled at my partner to watch that beak. But just then the bird wilted.

We had hardly taken our original positions on the ridge when a high loner swung over and Casey neatly brought it down. By now the light was bright and most of the birds had left the lake. Some swung back around occasionally, but most were too high.

Pass-shooting near a roost lake is best during the first hour of shooting time in the morning. After that, it is usually all over. On occasion you can get good evening shooting at the same location, but it is better to leave the birds alone then, letting them come back to roost. Otherwise they will forsake the roost lake, especially in years when water is plentiful.

Casey and I were about ready to call it a day. John had a limit, and I had two birds. As I reached for my camera case, John muttered, "Down!"

I dropped. A trio of cranes was coming from the flat toward the ridge. They lowered, apparently bent on gliding across the ridge and down to the lake. I followed with my gun barrel as they moved into range, and brought my last bird tumbling to within a few feet of us.

John and I went to the car and drew our birds. Cranes are exceedingly difficult to pluck. The undercoat is a kind of cross between down and feathers, and it absorbs water. That's one reason cranes cannot sit on water. Some hunters skin their birds.

We hung the drawn birds on a fencepost to drain and then fixed a cold midmorning lunch. While we ate I told John some of the lore I had learned from my previous crane hunts.

A roosting lake such as Coyote can provide good shooting for a couple of mornings, but by the third day at the latest the birds will begin to rise from the lake and spiral up and up until they can head overland without being shot at. Often the birds, after their morning feeding, will go to a windmill where there is a trickle of water. This is especially true when water sources are scarce. A well-camouflaged hunter who hides at such a spot can get shots.

Shooting in feeding fields, much as for geese, is the most common crane-hunting method. But it is tricky. For example, on my first hunt, in New Mexico, we selected a field in which several hundred cranes had been feeding for several days. We made tumbleweed blinds against a fence and waited for the birds to come in after daylight. They did. But our blinds were apparently too large and obvious, for the wary birds flew wide.

The next morning, at another field, we succeeded in bagging a couple. But we also learned that once a feeding field has been shot over, you may as well find another. The same birds will not return.

"A stiff wind," I told John, "would help us tomorrow. Cranes tend to fly low when it blows hard. But they're not like geese, which take off into the wind and usually keep heading into it. Cranes will launch into the wind but are unpredictable after

that."

Many hunters try to make a sneak on cranes. This tactic is seldom successful. There are just too many long necks stuck up, and the birds are always alert.

If a party of several hunters can find a field full of cranes and approach from several directions, a couple of the hunters might be able to flush the birds so that they fly within range of others who remain concealed. However, even this procedure is tricky, for cranes soar out of range in a hurry.

Also, sandhills habitually fly much higher than geese. It is common for them to spiral upward during the day, sailing around and around for hours until they are mere specks or are actually too high to see.

Casey was eager to observe how crane hunters worked with decoys. I had told him how friends of mine in New Mexico, anticipating that first open season, had fashioned silhouette decoys five feet tall. The technique they used was to set out the decoys in a field in which birds had fed for several mornings. The plan had worked quite well.

"Today," I told John, "most experienced crane hunters use decoys."

We had none, but I knew that Larry Merovka, recently retired from the U.S. Bureau of Sport Fisheries and Wildlife in Albuquerque, was staying at Portales, just across the state line in New Mexico, and that he was hunting nearby Arch Lake. Larry had fashioned a large number of shell-type full-form crane decoys and had perfected a method of hunting out in the middle of grainfields.

So Casey and I drove across the border and spotted Larry's car. He had just selected his spot and was putting out decoys.

In the soft earth Larry dug a very shallow depression that was long and wide enough for him to lie in on his back. He would use the edge at one end as a head rest. He gathered a few grain stalks and scattered them along the edges of the "pit." Then he set decoys nearby around the depression.

Larry was carrying his shotgun and an earth-colored blanket of heavy material woven like thermal netting. He had attached lead weights along the blanket's edges. He stretched out on his back in the shallow depression and laid the gun along his left side so that his left hand would be able to grip it. Then he drew the blanket over himself, leaving only his eyes showing

Larry Merovka demonstrates how he hides among decoys, then hurls off cover and sits up ready to shoot as decoying birds come in.

beneath his camouflage hat.

"I can use a call from this position easily," he said, "so long as I make no quick motion. Often, though, I call from a sit-up blind. I use a regular goose or duck call since I know of no crane call on the market. You have to pick a call and tune it and learn to imitate the cranes."

The important thing, he went on, was that without movement he had full view of the sky and could spot any birds coming in. He faces downwind because cranes circle and land against the wind.

"When birds are in range," he said, "here's what I do." With his right hand gripping the blanket from underneath and on the left edge, he hurled it aside, the weights carrying it well away. His gun was already in his left hand, and he came to a sitting position ready to fire. It was an intriguing idea.

Casey and I drove a quarter mile away, parked, and watched with binoculars. Presently a small flock came near Larry's spread. The sound of his call, and the bird voices, drifted downwind to Casey and me. The cranes circled, set their wings, and sailed right in. We heard the guns of Larry and his partners boom, and we saw three cranes go down. Several of Larry's cronies shot the setup that day and told us later that they'd collected 11 cranes.

"So little is known today about crane hunting," Larry said, "that a hunter has to make it up as he goes. This is the best bet I've found so far."

Over the years since that hunt, a few specialists have learned much more about crane hunting. Guides in the Texas Panhandle discovered a few seasons ago that rags dyed the general gray-blue color that cranes at a distance appear to be, make excellent decoys. They fashion large spreads by draping the rags over milo stubble and other crop-harvest debris. These are easy to carry in quantity, can be placed quickly, and, along with calling, have worked very well. The hunters, however, must conceal themselves carefully.

One guide from Plainview, Texas, told me that when a stiff breeze blows, often the case in the Panhandle, he places stakes here and there among his rag decoys, each with a rag tied to its top. These flutter in the breeze and apparently appear to passing cranes as birds landing or rising.

Next dawn John and I were in the same good spot above Coyote Lake. However, perfect setups seldom repeat.

It had snowed during the night, and I shivered as I knelt behind my bush. When shooting time came, a flock appeared as if on call, headed directly toward us. Imagine our astonishment when, from a clump of bushes near us, two guns began blasting away. We'd had no idea that other hunters were anywhere nearby.

The cranes had been three shotgun ranges away when these hunters began shooting. Another flock followed, and the same thing happened. Skybusting at cranes is even worse than skybusting at geese. There was an awesome clamor, and great masses of birds, already wary from the opening-day shooting, rose from the lake and spiraled up and up, staying over the water. At least 5,000 birds, we estimated, moved from the lake's lower end at altitudes of 200 yards or more.

One of the skybusters came over to us. "I forgot to get a duck stamp," he said. "Reckon I'm taking too big a chance?"

I had a good notion to tell him he'd better leave. Plenty of enforcement people, both state and federal, were in the area. But the fact is, you don't need a federal duck stamp to hunt cranes, though many crane hunters are under the opposite impression.

I explained that to him, and could not resist adding that what he did need was a better judgment of range. What is also needed presently is a so-called crane-hunting permit. There is no fee. It can be obtained from the game department of the state where you hunt. The purpose of the permit, explained on it, is to keep an accurate tally on the number of crane hunters and how many birds are bagged each season.

During one recent season, incidentally, less than 12,000 permits were issued throughout the entire open hunting territory. The harvest that season was an average of about one crane per hunter. That's an indication of the game qualities of these birds. Another statistic from the survey of that season points to where the prime crane hunting can be found. Texas crane hunters numbered 1,353, and each bagged four or more birds. The crane kill in Lynn County, south of Lubbock, was 15% of the national total.

Casey and I went on down the ridge and tried another stand. But hunters had moved in along the opposite shore at water's edge and were firing indiscriminately. We hunkered on the side of the hill and watched the birds fly. At last each of us got a chance, on a pair of birds that swung barely within range, and we managed to bring both down.

"You know," Casey said, "we should quit right now while the flavor of the hunt is still good."

We did. We slogged down the hill, watching high-flyers pass above and listening to their thrilling voices. Here, I reflected, was sport that many other hunters should be trying.

I had the same thought several days later as I sat at the dinner table at home with my family and carved a roast crane. Delectable!

29

The Wackiest Game Bird

One gets you 10 that less than one hunter per 100 has ever heard of the chachalaca. And one gets you 100 that not a single hunter per 1,000 has ever seen or shot this bird. Only one state claims it, Texas. Even there it is present in only a few counties of the lower Rio Grande Valley.

Everything about the chachalaca is a little bit wacky. Yet even at its most ridiculous it is a delightful and appealing feathered character of the dense thorn jungles along the lower Rio Grande River and a brief distance northward.

Basically it is a Mexican and Central and South American bird, with its northern fringe of range spilling over into extreme southern Texas. Distantly related to the quail, grouse, and other uplanders, it is the smallest member of the family *Cracidae*, to which the tropical, much larger guans and curassows, also game fowls, belong. It is, in fact, the only member of that large family that breeds north of the Mexican border.

Long ago it was extremely abundant in far-south Texas. Hunting didn't harm it. You'd be hard put to find a Texan who has ever shot one. Clearing of the mature mesquite forests, the thornbrush, and the cactus for citrus and truck gardening—and for the burgeoning human population there—has wiped out most of the chachalaca's prime south-Texas habitat. In the modest expanse remaining, the birds are by no means rare—but you can bet your last buck that in the awesome thorn-tangle the birds call home, hunters are!

The chachalaca is as unprepossessing in appearance as it is provocative in personality. It is one of the chicken-like birds, shaped, in fact, much like a small, slender pheasant but utterly drab. Body and wings are dark shades of grays and browns that

The chachalaca even at its most ridiculous is a delightful and appealing feathered character.

match the low-light tangle of brush, tall trees and vines through which it slips and climbs, seldom flying farther than from limb to limb or treetop to ground. The long, dark tail has faintly iridescent glints, and each feather is tipped with a white blotch. Breast and belly are paler, buffy. The only true color the bird wears is a minor daub of reddish-orange bare skin under the lower bill and on the upper throat, noticed chiefly when the males "sing."

An eyegrabber the chachalaca is not. When one perches on or slowly walks along a slanted tree trunk, it's just a bark-hued blob. So how on earth does the chachalaca rate as a game bird? Chachalaca shooting might be wryly billed as a new concept in the meaning of "sporty." The sport part has little to do with firing a gun. The challenge of worming your way into the awful, threatening net of vegetation they inhabit is a sport in itself. Getting back out doubles the job and satisfaction – or relief.

Bird dogs? You don't get a chachalaca to lie tight for a dog. Any hunting dog would have better sense than to get into such a situation, and you couldn't find a dog in the cover even if you could use one. Further, it would have to be a tree dog. An old bor-der-jungle Mexican, asked by a tyro upstate Texas hunter how one goes about shooting these birds, is quoted as having replied: "Shoot 'em ona wing, ona foot, ona leem, ona ground – but *andale! andale!*"

True enough. You have to be quick when opportunity is presented. If you wait for a shot at a flying chachalaca, you may be an authentic *viejo* before you get one. They run on the ground, darting through cactus and thornbrush, hop onto a limb, scurry up the tree, slither along vines, zip like oversized squirrels along a top branch – and suddenly go airborne with wings spread and tail fanned, often yelling their heads off. But they fly only to the next tree, or scale down through the mess to hit the ground running and hop into another tree. All this time, of course, heavy vegetation blocks your sight, entangles your gun, and hooks into your clothing.

When you watch a chachalaca walk down a slanted tree trunk, as this one is doing, you wonder why it ever earned its game bird rating.

Worming your way around in the thorned and spiny vegetation is the "sporty" part. Here a hunter on the Mexican side of the border actually gets a shot at a chachalaca during one of its brief flights.

If the wingshot will but camp for a couple of nights among chachalacas, especially in spring when they "sing" most vigorously, he will readily concede that killing one in any manner whatsoever is fair, and his aim in life will be either to get the heck out of there and catch up on his sleep or to strangle every one of the blighters he can reach with his bare hands.

What a chachalaca says is the first three syllables of its name—*cha-cha-lac*, *cha-cha-lac*—over, and over, and over. Not quietly.

No one would believe the volume that can erupt from a bird of such modest size. Prime time for singing is at daybreak. Males get into the tops of the tallest trees. Their voices are deep, with the grating timbre of an improperly adjusted chainsaw. Females get into the tops of other trees. They say the same thing. Their voices are not only grating but shrill.

When 30 or 40 are cranked up of a morning, the din is absolutely awesome. Then they quit. All at once. Then they

You have to be quick to grab any opportunity. But when you kill a bird or two, retrieving them may be a perfectly awful experience amid the jungle of cactus and thornbrush.

During mating season and occasionally at other times, chachalacas perch atop high trees and scream their name over and over. The din, when many are "singing," is awesome.

erupt again. Biologists have found the habit handy. They can make call counts and know quickly what the population is. Texas has been transplanting some birds a bit farther north, in suitable mesquite and thornbrush country on a Wildlife Management Area near the village of Artesia.

The mechanical unit that supplies chachalaca racket is intriguing. The windpipe of the bird doesn't pass from the throat immediately into the breast cavity. It reaches under the skin down the length of the breast in a long U, then enters the breast cavity on its return. This long pipe, pumped up, is what enables the bird to make such an infernal din.

Although their noisiest celebration occurs in spring, the chachalaca does some intermittent calling during the hunting season, too, much as turkeys gobble and visit in fall and winter. A sharp noise, such as the disturbance of a hunter, will set them

off. This leads the first-time hunter to believe everything is going to be easy. He hears the racket and starts to prowl to the source.

"Prowling" in chachalaca cover is seldom a straight-line endeavor. On some heavily grazed tracts there are openings so you can get around the close-spaced mottes of brush and trees or cactus patches. In these, you occasionally get a ground-sluice shot (fair!) at running birds, and at rare intervals may even catch one teeing off from the top limb of a venerable mesquite and sailing 30 yards to the next one.

In optimum habitat, however, hunting is a special anguish. Just as you get a noisy bird located and try to seek a snake-course to it, it shuts up. Suddenly, when you're close and perplexed, it flutters. There it is, running up a trunk and along a limb. No game bird on earth ever acted like this.

The hunter flings up his shotgun, catching the barrel in a grid of vines and brush. Trying to free it, he crouches, and three dozen varied thorns and spines from a maze of vicious species skewer his backside. The bird, perhaps for a moment almost within reach but immobile and unseen, gives a crowing commentary. It lets the air out of its inflated pipe with a sound of sneaky flatulence—*phooooooo*.

Curiously, hunting could be quite good still today, even with the habitat pared down. But Texans and others are so unaware of this bird that almost nobody tries it. The few who do usually are quickly chastised by the terrain, and throw in the towel. Even in Mexico, where chachalacas become more and more abundant the farther you go south on either coast, natives mostly eschew them except for unexpected opportunities. The going is just too tough.

The few who've hunted chachalaca and become hooked on it think of the bird as a kind of trophy. Collecting a few bloods a man—literally. A saving attribute is the fact that chachalacas are gregarious. Much like turkeys or pheasants, they consort in flocks, usually fairly small, up to perhaps a dozen birds. Once you get into a bunch, diligence—and a high pain threshold, one experienced Texan says with a chuckle—can sometimes result in a limit.

The Texas season usually runs through December and much of January, with a five-bird daily limit and 10 in possession. The open-season counties, which may differ from year to year, all border or are near the Rio Grande River, and are the southernmost in the state.

Hunting lands in chachalaca range are all certain to be privately owned. Although permission on most Texas lands is difficult to obtain, chachalaca hunters who track down a landowner and make a polite approach are likely to succeed. One land-owner, telling with amusement of such an approach, said, "I just reckoned anybody brave enough or dumb enough to fight the thickets those birds hang in should have his chance to suffer."

In searching out specific locations, one idea is to drive side roads at dawn and listen for birds sounding off. They can be heard a long way. There's no use looking for easy going. Pick the spots that appear all but impenetrable. They invariably sustain the best populations. If there are ranch trails cutting up such a thornbrush and cactus jungle, much effort can be saved by sticking to them. Groups of birds or singles commonly scurry across or walk along such trails. Even well-worn cattle trails are a good bet, if for no reason other than to help avoid the frontal assault.

Aside from seeing or hearing birds, you might look for communal dusting beds. The birds love to scratch out a dust bed, perhaps at the base of a big mesquite in a shady place, and fluff and roll in it. On occasion as many as a dozen crowd with little fuss or argument into the same dusting bed, lying ridiculously on their sides or almost with feet in the air. A well-used dust bed indicates a group living in the area.

There is no way you can tie the birds down to a feeding ground, as you can with most upland birds. Forage is everywhere—berries, buds, twigs, seeds, leaves, insects. The groups of birds seldom travel far. So once you locate the quarry, success depends on your own stubbornness.

In all of the chachalaca range, one emphatic caution must be sounded: snakes. This is some of the finest rattlesnake country on the continent, with some of the biggest snakes to prove it. Cottontails, squirrels, ground doves, pack rats, and other small rodents keep the snakes fat and abundant. Prime chachalaca cover is just as prime for rattlers, and a hunter's attention is often so involved with cactus spines and thorns that it's easy to forget watching the ground.

A shotgun, of course, is the practical arm. Gauge makes little difference. Choke should be fairly open, for most shots are short. Improved-cylinder is a reasonable choice. There are different opinions, among the few who have any, about shot size and load. The bird is by weight only about bantam-chicken size, averaging 1½ pounds. The only need for a punchy load is to ram it through the cover . . . although the pellets that do the ramming seldom are the lethal ones. Try No. 7½ high-base as a fair enough compromise.

A wonderful attribute of the chachalaca is evidenced during the post-hunt experience at the dinner table. The breast meat is white and savory, thighs and drumsticks about the hue of chicken. Don't attempt to fry these birds. The regional impulse to approach any game bird with cornmeal sack and lard bucket in hand is all too prevalent. Meager hunting means light pressure, and tough-gravy oldsters may be intermingled in the bag with birds of the year. Shake 'em in flour or meal, sear in a Dutch oven, then half cover with good red wine and water, adding a sprinkling of onion, rosemary, and some mushrooms. Then simmer oh so gently, covered, until tender. Your hunt's suffering will be healed, the birds' dawn "singing" will be forgiven—and you'll feel you too should ask forgiveness for your sinfully gluttonous indulgence!

Index

Some other fine hunting books
from America's Great Outdoor Publisher

Elk and Elk Hunting
Your practical guide to fundamentals and fine points.
by Hartt Wixom

Pronghorn, North America's Unique Antelope
The practical guide for hunters.
by Charles L. Cadieux

Badge in the Wilderness
My 30 dangerous years combating wildlife violators.
by David H. Swendsen

Grouse Hunter's Guide
Solid facts, insights, and observations on how to hunt the ruffed grouse.
by Dennis Walrod

Art and Science of Whitetail Hunting
How to interpret the facts and find the deer.
by Kent Horner

Hunting Rabbits and Hares
The complete guide to North America's favorite small game.
by Richard P. Smith

White-tailed Deer: Ecology & Management
Developed by the Wildlife Management Institute. Over 2,400 references on every aspect of deer behavior
edited by Lowell K. Halls

Bowhunting for Whitetails
Your best methods for taking North America's favorite deer.
by Dave Bowring

Deer & Deer Hunting
The serious hunter's guide.
by Dr. Rob Wegner

Spring Turkey Hunting
The serious hunter's guide.
by John M. McDaniel

How to Plan Your Western Big Game Hunt
All you need to know to plan a do-it-yourself or guided hunt in the 11 Western states.
by Jim Zumbo

Available at your local bookstore, or for complete ordering information, write:

Stackpole Books
Dept. BHD
Cameron and Kelker Streets
Harrisburg, PA 17105

For fast service credit card users may call 1-800-READ-NOW
In Pennsylvania, call 717-234-5041